PRAISE FOR
SOUL AUTHORITY

Dr. Van Tuyl's highly readable book is exactly what the world needs right now. Her Soul Authority system has offered me the tools and the robust yet malleable framework I need to reconnect to my core self, heal intergenerational trauma, and move through life feeling more grounded, centered, and empowered.

SHARLINE CHIANG, writer, activist, and co-host of *Democracy in Color*

Dr. Van Tuyl's provocative deep dive into the tremendous upheaval caused by today's social, environmental, and political tsunamis lays a solid foundation that will inspire readers to transform from passive spectator to committed change agent. Her seasoned professional experience shines through as she takes the reader on a journey to release buried shackles of old trauma and heal soul wounds. Her pitfall alerts, relatable examples, research-based nuggets, highlights of Soul Authority sessions, and step-by-step meditation scripts to reconnect with the elements made me feel as if I was being accompanied by a trusted guide while exploring a fresh and unorthodox path of transformation and realignment.

MIRELLA BAKER BEMMEL, EdD, sociology professor, founder of Next Level Educators, and author of *Building Blocks to an Abundant Life*

Soul Authority is incredibly rich, complex, and nuanced in both its breadth and depth, yet approachable for readers of diverse backgrounds and all levels of contemplative practice. Van Tuyl's innovative approach is grounded in her professional, spiritual, and multicultural histories and informed by current-day events that readers will recognize as touchstones of their own. Rather than follow a specific program to arrive at a specific conclusion, I felt invited to pull from a rich compendium to discover and develop my own innate wisdom and "soul authority." Parts of this book skillfully anchored me in familiarity and parts invited me to explore, stretch, and grow.

PEGGY ACOTT, certified life-cycle celebrant and co-author of *Portland Made*

The Soul Authority methods that Loraine Van Tuyl has streamlined in her book provide an essential key to unlocking emotional resiliency and are helping me to tackle every challenge in my life and career. I recommend it to other empaths in search of healing and intuitive insight on how to uncover the dazzling potential and inherent power present in their sensitivity.

LILY ROBERTS, MA, JD, attorney

Loraine Van Tuyl's *Soul Authority* provides a road map to the spiritual solace and strength we all need to shed our chains of internalized oppression. Now more than ever, we need the teachings highlighted on these pages to repair and empower our individual and collective lives. As someone who was seeking their Soul Authority and found it with the guidance offered in this book, I cannot recommend it enough!

ESPERANZA PADILLA, co-president of Spectrum: Autism at Cal

In this exquisite guide to personal and planetary healing, Dr. Loraine Van Tuyl has crafted a warm invitation to explore our own soul authority and showcases how this deeper work can build a better, more equitable and just world. Reading her book was a deeply transformational and emotional experience for me. It was both refreshing and relieving to feel immersed in a vast community of like-minded folks committed to this internal healing and external work. *Soul Authority* is essential for those of us doing both spiritual and social justice work, and is an absolute joy to read! I am so grateful to have these tools at my disposal and feel energized to continue sharpening my soul authority using the wisdom of the Earth's four elements and the brilliance of my own inner sanctuary.

JESSICA CALVANICO, PhD, feminist and racial justice researcher, educator, and writer

Dr. Van Tuyl's book will take you on a rich and courageous journey towards a path of discovering your own soul authority and potential. I gained much insight into our personal connection to the environmental, political, and social challenges we face in today's world. As a sensitive soul, I found myself intimately reflected throughout her book, and saw it as a call to action. The action of coming home to myself, with the deep understanding that renaturing myself is essential in living my soul's purpose to help heal our world. I found myself filled with hope and equipped with expansive tools to open up to the inner wisdom provided by nature and ancestral guidance. This book has empowered me to step into the truth of who I am—divinely guided, loved, and supported in all directions.

LAVIZA FUENTES, Master's student in counseling psychology

SOUL
AUTHORITY

Liberatory Tools to Heal from Oppressive Patterns and Restore Trust in Your Heart Compass

Loraine Y. Van Tuyl, PhD

North Atlantic Books
Huichin, unceded Ohlone land
aka Berkeley, California

Published by North Atlantic Books
Huichin, unceded Ohlone land
aka Berkeley, California

Cover art © gettyimages.com/Ju-Ju,
gettyimages.com/guvendemir,
DaisyArtDecor/Shutterstock.com
Cover design by Jasmine Hromjak
Book design by Happenstance Type-O-Rama

Printed in the United States of America

Soul Authority: Liberatory Tools to Heal from Oppressive Patterns and Restore Trust in Your Heart Compass is sponsored and published by North Atlantic Books, an educational nonprofit based in the unceded Ohlone land Huichin (aka Berkeley, CA) that collaborates with partners to develop cross-cultural perspectives, nurture holistic views of art, science, the humanities, and healing, and seed personal and global transformation by publishing work on the relationship of body, spirit, and nature.

North Atlantic Books' publications are distributed to the US trade and internationally by Penguin Random House Publishers Services. For further information, visit our website at www.northatlanticbooks.com.

Library of Congress Cataloging-in-Publication Data

Names: Van Tuyl, Loraine Y., 1969- author.
Title: Soul authority : liberatory tools to heal from oppressive patterns
  and restore trust in your heart compass / Loraine Y. Van Tuyl, PhD.
Description: Berkeley, California : North Atlantic Books, [2022] | Includes
  bibliographical references. | Summary: "Reconnect to your soul's innate
  wisdom with ancient healing practices, nature-based wisdom, and
  psychological principles-live authentically, nourish your inner power,
  and be a force for personal and collective liberation"— Provided by publisher.
Identifiers: LCCN 2021034562 (print) | LCCN 2021034563 (ebook) | ISBN
  9781623176938 (paperback) | ISBN 9781623176945 (epub)
Subjects: LCSH: Psychology, Religious. | Psychology and religion.
Classification: LCC BL53 .V36 2022 (print) | LCC BL53 (ebook) | DDC
  204/.42—dc23
LC record available at https://lccn.loc.gov/2021034562
LC ebook record available at https://lccn.loc.gov/2021034563

1 2 3 4 5 6 7 8 9 KPC 27 26 25 24 23 22

This book is dedicated to
Jade, Terrance, and Robert Van Tuyl,
my ancestors and descendants, and all
the brave hearts, change catalysts, and
wise old souls who live each day
with intention and determination
to meet the challenges of
their generation
and time.

CONTENTS

Step 5. Water: Unable to Keep Your Head above Water or Prone to Compulsively Rescue Others Downstream Instead of Stopping the Dumping Upstream?

THE WATER GUIDE AND CIRCULATION TEACHINGS

Topics: How to clear emotional dams and transform fear of flooding and drowning into creative flow

> *How to identify and nurture subtle and intense emotions without overidentifying with them*

Alchemy Action Steps: Soothe your heart and soul with compassion.

Step 6. Heart Compass: Is Your Inner Compass Giving You the Runaround Instead of Guiding You to True North?

THE HEART COMPASS GUIDE AND TRUE NORTH TEACHINGS

Topics: How to dethrone your trauma-body with your truth-body and ground in self-love

> *Fierce compassion versus compassion fatigue: guerrilla self-care and serving others from the inside out*

Alchemy Action Steps: Transform self-doubt into confidence.

Step 7. True North Living: Are You Breathing, Healing, Loving, and Leading with Soul Authority or Taking Yourself Too Lightly (or Too Seriously)?

TRUE NORTH LIVING AND IMPACT AND VISIBILITY TEACHINGS

Topics: Get out there and share your message, because it is and isn't about you

> *Why renaturing your denatured mind heals our nation, humanity, and the Earth*

Alchemy Action Steps: Fulfill your soul's mission with commitment.

Acknowledgments

I feel blessed to be alive during these challenging, catalytic, and promising times because of the many opportunities I've been given to cultivate my innate gifts and fulfill my soul's mission. I'm humbled by and indebted to so many wonderful souls who have, over the decades, made it possible for me to grow, refine, and impart my offerings to those who'd benefit from them the most.

I would like to start by honoring and thanking our sacred Earth Mother, my parents, and my ancestors, who've not only given me the gift of life but have nourished and guided me along an often arduous, but ultimately fruitful journey. I hope I've satisfactorily channeled and distilled the teachings that were mine to share and have done justice to their wisdom, courage, brilliance, and fun-loving nature.

I hold the same deep gratitude for the dozens of nature, animal, archetypal, and ascended guides and masters who've been by my side, probably protecting and guiding me long before this lifetime. That's the only way I can explain my clear sense that they've provided me a head start and foundation upon birth that fast-tracked my transformation and helped me to make sense of, regulate, and articulate intense periods of suffering, struggle, and creative inspiration throughout my life. I'll never take these blessings for granted.

Most of 2020 was heavily weighed down by heartache, fear, and grief due to the widespread loss of life, health, work, and social interaction caused by the global pandemic. Reckless disregard about the well-being of humanity and the planet—which flared up during the last administration—added powerful resistance and sociopolitical movements, such as the Black Lives Matter protests, and astronomical climate crises, such as the wildfires in California, to this upending mix. Long-ignored sirens suddenly became unbearable, motivating a growing number of us to recalibrate and reprioritize what matters most.

Against this backdrop, it was easy to spend more quality time with my partner of thirty-two years, Robert, and our two children, Terrance and Jade. Being there for each other during this stressful, uncertain, and emotionally taxing year definitely deepened our connection, love, and appreciation for one another as well as promoted growth spurts in each one of us. I was able to birth this book thanks to their unwavering support and understanding that taking care of my most vital and primal self over the course of this turbulent period required giving voice to the ancestral guidance that was coming through.

While sheltering in place, all of us experienced much more than the usual overwhelm that sensory and news overload, social media, and nonstop internet connectivity often cause. Even though Zoom fatigue became a new household term in 2020, our virtual connections offered many of us the only lifeline and way to do our work and remain connected with family (for many months, the only way to connect to my mother in a nursing home was through FaceTime), friends, sangha members, clients, and colleagues we could not meet with in person. For that, I'm grateful.

Some of the circles and communities that sustained me socially, emotionally, and spiritually in these ways include siblings, in-laws, extended family, and lifelong friends (many overseas in Suriname and Holland). They have been there through thick and thin. I'm thankful for my "Cool Moms" friends who provided sisterhood and a space to share parenting trials and triumphs; my fellow practitioners from the Circles for the Earth, the Space Clearing Society, and the Mind & Life Institute with whom I enjoy serving those in need; my fellow questers in the Tracking Wonder online group who show interest in and celebrate progress about any and all soul projects; and my fellow yogis and yoginis at Joya Yoga who keep me sane and fit. These social connections helped me to get through some of the toughest times and will always have a special place in my heart.

I'm beyond grateful for the devotion of and brave and astute guidance from Isa Gucciardi and Laura Chandler, my Depth Hypnosis teachers and mentors from the Foundation of the Sacred Stream, and the rest of my soul sisters and brothers at this sangha who've offered me top-notch care, guidance, and company. They've inspired me and taught me so much about soul integrity and healing over the last fifteen years through their own rigorous practice and example. They and so many other unstoppable and dedicated anti-racist and anti-sexist activists and social and Earth justice movers and shakers have kept my spirits up and offset the discouraging forces and voices that were and are deliberately sabotaging progress.

This book would not have been possible if it weren't for the incredible clients, students, readers, and online supporters of my work. I had an inkling that they mysteriously and synchronistically began to cross my path more than twenty-five years ago when I was just a fledgling in graduate school. In my attempts to guide them to the best of my ability, I ended up embodying my own soul authority and eventually quantum leaping. In my memoir, I unpacked and detailed the powerful impact that my transformative relationship with my client Paloma had on me and my work. It was delightful that this time around, my client Maria entered the scene at the tail end of writing this book. She portrayed over a period of just four sessions—as if she'd been reading and taking notes over my shoulder or had been in deliberation with my guides—a compact account and reflection of the core lessons I tried to convey. It was an undeniable testament that my Soul Authority framework now has a life of its own in the mysterious ether. With minimal guidance and setup, it can be intuitively accessed and practiced in the profound and effective ways it was designed for.

I'm most grateful for this gift of elucidation, and for the magnificent reflections, natural genius, and generosity of clients and students (most using pseudonyms to protect their privacy) who've trusted me with their hearts and lives over the years and made many invaluable contributions to this book. Our symbiotic relationship of mutual discovery, learning, trailblazing, and healing has been magical and deeply rewarding. I don't say this lightly, but they truly are the blood, flesh, and bones of Soul Authority. They give me hope about the future and give my life meaning on a daily basis.

Last but not least, I'm so pleased and thankful that North Atlantic Books offered to take *Soul Authority* under its wing. This was all set in motion thanks to one of my advanced students, Sharline Chiang, who trusted the hunches she was getting from her guides to meet with Tim McKee, North Atlantic Books' publisher. This resulted in an enthusiastic discussion of my work and my book in progress. It felt as if all the stars in my life had miraculously aligned when Tim read over my materials and felt excited about supporting and publishing my book. I've collaborated with North Atlantic Books for several months now, and I can't imagine a more suitable, progressive, and nourishing home for *Soul Authority* than this publishing house. I so appreciate the excellent developmental editing, clarity, attention to detail, and competent care that Tim, my acquisitions editor Gillian Hamel, and the whole North Atlantic Books team have offered me throughout this book writing and production process. It's been a real treat to watch the book improve and shine brighter each step of the way thanks to so many helping hands, minds, and hearts invested in presenting and packaging the material as superbly as possible.

May you enjoy and reap all the love, wisdom, and gifts that so many bestowed in this book, and may it inspire you to wholeheartedly pursue your callings, commit to your mission, and share your joy and offerings to the world—all the while standing solidly and basking confidently in your soul authority.

Foreword

If you've gotten unmoored by 2020's perfect storm of pandemic, political, and planetary woes and its tumultuous aftermath, allow Loraine Van Tuyl to show you how to reconnect to your core self and stay grounded. Her brilliant book, *Soul Authority: Liberatory Tools to Heal from Oppressive Patterns and Restore Trust in Your Heart Compass,* will guide you back to center with clarity and courage. This is your best defense in meeting and integrating the intense feelings that threaten to flood and overwhelm us during these catalytic times.

In my roles as clinical psychologist and neuropsychologist at the Summit Center in Walnut Creek, California, as a functional diagnostic nutrition practitioner, and as a student of the Intuitive Way, I've identified and assisted hundreds of gifted individuals with the unique challenges they face in navigating their academic, emotional, social, and spiritual paths within society. These professional experiences have deepened my appreciation for Loraine's skills, dedicated service, extraordinary gifts, and multidimensional "rainforest mind" since meeting her twenty-five years ago in graduate school.

I've celebrated Loraine's amazing growth and the development of her Soul Authority solutions for sensitive and gifted people up close and personal over the years. I can attest that the solutions that Loraine shares in this book are cutting-edge, powerful, foundational, and ideally suited for change agents and activists like us. They will boost your confidence, especially if you are a highly sensitive empath, a natural-born leader, healer, or wisdom keeper who doubts your gifts and ability to help create a more socially just, environmentally sustainable, and peaceful world.

If you have been hurting, hiding, or holding back, now is the time to step up your self-care and stretch as a leader. We need you! Loraine's transformational toolbox will fast-track your growth by enhancing your clarity, intuitive resilience, and self-trust. Her tools are practical and aim to deliver immediate results at home and work, while guiding children, clients, or teams, in activism forums, and when speaking up in your social circles, sharing your bold vision in writing, and designing the progressive programs and policies that we need for true reform.

It has made me even more grateful that Loraine ultimately found her way here after a military coup in her native Suriname uprooted her family. Her courageous journey of healing and spiritual awakening—which included a spontaneous initiation in our clinical psychology graduate program—helped to scaffold the earliest iterations of this new book, *Soul Authority*. The fact that Loraine's focus is just as relevant today as it was more than two decades ago speaks volumes. She has a good eye for identifying universal patterns that exist within every human, without diminishing their individual story. You're going to love this book and learn so much from her hard-earned wisdom.

Loraine's mastery in grounding overwhelm, fear, and self-doubt during trying times like these is unparalleled because of the many losses and similar tests she has already overcome. Her devoted spiritual practice and natural gifts in doing deep soul integration work have furthered her effectiveness. She is able to immediately put clients at ease, no matter how distraught they are or how intense the issue at hand, because of her grace-under-fire disposition, fierce compassion, and expertise in grounding and harmonizing imbalanced energy and unruly emotion. She has touched and uplifted countless lives in her holistic practice, in her online courses, and through her participation in shamanic healing and clearing rituals for the Earth and the community—ranging from hospitals, schools, government buildings, and social services agencies to offices and homes of healers and public servants in Oakland and the greater San Francisco area.

I highly recommend Loraine's clear guidance, especially if you feel overtaken or overwhelmed by intense emotions that won't let you rest or recharge. She will help you to tackle obstacles that seem insurmountable, and transform self-doubt and setbacks that are zapping your vital energy and creative ideas. Loraine's aligned strategies and action steps will infect you with a can-do attitude and renewed passion to regain your soul authority so that you can finish your important work with greater ease and enthusiasm.

I'm so delighted that Loraine has infused her game-changing methods, one-of-a-kind tools, and signature sharp focus into a compact, easily digestible book. Her strategies have empowered hundreds of transformation agents in her practice, her online forums, and her Soul Authority and Natural Genius courses, but through this book, so many more conscious leaders and readers like you will get to explore and expand your soul authority and highest potential in service of the greater good. This is precisely what's needed at this critical juncture in history to transform today's world into the boldest and brightest vision of a healed and peaceful tomorrow—for future generations and the planet.

Jeannie Lopez, PhD, FDN-P,
licensed clinical psychologist and neuropsychologist
Summit Center, Walnut Creek, California

CHAPTER 1

Is This Book Right for You?

Never underestimate the empowered empath. Our kindness and compassion is too often mistaken for weakness or naivety, while we are in fact highly calibrated human lie detectors ... and fearless warriors for truth and justice.

—ANTHON ST. MAARTEN

Ours is not the task of fixing the entire world all at once, but of stretching out to mend the part of the world that is within our reach. Any small, calm thing that one soul can do to help another soul, to assist some portion of this poor suffering world, will help immensely. It is not given to us to know which acts or by whom, will cause the critical mass to tip toward an enduring good.

—CLARISSA PINKOLA ESTÉS

To quote Alice Walker: we were born for these times. We know that the political spectacle and dysfunctional power plays that took place during the 2020–2021 presidential transition have been operating for a long time in various forms throughout history in the highest levels of government and in every institution and social system that we're a part of. We feel called to restore trust in the truth, each other, social and Earth justice, and our most powerful leaders and institutions because we intuitively get how much our personal health is influenced by our collective well-being and wholeness. We're best suited to tackle these issues because we're most shaken up and uprooted by neglected emotional, social, and environmental wounds and imbalances that are not addressed in society and that cause a lot of harm. We are also good at surfing the waves of historical pivots, and know when the tides are turning. We're going through one of those major transitions.

We go by many names. Call us consciousness pioneers, highly sensitive wise souls, transformation trailblazers, starseeds, holistic healers, freedom fighters, thought leaders, social justice activists, renewable energy and climate warriors, nature lovers, natural-born leaders, modern-day bodhisattvas, spiritual gangsters, seekers, and teachers. This is what we do best: trailblaze liberating paths of transformation for ourselves and others. We ache to contribute to meaningful movements that benefit all sentient beings, including our planet, because we recognize the urgent need to restore humanity's soul, overall health, and integrity. We come from all walks of life and from every region of the planet. This is what we have in common: many of us were born awake. That means that our clarity and vitality have defined and energized our sense of self and our true nature for as long as we can remember. We often didn't realize how precious this was until growing social pressure to belong and survive caused fear to seep in and occupy our minds, hearts, and bodies.

What's perhaps different between us and other children—who were similarly awake but more readily dimmed their light, natural genius, and vitality as they got older—is that this solution tends to create considerably more inner conflict, objections, and unbearable symptoms in us than in them. Therefore, our sensitivity to social pressures doesn't necessarily mean that we immediately succumb to them. Many of us challenge outdated, patriarchal, and oppressive norms within our birth families with our sheer presence and stubborn symptoms, even as school-age children. We're often the reason why our families finally seek outside help for long-standing issues: we make it really difficult to remain in denial, because the truth is often the only thing that grounds us and releases us from suffering. We learn to honor our bodies and symptoms more as we grow older, often because it's the only way we can truly be at ease: by setting fierce limits with all imbalances that cause dis-ease.

AUTHENTIC AND FREE

Our disposition explains why we are driven by a deep need to be authentic and free. We are by nature extraordinarily loyal to our inherent joy, wholeness, and integrity (after all else has failed), and are willing to withstand numerous trials by fire when tested. We're also very passionate about social, political, and earth justice causes and are devoted to serving people and movements in need of our help. We discovered, often the hard way, that our well-being, physical health, and soul fulfillment require us to take a stand for humanity's highest good, which means empowering the disenfranchised and silenced. We thrive when engaged in meaningful missions and acts of compassion that heal others and the planet. When we boldly own our natural genius, healing wisdom, and gifts, we're magnetic, unapologetic, and exponentially impactful. When we dare to trust ourselves and our daunting missions, we transform the circles and communities that we're a part of with our brilliance and big hearts. In our element, we're capable of leading consciousness revolutions with fierce compassion and clear plans of action. Unfortunately, we face far more pushback than most for willingly and unwittingly rattling the status quo. We need all the support we can get not to betray our souls and missions in exchange for safety, belonging, thwarted love, financial security, and other promises of conventional or misaligned success and power.

DEMOGRAPHICS AND PSYCHOGRAPHICS

We are very diverse in regard to age, gender, class, sexual orientation, education level, physical ability, spiritual and religious affiliation, national origin, ethnic ancestry, racial background, and many other qualifiers that can box us in. Students and clients in my Soul Authority courses, retreats, and private practice represent every decade (their ages range from nineteen to seventy-four), but the majority of them tend to be between thirty and fifty-five years of age. The professions and careers that seem to provide the best structure and public interface for their deeper soul missions involve academia, social work, holistic healing, coaching, the arts, humanities, conservation, renewable energy, renegade economics, yoga and mind-body practices, spiritual entrepreneurship, nonprofit services, social and earth justice, law, politics, and psychology. As a group, we tend to have well-developed intuitive gifts and emotional and spiritual intelligence (EQ and SQ) that help us to see through facades, social conventions, and lies more easily than others, starting as early as childhood. Parents, teachers, and other adults may appreciate us and recognize us as revolutionary old souls or as nuisances that threaten their worldviews, biases, or social privileges.

My mother was often exasperated when I stood my ground, and often called me *eigenwijs*—a Dutch expression that has an ambiguous meaning.

The literal translation is "own way/wisdom," describing an admirable strong person who follows their own wisdom. When that wisdom goes against the preferred grain, it means "being as stubborn as a mule." I was astute enough to notice the flicker in my mother's eye when she admired how *eigenwijs* and resolute I was, versus when she believed that I was being annoyingly difficult just to get my way. Because of her reactions to me, I questioned throughout my life whether or not my intense *eigenwijsheid,* my "own wisdom," was ego- or "indigo"-powered, the word I used after reading the book *The Indigo Children: The New Children Have Arrived,*[1] to help me to assess whether or not my impulses were ego-ecosystem aligned (indigo-driven) or misaligned (ego-driven and influenced by modern-day values and priorities that are lacking integrity).

HOW WE PLAY SMALL

Being a catalyst of transformation is very challenging in today's world. These are a few of the creative solutions that we default to when unable to be both authentic and attached (fully accepted by our social groups):

1. We disconnect from our inner wisdom and play a smaller, conventional, and more demure role to fit in and fly under the radar.

2. We withdraw into our own world, and end up identifying as quiet, countercultural, or dark with a very active imagination and an unfair share of mental health challenges.

3. We assume the warrior role, openly resisting being boxed in by external pressures. We willingly risk being misunderstood and pegged as being too precocious, particular, meticulous, stubborn, difficult, or righteous, or an old soul, outlaw, maverick, scapegoat, or devil's advocate who's a pain to be around.

4. Even as a rebel, we may have knowingly or unknowingly taken our big mission and important soul callings underground, and have scaled them way down to minimize harm and hassle.

5. As (older) undercover agents, wearing whatever disguise or hat necessary not to draw unnecessary or harmful attention to ourselves, we may try to do our work as safely and easily as possible.

We do this within a demanding modern-day context while often juggling many other responsibilities. It can be a lonely and hard journey that causes us to lose sight of our callings.

BEING IN THE WORLD
BUT NOT LIMITED BY IT

Clearly, we feel and behave like a hot mess at times. This doesn't mean that we are to drop our missions. On the contrary: the symptoms of dis-ease most of us struggle with include complex PTSD and stuck, old, and layered grief that is at the root of our depression, anxiety, bipolar symptoms, addictions, interpersonal distress, and many stress-related and autoimmune physical symptoms. PTSD and grief stem from a wide variety of relational abuse and messy boundaries that are repeatedly aggravated by "dirty pain" (unhealthy and avoidant) coping patterns that perpetuate intergenerational, ancestral, planetary, and large-scale societal violence and devastation. Recent triggers that trouble many of us include the pandemic, climate change, the Capitol siege by radicalized extremists, and domestic terrorists wearing or waving Confederate, white supremacist, and Nazi-related symbols and propaganda, incited by former president Donald Trump, and the homeland security threat that they now pose.

TRAUMA IMPRINTS

We have ancestors from around the globe. The wide range of undigested traumatic residue and psychic imprints that often emerges during deep Soul Authority healing sessions includes tribal warfare, massacres, genocide, imperialism, the Holocaust, feudalism, crusades, witch hunts, the Chinese Cultural Revolution, the enslavement of Indigenous and African people, colonization, segregation, lynchings, ethnic cleansing in eastern Europe, drug cartel terrorism in Latin America, sex trafficking, and patriarchy and misogyny in the form of religious, physical, sexual, political, and racial violence everywhere. These imprints often intersect with their current issues and the subcultures and regions where they are from, still living in, or escaped from—if residing in the United States, some examples of these areas are inner cities, Native

American reservations, well-to-do but soul-impoverished suburbs, Bible Belt areas, religious cults, and the Deep South. Despite carrying a heavy load of emotional labor, we are still best suited to forge new paths of liberation and to inspire others to embark on their own journeys of healing. Those close to us know that we remain shaken up and off unless we recalibrate our energy and emotions as quickly as we can when out of alignment. After a lifetime of diligent practice, we have become quite good at this. In that sense, we are pleasure activists[2] through and through.

THE CENTRAL ROLE OF HOLISTIC HEALING

We have a lot of practice and know-how in tending to our neglected and bypassed needs through meditation, writing, psychotherapy, and heart-to-heart talks with friends, loved ones, and colleagues. Learning to set fierce and compassionate limits challenges our bighearted disposition but is key to our well-being. We often unlock our inner strength, refine our clarity, and protect our innate gifts by exploring holistic healing modalities and courses in plant medicine, mindfulness meditation, shamanic journeying, art, journaling, and energy and body work, such as acupuncture, massage therapy, craniosacral healing, yoga, qigong, and tai chi. Psychotropic drugs in low doses can at times offer inner support and stability that's hard to access or sustain in other ways. These healing methods help us realize just how much interpersonal, sociopolitical, historical, and ancestral oppression and inherited trauma have shaped us into the people we are today. Many of us have built armor around our hearts and souls for protection, and pushed scary truths out of our cognitive awareness. This may have helped us to succeed and even thrive in some areas of our lives but it is nevertheless blocking our greatest potential. In many instances, our self-soothing and self-medicating habits, distractions, consumerism, pervasive fear, rigid indignation, and crisis management have become all-consuming. Unfortunately, or perhaps fortunately, the pain and turmoil that widespread intergenerational denial represses is difficult to keep under wraps. The alternative to this is learning to radically accept past trauma and to alchemize it into creative fuel to deal with today's problems. We do this by being double-minded: learning how to be in the world but not limited by it. It requires learning to be one degree more in the deep *now* while staying simultaneously attuned to the deep *mess* so we can transform it with energy from the infinite Source of love and healing that we're tapped into, instead of infinitely toggling between these two.

GENERATIONAL DIFFERENCES

Nature and mystery are far more omnipotent than we are. Especially when we resist, we're more likely to come face to face with our denial and disowned parts in increasingly more dramatic and painful ways to shake us awake. I've seen a trend in my practice where the youngest generations, Gen Y and Gen Z, are supporting this evolution in consciousness and have diametrically gone against misaligned values that their parents have passed on to them to get ahead in life. If you as the parent have slacked a bit in your own growth, they will certainly get you to reprioritize all the issues and overwhelming pain on the back burner, regardless of whether it's a good time or not. They are not seduced or derailed by dirty pain patterns, and are strongly motivated by multicultural ideals, social equity, spirituality, civic responsibilities, and authenticity. They are tech-savvy, are globally aware, and will dive headfirst into all the complex and emotionally charged topics and unjust situations that their parents have spent a lifetime avoiding. Their love and courageous advocacy for the truth is inspiring and refreshing, and they seem more willing to go through an "ego death" to protect their integrity than older generations.

ALIGNING OUR EGO WITH OUR ECOSYSTEM

They are technically not killing their ego-selves—they are less likely and less willing to stray and build it up into something it isn't, only to have to break it down again. They are also not demoting the ego-mind into a role of lesser importance, as some traditions describe this transformational shift. I see it as a lateral move, absolving the ego-mind of visionary responsibilities that are over its head and finessing its focus and skills in what's most crucial to master these days. Steve Taylor, author of *The Fall: The Insanity of the Ego in Human History and the Dawning of a New Era*, explains how an awakened self differs from our usual self: "You could say that awakening doesn't mean no-self so much as a new self. Awakening means the emergence of a new self-system."[3] This new self-system is what I call an aligned ego-ecosystem and best prepares us to exercise our soul authority.

Taylor provides great imagery in describing this optimal alignment:

> Our normal self-system is like a city with thick walls around it; it seems to exist as an entity in itself, in separation from the rest of the landscape. But in the wakeful state, our self-system is like a small unobtrusive settlement—an eco-village, perhaps—that is so well-integrated that you can hardly tell it apart from the landscape as a whole. It has clearly emerged from the landscape; it's made of the same materials as the landscape and merges into it without any sense of separation. The key point, again, is that there has to be some kind of self-system within our being. There has to be some kind of organizational or administrative center within the landscape, even if it only plays a minimal, unobtrusive role. And a self-system implies some degree of identity, a sense of being someone who inhabits the landscape of our being.[4]

Within my Soul Authority framework, this self-system assumes the roles of a central operator and administrator who takes aligned and alchemical action based on input from four essential human qualities—mind, body, heart, and soul—and their corresponding elemental guides—Air, Earth, Water, and Fire. In an elementally harmonized inner state, we experience considerable relief as soon as we are able to sense and trust that our heart compass is aligned with a higher self when offering us guidance and direction. Our bodies feel safe and are able to relax when we function in this synchronized, truthful, and integrated manner.

MY MISSION

We're brimming with potential to change every social system, government institution, and organization that we're a part of just by embodying more of our innate genius and authentic selves. With one foot out and one foot in the troubled world and armed with savvy soul authority tools, it's possible to learn how to access sacred clear space and alchemize intense emotions into a bright torch that generates healing light, energy, wisdom, and transformational missions to remedy the troubles that have overwhelmed and stunted our evolution. My Soul Authority system will offer the guidance and support needed to reconnect to our core self, embrace our mind, body, heart, and soul *as is,* and cultivate more trust in our true nature and self-healing gifts. This allows our authentic self to experience and associate purpose, joy, soul authority, meaningful social connections, and true attachments—rather than social rejection and fear of abandonment—to our personal truth and inner guidance. This self-generates positive momentum in the right direction.

CHAPTER 2

My Liberation Story

The Predictability of Oppressive Patterns Versus the Creativity of Our Natural Genius

> *I don't do this to change the country. I do this so the country doesn't change me.*
>
> —A. J. MUSTE

I want to tell you my liberation story and the key highlights that contributed to the earliest discoveries of my own soul authority and the development of this system. May my story reveal how unoriginal and predictable oppression, domination, and divisiveness are compared to our natural genius.

Born and raised near the edges of the Amazon rainforest of Suriname, the most forest-covered country in the world (98.3 percent),[1] I have been rocked by the arms and rhythms of nature ever since I was a baby. While I was growing up, no one in the world understood my timeless soul yearnings better than Mowgli. Sensitive but rambunctious, I often pretended to be him and I looked like him too. As a hollow bone and an old soul, I was particularly attuned to relational conflict and to emotions that were never acknowledged or talked about at home or at school. I often felt pressured to deny my inner climate and ignore unspoken tension and harmful energies that acutely jarred my innate sense of harmony and wholeness. It stormed daily in my personal ego-ecosystem with no sign of calmer weather on the horizon. I regularly shed tears of overwhelm and frustration, and was teased for being a crybaby by peers or criticized by my mother, my aunties, and my teachers for overreacting to everything. I longed to be seen, heard, helped, and honored for receiving and running a lot of energy and guidance through my little body, and couldn't face the painful truth that this wasn't likely to happen in the near future.

FREE TO BE ME IN THE JUNGLE

Because I was so prone to absorbing toxic fumes and energy wherever I went, I dreamed of running away and of living in the jungle all by myself, just like Mowgli. His reservations about humans and the modern world mirrored mine and made me feel less alone. My adventures in patches of mystical Amazon rainforest all around our home, and weekend visits to acres of our mostly uncultivated farmland surrounded by jungle outside of the city, soothed my heartache and nourished my lonely soul. In the jungle, I could breathe freely and be my true wise self. I felt on top of the world, climbed trees, and played with intriguing insects, critters, self-made toys, and the wonders of the elements and nature until the sun went down and crickets indicated that it was time to go home. I was regularly on the prowl for creative solutions that could quiet my inner turmoil, and I soaked up like a sponge the intuitive guidance that I picked up from ancient living traditions I was exposed to. My survival instincts, wisdom, and sixth sense developed most rapidly in the jungle, where my mind had lots of space to wander and daydream as I, armed with a rusty machete, roamed around with my pant legs stuffed in hefty black rubber boots. My free play caused the profound information I'd read in my favorite library books to bubble to the foreground and match up with lessons I was picking up from nature and ancestral guides through spontaneous inquiry and introspection.

IMAGINARY SOUL MATES AND SPIRIT GUIDES

I had relatable, imaginary soul mates, like Anne Frank, Joan of Arc, and Helen Keller, who became my first spirit allies. Their stories gave voice to intangible energies and offered me insight into hard concepts like injustice, patriarchy, anti-Semitism, ableism, precognitive awareness, misogyny, religious oppression, inner freedom, wisdom versus intelligence, courage, compassion, self-trust, and nature as refuge. As if preparing me for what was yet to come, they provided evidence that young girls and women could be leaders, could be wise, could be warriors, and could be inspired by their mysterious connection to nature and a divine Source of guidance. It implied that there was nothing wrong with me. Like Helen Keller, I had an extrasensory gift, and this was a good thing. I needed to understand that this gift was prone to evoke self-doubt and denial because the people who didn't like the painful truths I might unwittingly or clumsily expose would try to shut me down. These kinds of objections trapped me in an irreconcilable double-bind: either be awake and alone, or asleep and accepted. I figured out how to use my intuitive gifts to creatively resolve this inner conflict. My wise guides inspired me to write a book to tell my parents and other grown-ups what was really going on in the minds of children, on my terms, just like Anne Frank had done (I had no journal or diary, so I mostly imagined doing this and filed key book ideas away in my head). They made it okay for me to know things and have secrets that some adults didn't understand. I could decide when to share them and to whom. I woke up to an unshakable knowing that I was the sole author of my life, even though I had no words for this epiphany.

FROM DOUBLE-BINDED TO DOUBLE-MINDED

This double-minded solution, the earliest roots of soul authority, gave me hope that I would be accepted for who I was, even if it didn't happen immediately. The support of my dream triad of friends meant a lot to me and made the delay feel okay. Before I was presented with this possibility, not being heard, seen, or understood by those who were supposed to, like my mother, tormented me to no end. Not having any space where I could exist and simultaneously connect to other living humans, in particular my immediate family, evoked intense feelings of annihilation, terror, and rage. I was relentless in my attempts to get through to them, and had exhausted all possibilities that were available to me at that age. I'd once even blurted out to my mother that I wanted to run away and live in the jungle. It was meant as a threat that I hoped would make her stop and think about her harsh parenting. She sharply retaliated with, "Go ahead. Who's stopping you?" and fiercely stared me down until I acquiesced. I may have been seven or eight. I decided that day to *never* ever tell her or anyone else about my painful feelings or plans again. The audacity to trust my soul authority and guides was my only protection from crushing self-blame and emotional abandonment, especially when my mother didn't get or support me, and my father wasn't home during the day to get what was happening. I didn't know yet that a near-death experience in a past life had contributed to my precocious soul authority inklings as a young child, but I did know that I needed to record my wise insights in a book to help inform people like my mother.

LOSING MY RAINFOREST SANCTUARY

The natural world served as my go-to safe haven and sanctuary until a military coup uprooted my life at the tender age of ten. There were bombings and fires, kidnappings and protests, and disappearances and killings of those who dissented. My parents had the stern talk with my brother and me. We were warned not to ever say anything that could put our safety and lives in jeopardy. I was already well trained in keeping my mouth shut, and went on with my life as usual. Three years later, at the height of ordinary adolescent mayhem, my family emigrated to Miami, Florida, to flee the ongoing chaos and political unrest that was only getting worse. Not until my daily sanctuary was completely gone did I realize how lost I was. Fortunately, my deep connection to the rhythms and wisdom of nature that my childhood spirit guides had awakened in me never left, and helped me to rebuild an inner soul sanctuary that resembled the outer nature sanctuary that had soothed, protected, grounded, and guided me during all my years of everyday forest bathing. This connection became my new spiritual lifeline and served as my True North in the concrete jungles of the United States. My inner compass at the heart of my sanctuary helped me to navigate a whole new set of challenges—self-doubt, survivor guilt, grief, culture shock, racism, selective mutism, second-language anxiety, PTSD, rebellious behavior, being blackmailed by an abusive teenage boyfriend, panic attacks, hearing things, fears of going crazy, uncontrollable crying, and everything in between—well into adulthood. My True North compass guided me toward a professional career in clinical psychology, and got me through a spontaneous shamanic initiation and several soul authority tests while in graduate school. It also helped me stay the course while undergoing rigorous study in Depth Hypnosis, Buddhist psychology, shamanic counseling, and energy medicine after receiving my doctorate. The profound protection, healing space, and guidance that my soul sanctuary provided me served as the foundation and premise of my Soul Authority system later on.

MY ENDURING CONNECTION
TO THE ELEMENTS

Growing up, I was fascinated by Taoist Chinese teachings of the five elements—Wood, Fire, Earth, Metal, and Water—and their regenerative and constricting properties. I learned about their qualities from booklets and drawings, and informally from elders. This helped me to intuitively discern what elements were out of balance when my parents were in conflict or when I butted heads with my mother. My mother, a junior high school principal of Dutch, Jewish Portuguese, and African ancestry, became raging Fire and hardened Earth when angry; and my father, an architect of Chinese ancestry, responded by turning into peaceful, flowing Water. He liked to say, "The body is weak, the spirit is strong." I got that it was his way of teaching us not to take my mother's and our own temper tantrums too seriously, but it seemed at times that he cared too much about invisible matters of spirit that were as illusive as Air. Perhaps the body felt pain and weak because it needed more strength and support. I saw how they each needed what the other had in excess, but they ended up triggering and polarizing each other instead.

You could say that this gift and my soul's mission were sealed by my given names: my Chinese name, Gam Lan (which means "Golden Flower" in Hakka), and Loraine (Joan of Arc was from the French region of Lorraine, and bore the cross of Lorraine on her freedom flag). At the most opportune times along my journey of awakening, my guides revealed the special significance of these names. The cross of Lorraine is the hermetic symbol for As Above, So Below. It gave a name to the guiding power that fueled the liberation efforts of Joan of Arc and the mission she had been preparing me for since childhood. *The Secret of the Golden Flower* is an eighth-century Chinese book and Taoist alchemical tract. Carl Jung took a fifteen-year hiatus from conventional psychiatry and credited this book for his maturing and return to the field. Both Jack Kornfield (in a seminar on Mindfulness and the Brain) and my tai chi teacher at the time, Michael Mayer, casually mentioned it two weekends in a row, when I was particularly down and discouraged by how long it was taking me to write the memoir that had been sown in my conscious mind decades before. I was frustrated that I wasn't able to just bust it out like my dissertation, a structured project that was much easier for me to capture in words. I felt loved and encouraged by my ancestors when this book with my name, Golden Flower, crossed my path at the exact right time and inspired me to keep going. This is what I wrote about this magical moment in my memoir: "I reminded myself that bridging Western psychology and holistic, indigenous, and non-dualistic worldviews was no easy task, not even for Carl Jung, and to be kind to myself.... The alchemical symbolism of gold—the transmutation of base metals and matter into a precious metal—and the symbol of the flower or lotus—the uncontaminated truth-body rising out of mud—were beautiful and profound."[2]

DELIGHTFUL DISCOVERIES

While researching the specifics of this ancient script for this *Soul Authority* book, I found a link to the whole book online. It felt as if my Taoist ancestors invited me to play with them in the big leagues, albeit in a "the joke's on you" slapstick comedic way. I grinned when I read that some of their key ideas, such as "preserving in a transfigured form, the idea of the person," already contrasted with Buddhist thought many centuries ago—where "this return to Nirvana is connected with a complete annihilation of the ego."[3] I'd assumed all along that the unconventional component of Soul Authority—the deliberate preservation of the ego-self, as described earlier by Steve Taylor—had been influenced by my own indigo-ego hang-ups and *eigenwijze* ways, by data I'd collected in psychotherapy sessions, and by my training in Western psychological theory. Ha! An excerpt from the book suggested that my Taoist Chinese ancestors had steered me in these directions without my knowing:

> Eternal is the Golden Flower only, which grows out of inner liberation from all bondage to things.

> Through the union of Heaven (yang) and Earth (yin), and through the activity of the two primordial forces within this scene (an activity governed by the one primal law Tao), there develops "the ten thousand things," that is, the outer world.

> A man who reaches this stage transposes his ego; he is no longer limited to the monad, but penetrates the magic circle of the polar duality of all phenomena and returns to the undivided One, Tao.

> Herein lies a difference between Buddhism and Taoism. In Buddhism, this return to Nirvana is connected with a complete annihilation of the ego, which, like the world, is only illusion.

In Taoism, on the other hand, the goal is to preserve in a transfigured form, the idea of the person, the "traces" left by experience.

That is the Light, which with life returns to itself, symbolized in our text by the Golden Flower.[4]

—*The Secret of the Golden Flower,* translated by Richard Wilhelm

RAINBOW CRYSTAL WOMAN

In 2001, almost a decade before running into this ancient text, I had a full-bodied, soul authority breakthrough during an intense ceremony in a womb-like sweat lodge where I drummed so vigorously, I felt like I'd become the drum and was channeling Gaia's heartbeat. Right before the ceremony, I'd balanced an amethyst egg, representing my spiritual rebirth, in the center of a medicine wheel that was sitting on a drawing of a *kapemni,* the Lakota symbol for As Above, So Below. Right after, I received the earth name Rainbow Crystal Woman from my guides, but didn't understand yet how it related to my Soul Authority system or mission. A few years later, during an intense vision-quest on ceremonial grounds, I found a stone that had been naturally worn into the shape of a white buffalo. According to Brooke Medicine Eagle, Rainbow Crystal Woman is the modern incarnation of White Buffalo Calf Woman.[5] She had come to Brooke and some of her students as a guide, and shared similar teachings with them as she's done with me. I gave the buffalo stone to the ceremony leader, who lived on the land. He didn't trust me, because I'd unintentionally invoked a near-death experience, provoked by fears that my spiritual explorations were going to result in professional suicide. I sensed my overarching higher self and my Rainbow Crystal Woman guide goading me on and saying, "So be it. Bring this professional death on if this is what needs to happen" (I learned later that a near-death experience right before getting persecuted as a witch in a past life left an energetic imprint that allowed me to transcend my ego entanglements with ease during peak moments like this). The ceremony leader scratched the brittle totem and seemed more spooked and bewildered when he realized that it was not a store-bought stone fetish and that I was not trying to trick him.

I felt very conflicted and didn't know how to speak about the deep Soul Authority teachings I'd received about the seven directions and medicine wheel until I met Inuit medicine woman Mary Attu. She had worked on a Lakota reservation, and had felt strongly guided by fierce Lakota leader Crazy Horse. She explained to me that Rainbow Crystal Woman was another As Above, So Below name. The seven rainbow colors of light represented infinite earthly forms and the spirit and light of Gaia after passing through her pristine crystalline body. Mary quieted my concerns about culturally appropriating (for strongly resonating with and wanting to use the four-directions medicine wheel—Air, Fire, Earth, and Water—instead of the Chinese five-elements model), and my chagrin at why on earth my guides picked this framework out of my many ancestral and cultural lineages to choose from. She said that this one was right for me and that "the people" depended on me to guide them. The long history of pillaging has left deep wounds of mistrust toward spiritual teachers and ceremony leaders claiming to be called to make good use of these teachings, but Mary reassured me that I had the right intentions and that I was being guided by the spirits to be of service and heal the dis-ease that is harming oppressed and disenfranchised people as well as our Earth Mother.

THE TRAP OF RIGHTEOUS INDIGNATION: A PROMINENT DIRTY PAIN PATTERN

I realize now that my journey needed to unfold in this precise manner so I could learn important lessons about undigested wounding and our sensitivity to the defensive and harmful weapons that people with powerfully activated trauma-bodies revert to when triggered. PTSD and painful memories of grave injustices can fuel righteous indignation, rigid ego-attachments and beliefs, and lower-self, misaligned coping that worsen instead of improve the situation. My lessons in regard to these kinds of misalignments went as far as having to remove a curse that a bitter medicine woman set on me when undermining my authority with snide remarks at a book talk. She hated the term "shaman," she hated "neo-shamans," and, based on what she'd read in my memoir, she had concluded that I was a fraud. I had no Native blood, and my instant downloads (passed down from other lifetimes and other dimensions) sounded like a joke to her. My heart hurt and burned for months after her comments. I could feel the hatred shooting out of her heart into mine, and I learned to neutralize and heal it, empathizing much more with her and her tribe's suffering throughout the process. I needed to stop contracting and bracing myself in defense, and was able to stretch big and wide enough to dissolve her wrath and the curse with fierce compassion.

From then on, I was no longer afraid of or controlled by anyone's righteous indignation. I discovered through the decades that our ancient soul structures are as similar as the makeup and the color of our blood and the bones in our bodies. Very diverse clients from all over the world, some with no prior exposure to esoteric teachings or meditation, are more similar than different when we dig deep enough. Their past-life bleed-throughs (and my own) crisscross the gamut and planet, as if mystery has a wicked sense of humor and is constantly cross-pollinating us to keep challenging our artificial walls and borders. It behooves us all to explore how these gifts can give us a head start and improve our chances of healing and collective survival if we no longer insist on reinventing the wheel. Some of us may very well be able to directly download clear guidance and profound teachings from spiritual guides, past lives, and other dimensions, but are perpetually undermined when written off as New Age charlatans. It's important to be able to discern what's what and who's who in regard to yourself as well as others, lessons I'd integrated years ago with the help of my Soul Authority system (we will do this together in the last meditation in the book) and hadn't given much thought to these struggles until considering how to acknowledge the different streams that influenced this model.

PASSING ANCESTRAL TESTS

My Taoist ancestral guides reemerged and seemed to think it was time to let me in on a secret. In skimming *The Secret of the Golden Flower,* I ran into this passage: "Man is spiritually reborn out of water and fire, to which must be added 'thought-earth' [Air—mental and Earth—physical dimensions], as womb or tilled field [Earth]."[6] No wonder it felt so natural to work with these four elements: these elemental ideas were central to my soul callings as well as foundational teachings within my own Taoist Chinese lineage. My ancestors got a big wicked kick out of the joke they'd pulled on me (not showing me this much sooner). They winked at me for sticking with the four- instead of five-elements model and trusting myself, even when things got very heated and hard. It wasn't funny at the time, but I could appreciate their trickster humor after learning through a talk by Dr. Leslie Gray that highly respected and rigorously trained Indigenous clowns apparently also practice this kind of wicked humor when ceremonies and the sacred are getting a bit too serious.[7] I felt reassured through this discovery that if we deeply trust our innate wisdom and natural genius, no amount of modern-day arguments and pressures can thwart our path, and that our guides and the Universe come through for us when it matters most.

OUTREACH AND SERVICE

In recent years, I've tweaked and finessed my Soul Authority system and strategies even more with the guidance of master teachers in mental health and ancient healing traditions. In published articles and in my memoir, I chronicled how I obtained them, and how I used them to empower hundreds of change catalysts, agents, and leaders in holistic health, academia, the arts, social entrepreneurship, and renewable energy in my practice and online. I shared my techniques and tools in trainings and talks at the UC Berkeley counseling center, the Native American Health Center, and professional conventions in psychology and spirituality, and enjoyed talking about their effectiveness as an expert guest in women's circles and on podcasts and radio shows across the United States. In reviewing my journey of transformation, it's hard for me to wrap my mind around the fact that the same withdrawn young girl who hid in the rainforest and was selectively mute for almost a year as an adolescent (in a cold war with my American peers, pretending not to speak English) has shared her truth in front of cameras, with radio and podcast hosts, in articles and blog posts, on virtual platforms, and to live audiences and groups of more than seventy people. It feels surreal, but it's the truth. By healing my fears and daring to speak up, I have inspired and helped thousands of other sensitive souls with my story and intuitive grasp of deep healing and soul integration work.

CB EO

My Biggest Takeaway: We are the ones we have been waiting for, and our self-doubt is robbing ourselves and the world of our powerful gifts and hidden talents. If you've read this far, you are a rare treasure chest filled with dormant old soul wisdom and potential that those in your circles of influence need more than ever. So let's dive in. There is no better time to empower yourself and the world with the help of the following Soul Authority tools and strategies.

CHAPTER 3

Why This Book Is Right on Time

Hearing the Calls of My Ancestors and the Wild

Walking, I'm listening to a deeper way.
Suddenly all my ancestors are behind me.
Be still, they say. Watch and listen.
You are the result of the love of thousands.

—Linda Hogan

Hearing and honoring the calls from my ancestors and the wild propelled me to write this book. I'm used to listening and surrendering to their guidance, but the degrading, cowardly, and callous way in which George Floyd was killed on May 25, 2020, shook me to the core and took the volume of their calls to a whole new level. It didn't take long for me to realize that the intensity of my rattled inner state wasn't going to release its grip on me until I explored and made space for what needed to come through. It all felt deeply personal to me, directly threatening my core existence and racial ancestry, even though I don't look Black nor need to deal with the anti-Black racist slurs, microaggressions, institutional racism, or serious assaults to my psychological integrity and physical body that those with Black racial features and darker skin color grapple with on a daily basis. I was overcome by anguish and rage every time I imagined the psychological agony, exhaustion, and fury that this atrocious hate-crime was stirring up within Black homes and communities, probably landing like the last drop in buckets full of daily racial trauma and denied injustices. This is how George Floyd's murder and the upsurge of the BLM movement became the blaring siren and impetus I needed to capture what my ancestors for a while had wanted me to prioritize.

Their request was undeniable. I needed to pivot during this crucial turning point in history and start book two: the how-to book that I'd left on the back burner of my to-do list while designing and offering my Soul Authority courses.

ANCESTRAL BLEED-THROUGHS

I suspected that my maternal great-grandmother, a descendant of enslaved Ghanaian people and my central ancestral guide, was most active and invested in this new chapter of my life that was quickly taking shape. She'd protected and guided me in spirit throughout my childhood while playing in the Amazon rainforest and was the first spirit guide to come through when I was a clinical psychology student at risk of losing my core self in graduate school. In my ethics classes, while contemplating the competency guidelines of my profession, I started to hear familiar drumming sounds in my inner ear (kind of like a song stuck in your head). They sounded like the drumbeats that I often heard on radio Apintie and on television. I also started to see flashes of the Maroon people who were dancing to the sounds of the Apintie drum at my elementary school during a powerful and magical healing ceremony. My feelings about the relentless drumming were all over the place, strangely evoking a dire sense of extinction that I'd initially linked to rumors of large-scale logging of Suriname's rainforest.

FEARS OF GOING CRAZY

Because of the traditional clinical psychology setting I was in, it was easy to work myself into a paranoid frenzy. I was constantly worried about going crazy or of being perceived and diagnosed as crazy, psychotic, or unfit to become a psychotherapist, should any of my mentors and peers find out about my state of mind. I was relieved when I discovered that the jungle was not at risk of being cut down nor that I was losing my mind. I realized that I was, however, at grave risk of losing my soul and my connection to my true nature and the heartbeat of the forest. The modern world was encroaching upon us and suffocating the ancient and Indigenous ways. Not only did I need to note this; I apparently needed to do something about it. I'd assumed that the mental health field was one of the last safe places in the world, a sanctuary where I could finally take my guard down, but the pressure to rely on evidence-based practices (that didn't represent people like me) was messing with my mind and creating a great deal of inner turmoil. During a hypnosis session years later, I learned that the drumming sounds were the alarm bells and rallying cries that my great-grandmother used during this phase of my life to get my attention and wake me up. Even though my body and soul instantly knew what was up, it took my scrambling mind quite a while to connect all the dots and trust the process.

SUMMONING POWER

When I was a child, I was blessed to experience the power of the Maroons' rituals and energy firsthand during unforgettable, life-altering close encounters with these descendants of escaped enslaved people who'd set up small, intriguing homes on patches of communal land around the edges of the capital—the only "city" in Suriname, inhabited by a few hundred thousand residents. They'd formed six distinct tribes, and most of them remained hidden in the dense jungles of Suriname from the late 1600s until the late 1900s, preserving their distinct languages, wood-carving skills, architectural styles, and traditions. What I learned through my mysterious connection with them was that escaped enslaved people vigorously beat their drums to summon power and protection from spirit allies and to instill fear in plantation masters when the escaped enslaved people were about to attack and burn a plantation to free more enslaved people. They were trying to rescue me and pump me full of courage before it was too late. I didn't know how to stand up for myself because I'd intuitively lived by my convictions and inner knowing without ever needing to conceptualize or articulate them. My innate wisdom was at risk of getting bulldozed over and buried by an authoritative body of knowledge that I couldn't compete with.

THE WAY OF THE SPIRITUAL WARRIOR

My ancestors stopped me in my tracks before I could cut myself off from a lifeline that had guided and protected me my entire life. I needed to consciously choose which path was right for me instead of passively submitting to a professional perspective that wasn't aligned with my inner wisdom and that would continue to make me feel out of sorts, confused, and unwell. When I could finally see what was happening and felt the support of my ancestors, it was a no-brainer that the ancient ancestral path, the way of the spiritual warriors and earth wisdom keepers, was right for me. This path began to feel less of a choice and more like relinquishing and relaxing into who I truly was, who I had always been, and who I could never desert, even if I wanted to. After I regained my footing, my great-grandmother helped me to renature myself and revive my inner wisdom and shamanic gifts. In spontaneous trance sessions, I assisted with the soul healing of our ancestors who'd endured the horrors of slavery. It involved recognizing their powers and honoring them for who they really were, even when they were stuck for life in a social system that did not. I not only helped to release them from their shackles in the afterlife; I also freed my own hidden powers, my shamanic inklings, and my true potential.

MY LARGER SOUL MISSION

Through a great deal of me-search and cross-national dissertation research into my ancestral roots, I discovered that my path had another layer. I couldn't just turn my back on my dreams of becoming a psychologist, and simply decide to become a shamanic practitioner instead. That would've been too easy. The imbalances and biases in the mental health field were like a thorn in my side and would eventually burst my bubble of isolated well-being. My soul purpose was to reveal the compartmentalization and overpathologizing that were so prominent in the mental health field and to help reform them before they harmed more people like me. I also needed to own and dissect why I felt so disillusioned, distraught, and mystified. My most authentic and whole self had been robbed from me. Why did I feel least supported and most misunderstood in a helping field that encouraged so many vulnerable souls to place their last shreds of hope and trust in its care? I'm sure that I wasn't the first and wouldn't be the last to feel wedged apart from my healing intuition and the wise teachings of my ancestors. I had no idea how to resolve this systemic issue. I had insider privileges and more power than most to do something about this, and yet I felt utterly helpless and out of my mind for wanting to confront a giant a hundred times my size.

SELF-TRUST AND CLARITY

Desperate for answers, I retreated and consulted with my wise guides, something I learned to do as a child while roaming in the rainforest. I grokked that my mission was to immerse myself into this problem and profession, like a journalist, and expose all the roadblocks, dead ends, and tight knots that made it so challenging for me to be present. I surrendered to the guidance. I wrote in secret about my doubts and the many inner and outer conflicts I wrestled with while traversing uncharted territory. I didn't trust anyone, but I was used to trusting myself when defying authority figures as a child. By regularly sorting out my thoughts and feelings with the help of nature and spirit guides in my imaginary parenting book, addressing adults who didn't get it, I taught myself how to be mindful and reflective. I figured out throughout the course of my life how to remain devoted to the truth, no matter how painful, by being an observer, by *not* taking everything personally, and by finding meaning and openings in hardship and closed doors. To my delight, my self-trust and clarity were coming back full force. I discovered while writing that my reflections were finally ripe and seasoned enough to be compiled into a spiritual memoir. While it was an arduous challenge to integrate my premonitions and intuitive insights as a child with my awakening journey, professional training, and cross-national dissertation data as an adult, it allowed me to realign and ground myself.

ROUND TWO OF ANCESTRAL BOOK GUIDANCE

I recognized that a similar awakening and writing process was taking root within me during this catalytic moment in history, bookended by the chaotic rise and fall of the Trump administration. Because of what I'd experienced in round one of book writing, I anticipated that this creative undertaking would provide me the best possible buffer during this turbulent and triggering transition; and vice versa, this trying time would serve as the best creative muse to dig up and reckon with our nation's biggest blindspots and skeletons for greater accountability, healing, and trust building. The rich and promising golden thread that moved through me felt familiar. I traced it to a universal theme that I've struggled with throughout my life as a highly sensitive and intuitive empath. I would describe it as an overwhelming yearning to integrate and resolve the tension between two powerful forces that were at opposite ends of the spectrum:

- ○ Unresolved intergenerational pain and social conflict that I couldn't harmonize and balance
- ○ Mysterious and determined ancestral, spiritual, and nature-centered guidance I couldn't fully absorb or put to use

Back in grad school, I realized that the clients who were drawn to me reported similar challenges and that I wasn't alone. I felt an obligation to protect them and their missions but had no idea how. The desire to bridge these two extremes—which were heightened by graduate school splits and callings from other guides, like my Taoist Hakka Chinese and Portuguese Jewish Dutch ancestors—eventually inspired me to design emotional regulation systems that effectively integrated these polarities within myself and those I served. Since then, I have tested and refined these models in my professional roles as a holistic clinical psychologist, multicultural researcher, diversity, inclusion, and racial equity specialist, Depth Hypnosis practitioner, shamanic ecopsychologist, ordained minister, and meditation teacher. For more than two decades, all seemed to move along smoothly in my practice until this screeching halt.

STRETCHING DEEPER, WIDER, AND HIGHER

Because of my in-depth prior work, I was surprised how much George Floyd's heinous death unraveled me. It revealed a buried layer that I didn't even realize was there. Underneath my heartbreak and outrage were feelings of hopelessness, shame, and utter defeat about our ineffectiveness at and resistance to fighting racism as a nation and as a human race.

- ○ All of a sudden, my dedicated practice, convictions, and sense of spaciousness around "being the change" evaporated into thin, toxic air.
- ○ I started to have serious doubts about our ability to make any meaningful social and racial justice strides as a global human family.
- ○ The future looked futile and bleak, because the most basic human rights—let alone the long list of unmet higher-level needs—of a large

segment of our BIPOC (Black, Indigenous, and People of Color) relatives were still rampantly violated.

- Anti-Black injustices in particular were occurring on a widespread, blatant, and systemic level. Their diminished health, nutrition, and resources were the reason why disproportionately more Black people were susceptible to COVID-19 and dying during the pandemic.
- Donald Trump's divide-and-conquer tactics and propaganda—the racist subtext of MAGA, Make America Great Again, his overt and covert undermining of policies, positions, and programs that support inclusion, diversity, and racial equity, and his dog whistles to white supremacists and QAnon supporters during tragic moments like these—were exasperating and becoming a dangerous pandemic in their own right alongside COVID-19.

MY TIPPING POINT

The resurgence of the BLM movement gave me the courage to reach the boiling point that I'd been avoiding. When every cell in my body culminated into a hard "No!" from one day to the next, it registered how much fear and extra baggage I'd been carrying. It was the hard stop and clear limit I didn't dare to set, despite being given many opportunities to do so while steeped in some form of anti-racism work since 1990. I never realized how much I was still haggling with fear and self-doubt that hadn't composted. These are some of the issues that were lingering in some far corner of my mind and blocking my fullest potential:

- I was afraid to take a fierce, uncompromising stand against anti-Black racism and confront the most charged social injustices head-on because of inherited persecution fear.
- I indulged a knee-jerk protective reflex that signaled that I'd be in danger and targeted if I came out of hiding and became more visible to an omniscient, invisible enemy.
- I was continuously adjusting my inner climate, expectations, and strategies by subconsciously catering to an external social climate that was always in flux, in charge, and used to monopolizing shared spaces.

○ The worldviews of those around me and the perceived threat that they posed to my inner safety shaped my behavior and unconscious thoughts, biases, and assumptions more significantly than I wanted to admit.

While my harmonizing talent has been a valuable asset in many contexts, it compromised my ability to anchor in my core values and protect my energy, soul, and integrity as well as they needed to be. This diminished my inner strength and wellness, and made it harder to remain focused on my mission and push the envelope further.

THE THINGS I CANNOT ACCEPT

Angela Davis challenged my take on things and helped me to up the ante with her battle cry: "I am no longer accepting the things I cannot change. I'm changing the things I cannot accept." For thirty years, I'd invested the bulk of my energy into who was ready to change and on what seemed manageable to tackle, just as the original serenity prayer suggested. Despite doing lots of good and powerful work this way, this approach didn't challenge white privilege nor my own—enough. Something continued to feel off within myself. How could it not, when considering the parts of our collective human body that are still riddled with pain and neglected every single day? BIPOC, and in particular Black and Indigenous people, continue to experience a disproportionately high degree of police brutality and murder, and poor access to adequate housing, education, nutrition, transportation, social support, and medical care; and they have extraordinarily high rates of incarceration, poverty, domestic instability, violence, substance abuse, and mental and physical health issues that are already disadvantaging future generations and setting them up for repeat. Those at the margins and most stuck in harmful situations will remain oppressed, and those driving the inequities for profit and selfish gains will remain in power and do harm for far too long, even if I and others do meaningful work that doesn't really get to the collective root of the problem. Complacency and privilege allow many of us to remain in denial and ignore these very disturbing facts because they're not causing us daily pain and frustrations. We can remain comfortably padded and sandwiched here for a few more generations if we don't dig deeper in understanding our contribution to these long-standing problems.

DAILY ANTI-RACISM ACTIVISM

It needs to become increasingly more clear that we either (1) endorse default racist claims and ingrained assumptions that entire groups of people are responsible for their own demise and driven by negative, self-defeating, or culturally or biologically inferior influences or intentions, or (2) recognize that those of us in historically dominant positions or with greater access to privileges, power, and resources are failing them on a daily basis while deliberately, obliviously, or quietly benefiting from our one-up position and hence their one-down status. Becoming an anti-racist activist requires taking a hard look at our past and our racist origins to dispel our modern-day myths and assumptions about the nature of reality, and to face the deceptive and destructive path that we've been on. Resmaa Menakem, racialized trauma specialist, healer, and *New York Times* best-selling author of *My Grandmother's Hands: Racialized Trauma and the Pathway to Mending Our Hearts and Bodies,* has us focus on two kinds of pain and coping patterns—"clean pain" and "dirty pain"—especially while navigating this tricky racialized terrain. This is how he differentiates clean pain (higher-self inspired) from dirty pain (lower-self inspired): "Healing trauma involves recognizing, accepting, and moving through pain—clean pain. By walking into that pain, experiencing it fully, and moving through it, you metabolize and put an end to it.... The alternative paths of avoidance, blame, and denial are paved with dirty pain. When people respond from their most wounded parts and choose dirty pain, they create more of it, both for themselves and for other people."[1] It is through dirty pain that we develop emotional problems and mental disorders. It's also the root cause of scapegoating, white supremacy, violence, and our long history of covert systemic racism, founded on centuries of overt racist brutality that has not been able to properly compost because of our ingrained and pervasive dirty pain patterns. The only way for us to come up with root solutions is by excavating the dark secrets and skeletons that we've dumped in mass graves or just left to rot without proper burials. We hold all of this denied history and suffering in our bodies and souls. Opening the channels of communication between them is what will alchemize them into a higher form and ultimately release them out of our bodies. Resmaa says, "Somatic Abolitionism is a living, embodied anti-racism practice and culture building that requires endurance, agility, resource cultivation, stamina, and discernment."[2]

CHAPTER 4

All Men Are Created Equal

But Not All Men, Let Alone All Genders, Are Treated as Equals

I never doubted that equal rights was the right direction. Most reforms, most problems are complicated. But to me there is nothing complicated about ordinary equality.

—ALICE PAUL

What's the problem with being "not racist"? It is a claim that signifies neutrality: "I am not a racist, but neither am I aggressively against racism." One either allows racial inequities to persevere, as a racist, or confronts racial inequities, as an antiracist.

—IBRAM X. KENDI

In writing the Declaration of Independence, Thomas Jefferson, enslaver of more than six hundred people and owner of several plantations,[3] proclaimed that "We hold these truths to be self-evident: that all men are created equal; that they are endowed by their Creator with certain unalienable rights; that among these are life, liberty, and the pursuit of happiness." He thought that it was powerful enough of a claim to ultimately end slavery. We all know how that went down. This proclamation was fought tooth and nail for nearly a century until it resulted in outright war. Roughly 750,000 Americans died in the Civil War, a fight that was, at its core, about granting Black Americans their equality—their voting rights, power, resources, possessions, culture, respect, and freedoms—versus continuing to exploit them for self-gain through racist institutions—slavery—and beliefs that justified their inferior status. Abolitionist Thomas Day, a transformation trailblazer of his time, was baffled by the widespread cognitive dissonance and denial that existed in 1776. Today, he would probably be considered a "radical social liberal" for pointing out the obvious: "If there be an object truly ridiculous in nature, it is an American patriot, signing resolutions of independency with the one hand, and with the other brandishing a whip over his affrighted slaves."[4] Even religious leaders endorsed white supremacist ideologies and racist practices while simultaneously and hypocritically preaching about peace and love. Some claimed that Black people were the cursed descendants of Ham, and therefore cursed forever into enslavement. Or they would claim that according to science, ethnology, or biology, Black people by nature were destined to slavery and servility. That this was God's will and nature's law, which absolved white slave masters of their savage mistreatment of people purely because of the color of their skin.

LIP SERVICE AND LOFTY IDEALS

In 1975, in an essay marking the approach of the nation's bicentennial, the eminent historian John Hope Franklin accused the Founding Fathers of "betraying the ideals to which they gave lip service … human bondage and human dignity were not as important to them as their own political and economic independence."[5] That America's founders gave lip service to their ideals in order to amass more wealth, land, and political power—above all in regard to the subject of race—is an enduring charge. Generations of political leaders followed suit and, to this day, discard these ideals in exchange for more wealth, land, and political clout. There has been a lot of speculation that Indigenous cultures and values influenced the lofty ideals that America took full credit for but could not live up to. Jerry D. Stubben examined the research presented by the critics and proponents of the Indigenous influence theory. In 2000, he wrote in the *Social Science Quarterly* journal, "This research analyzes the writings of historians and other scholars involved in the study of the indigenous influence theory, the writings and speeches of sixteenth- to eighteenth-century European political philosophers, the founding fathers, and indigenous peoples, and government documents. The scholarly debate has gone beyond proving that indigenous societies did influence the development of American democratic norms, values, and institutions to defining the degree of such influence."[6] Jefferson was indeed fascinated with Native cultures and languages, spending his spare time studying and reading about them. He believed Native American peoples to be a noble race who were "in body and mind equal to the white man."[7] Nevertheless, like many of his contemporaries, he believed that Native Americans were culturally and technologically inferior because they didn't exploit and take private possession of their ancestral land.

EUROPEAN PATRIARCHY AND ENTITLEMENT

Jefferson and European settlers and colonizers (many were political and religious refugees escaping poverty, persecution, disease, and misery at the bottom of the social ladder back home) felt entitled to take over the Natives' lands. They either assumed that the Natives "had plenty" or that these were public lands up for grabs because they were unmarked and unfenced. Their motives and attempts at emulating all that's "cultured," "civilized," and more advanced—their appreciation for the value of individual land and accruing wealth—were influenced by what they had endured at the hands of feudal warlords, religious tyrants, and rich aristocrats who'd oppressed them in the Old World.

Because of racist white supremacy norms, it didn't even register at that time that the empty democratic ideals and proclamations that were copied and portrayed as America's foundational backbone sounded empty and ridiculous amid slavery, colonial fervor, and pillaging of Indigenous life and land. Under the guise of "expanding civilization," the fury to acquire land, widen borders, and either enslave or eradicate "Native savages" or convert them to Christianity incited centuries of violence and death. Fewer than 300,000 Native people remained in the 1890s of what was once a vibrant population of 12–15 million, perhaps even more. The biggest killers were smallpox, measles, influenza, whooping cough, diphtheria, typhus, bubonic plague, cholera, and scarlet fever, killing off entire communities and villages in excruciatingly devastating ways. All of these diseases were brought over by European colonizers. As horrific as this was, the brutal savagery inflicted on Native tribes by early colonizers was much worse. Throughout the "500-year war," which some call the American Indian Holocaust or the Native American Genocide, Native people were subjected to more than 1,500 wars, attacks, and raids.[8] Hundreds of men, women, and children were tortured and murdered at a time. Most of these massacres were authorized by the US government.

NOT TAKING RESPONSIBILITY FOR OUR BARBARIC PAST

Pulitzer Prize–winning historian and Harvard educator Bernard Bailyn, who died at age ninety-seven, spent most of his life meticulously reinterpreting and clarifying America's blurred and barbaric early history. He has no qualms calling the countless massacres and ruthless obliterations of Native Americans a genocide. In his last book, *The Barbarous Years*, he portrays the 1600s as a grand drama in which the glimmers of enlightenment barely surpassed the rampant savagery. "Nobody sat around erasing this history, but it's forgotten," he said during an interview with Ron Rosenbaum from the *Smithsonian Magazine*. "Conveniently?" Ron asked him. "Yes," he agrees. "Look at the 'peaceful' Pilgrims. Our William Bradford. He goes to see the Pequot War battlefield and he is appalled. He said, 'The stink' [of heaps of dead bodies] was too much." "The ferocity of that little war is just unbelievable," Bailyn says. "The butchering that went on cannot be explained by trying to get hold of a piece of land. They were really struggling with this central issue for them, of the advent of the Antichrist."[9]

The majority of Americans don't know what occurred on that dreadful day in 1637 near present-day Groton, Connecticut. According to William B. Newell, a Penobscot Indian and former chairman of the anthropology department of the University of Connecticut, more than seven hundred men, women, and children of the Pequot Tribe had gathered for their annual Green Corn Dance, their Thanksgiving celebration. In the predawn hours, the sleeping Indians were surrounded by English and Dutch mercenaries—religious refugees escaping persecution—who ordered them to come outside. Those who came out were shot or clubbed to death while the terrified women and children who huddled inside the longhouse were burned alive. John Winthrop, the governor of the Massachusetts Bay Colony of about a thousand Puritan refugees, declared this next day "A Thanksgiving Day … For the next 100 years, every Thanksgiving Day ordained by a governor was in honor of the bloody victory, thanking God that the battle had been won."[10] Many of these massacres, including this one, didn't involve "any battle" or resistance.

IT'S TIME FOR TRUTHSGIVING

I wonder if we will sound as ridiculous to our descendants 250 years from now for making the claim "All men are created equal" while mindlessly partaking in hurtful and racist traditions and practices that portray huge cognitive dissonance, denial, and blindspots that we don't see or refuse to see. Indigenous activist Christine Nobiss coined and introduced the concept "Truthsgiving"[11] to dispel the lies and myths about our past, including the real story and meaning behind our most celebrated and observed holiday in the United States, Thanksgiving. Over the decades and centuries, our whitewashed minds and colonized bodies have learned to reject our own inner wisdom and intimate connections to ancestral pain and truths in favor of patriotic and sanitized stories that willfully omit or distort the facts. So much has been obscured and diffused in history books that sobering and important facts about the most heinous of human rights violations and war crimes that were primarily orchestrated and financed by European countries, royalty, missionaries, colonists, slave owners, and slave traffickers—such as the Native American Genocide and the trafficking, enslavement, exploitation, and torture of 12 million African people over hundreds of years, involving 45,000 horrific transatlantic voyages to the Americas—are still swept under the rug. Conveniently forgetting these horrors is irresponsible, racist, and privileged, but intentionally erasing them takes white supremacy and entitlement to a whole other level.

DELIBERATELY ERASING AND ATTACKING HISTORICAL WORKS

According to historian Bailyn, no one was deliberately attempting to erase our treacherous history: it was just conveniently forgotten … until Donald Trump arrived at the scene. He not only attempted to erase historical facts and truths that are crucial to those who've been lied to for centuries. He blatantly refuted them as untruths, slandering educational programs as toxic and divisive just months after criticizing and falsely portraying BLM protesters as antifa (anti-fascist) domestic terrorists who are trying to stir unrest and trouble. In September 2020, he specifically attacked the *New York Times'* 1619 Project, a Pulitzer Prize–winning endeavor by Nikole Hannah-Jones. Her goal was to cast a spotlight on the 400th anniversary of the first slave ship arriving in America and to illuminate how the legacy of slavery continues to impact our daily lives. According to Trump, her 1619 Project "warped" the American story. He claimed that the country's early foundational reliance on slave labor and the longtime disenfranchisement of racial minorities is a "web of lies" and that teaching it is "child abuse." He also called curriculum on race a "crusade against American history" and "toxic propaganda," an "ideological poison that, if not removed, will dissolve the civic bonds that tie us together" and "will destroy our country."[12] He threatened to cut funding to California schools that teach the 1619 Project and ordered the crackdown on federal anti-racism training, calling it "anti-American." During the closing days of his administration, he fulfilled his promise to issue a report that promotes a "patriotic education" about race and the birth of the nation. He released "The 1776 Report," on Martin Luther King Jr. Day no less, to refute teachings on systemic racism, critical race theory, and deeper examinations of how slavery has affected American society.

VIOLENT ATTEMPTS TO PRESERVE OUR RACIST PAST

According to Dr. Jonathan Holloway, president of Rutgers University, historian, and author of *The Cause of Freedom: A Concise History of African Americans*:

> Many of the insurrectionists who stormed the Capitol on Jan. 6 were driven by a belief that they were acting in accord with the principles fashioned at the birth of this country, that their protest embodied America's long history of patriotic rhetoric about freedom and citizenship.... This patriotic rhetoric fundamentally ignores centuries of efforts to make sure that only certain people are protected by the nation's laws, and that Black Americans, even if freed from slavery, remain second class citizens. Even for abolitionists who believed that slavery was a sin, the breadth of what was meant by freedom for enslaved Africans was a deeply contested idea."[13]

These ingrained, contentious, and ongoing power struggles and debates involving the lives and concerns of BIPOC—nowadays concealed as a political game and sport between dueling parties, especially when on campaign trails—emerged in full glory during the Capitol siege to "Stop the Steal," the alleged stolen election. This also explained the Republican senators' complicated relationship to their party, and their acquittal of Donald Trump, who'd been impeached for spreading the lies and inciting the insurrection. None of these events happened in a vacuum. And neither do the many incidents of anti-Black police brutality and the disproportionate imprisonment of Black people, for that matter. They are all the result of racist tension between two forces caught in an epic battle in the United States between "domination and privileges for a few" (white, heteronormative cis-males enjoying but denying others most of these privileges, now claiming that their freedoms are under attack, i.e., their historical position of dominance and superiority is at risk of getting toppled) versus "freedom and equality for all" (the opposing party trying to live up to the founders' claims of equality yet barely able to do so).

RACIST MADNESS ON STEROIDS

In just four years, Trump injected steroids into dormant racist madness and molded the party into a cult of personality, one likely to leave a long shadow in the historical record. Especially in the Senate, where smaller, rural states have had disproportionately more representation of white voters, his prominent influence can be curbed only by a deep understanding that our long-standing denial of our buried racist history has contributed to this frightening rise of deranged power. The demand of a growing majority to live up to 1776 democratic claims in the twenty-first century—thanks to the BLM movement—has significantly threatened the alternate reality of Trump and the members of a patriarchal, white supremacist universe. Political pundits have claimed that Trump has "majorly failed" because he received a much lower popular vote than Biden. They argue that the seven million vote gap is the biggest it has been in most prior presidential elections. It's all a matter of perspective. The nearly seventy-five million votes he did receive are the second biggest number of votes ever received by a presidential candidate, which is shocking, given what he openly stands for. Recent polls are no longer interested in what the majority of Americans think, but what the members of each party believe.[14] They've consistently shown that 80–90 percent of his followers and political pawns believe or support his boldest, most calculated, and transparent lies, regardless of how robust the counterevidence and contradicting facts are (these numbers are slowly dwindling).

NOW WHAT? NEITHER THE EMPEROR NOR HIS GROWING BASE ARE WEARING CLOTHES

It's one thing for everyone to pretend that the emperor has no clothes. It's another when almost half of the population is now also walking around naked, convinced to be wearing clothes and waiting for his return. All the legal elections and votes in the world won't make such a society a true democracy. We've reached the mother of crossroads and need to summon all of our power, clarity, and soul authority to inspire as many of our fellow brothers and sisters toward truth and out of the trenches of deception and manipulation. White supremacists getting officially elected to key posts by aggressive constituents is not just one party's problem—it's our collective problem. It took Hitler more than a decade to radicalize enough people and position them in key posts. Of course our situation is not the same, but it is similar enough for us to be aware of and concerned about what may be brooding behind the scenes and in the sewers. Today, it is as crucial as ever for all of us to cultivate the health, well-being, and integrity of all of our citizens and voters so they are in the best psychological position to choose their leaders wisely. Trump drove deep wedges in existing family conflicts and splits. His vitriol didn't only get to strangers from opposing parties who lived in either blue states or red states and could conveniently avoid each other if they desired. Almost all of my clients experienced painful fallouts and deep ruptures within their immediate families and close social circles during his presidency. Although the conflicts that tore them apart were there before (and mostly hinged around social justice–related topics: sexual assault, misogyny, nonconforming gender identity, homophobia, Islamophobia, racism, etc.), Trump fueled and fanned manageable flickers and transformational flames into raging fires and impenetrable firewalls during his presidency, and has added mask wearing, pandemic denial, absurd conspiracy theories, and mind control to the list of work, family, and friend strife. It will require all of us to salvage and repair what's left of our bonds and social fabric and especially support the brave trailblazers and change agents who are invested in the truth and in creating authentic bipartisan partnerships.

DONE WITH THE "FREE SPEECH" KOAN

May our nation's "one man, one vote" and "all men are created equal" empty democratic promises start to sound more problematic and hypocritical to all of us each passing day. Similarly, may racist brands, discriminatory policies, problematic propaganda, and conspiracy theories become more apparent and aversive to an awakening anti-racist majority. We've treated right-wing groups—e.g., the Proud Boys, and what they stand for—like a "free speech" koan. We've struggled to see clearly that those accustomed to privilege will experience equal rights as an impingement on their freedoms. They've trapped us time and again into analysis paralysis, afraid to trust our inner wisdom that it makes no sense for a political party or a president to rely on the support of, or openly support, extremists, domestic terrorists, and white supremacy groups in a nation that claims to be a democracy. Their slipperiness and offensive verbal acrobatics are getting more refined. Our confusion each time we are accused of wrongdoing helped to make it possible for these groups to wave their Confederate flags and display coded white supremacy and neo-Nazi symbols in plain sight, so they can do what they do best: wiggle through loopholes, exploit our democracy's weakest links, and embolden others, including influential supporters in powerful media positions, to employ their methods and argue that the freedom of speech clause of the First Amendment allows them to share their oppressive opinions. This misses the point of freedom of speech altogether: to protect the freedom and rights of all.

POLITICAL YO-YOING VERSUS SECURING A CIVIL RIGHTS BEDROCK ACROSS PARTIES

During the first hours of his presidency, Joe Biden overturned more than a dozen executive orders, many that undermined the civil rights of ethnic, racial, and sexual minorities during the Trump administration—e.g., he nixed "The 1776 Report," revoked the Keystone XL pipeline, abolished the Muslim ban, banned discrimination against LGBT and nonbinary employees, protected the Deferred Action for Childhood Arrivals (DACA) program, and proposed legislation making Dreamers eligible for citizenship. It was a statement that clearly showed where the main political divisions lie between our two parties.

Despite the great relief that Biden's reversals brought to many, we won't make real progress if the civil rights of BIPOC and other marginalized groups keep yo-yoing and being toyed with every time we change administrations and party leadership. Putting the civil rights of BIPOC on the chopping block—either blatantly or through coded terms, policies, and promises that boost white privileges and power, e.g., voter suppression—is racist. This bar is far too low in terms of diversity, inclusion, and racial equality standards. Treating BIPOC and other marginalized groups like equals means no longer treating our birth rights and civil rights as negotiable points of discussion. It means becoming more aware of painful undercurrents, dog whistles, and hidden jabs that deliberately poke into ancestral wounds and unhealed trauma each time our lives and rights are politically partied with, and not falling for the gaslighting that conveniently blurs and muddles past and present racism, white privilege, and inequities during these duels and debates. BIPOC are not only incensed and put in their second-class place by the harmful messages and energy that are sent out each time. The fact that this happens under so many oblivious noses is shocking. It's also frustrating to see so much privilege and power not being put to good use while others with so much less are scrambling around every day to squeeze every drop out of the driest lemons to catalyze change. Our ancestors, not just the ancestors of BIPOC, are not at peace. The racist practices and deranged beliefs that robbed them of their true freedom, well-being, joy, authenticity, and dignity are a sore point, but the shackles that still enslave all of our minds and hearts are a bigger one. They will keep rattling our cages and blaring their sirens until we wake up and take action.

RESTORING OUR SACRED INTERCONNECTEDNESS

Our trust in humanity, the truth, and our sacred connections with each other, our ancestors, and nature will be restored when we are no longer neglecting and harming any marginalized group. The civil rights of disenfranchised groups of people can no longer remain the brand of one political party and the butt of a joke of another. Meeting on higher, not just common, ground means coming up with innovative ways to set limits with unmetabolized trauma patterns within and outside of ourselves and dissolve ingrained and unjust social norms. The actualization of our egalitarian ideals is no small task but is possible as long as we allow guiding truths to lead the way. Our shared desire, focus, and determination to grant liberty, justice, and equity to all can be a powerful enough soul authority force, if exercised, to move the needle in significant ways during this optimal time for global transformation and consciousness shifting.

Start the journey by daring to be more authentic and present. It will open the doors to your highest truth. Once this power takes deep root in your body-mind, it will be impossible to contain it. Your clarity and integrity will inspire new anti-discriminatory policies and practices in family, work, school, political, and church environments, where soulful and holistic living, radical acceptance, clear boundaries, and compassion will eventually get adopted as a foundational baseline. Public opinion influences CEOs, NGO directors, politicians, investors, bankers, philanthropists, small donors, journalists, and consumers on a daily basis, and helps them to decide where and how to spend their dollars, days, time, and energy. The more people agree and laser in on what is unacceptable, the greater our success in replacing oppressive practices and policies with programs and solutions that promote racial healing, social justice, diversity, and inclusion. We are natural-born leaders and consciousness pioneers, continuously scouting what a socially and environmentally healthy planet needs in order to freely breathe and exhale for generations to come. Our biggest gift to the world is our unshakable commitment to our well-being and wholeness, and our hard-earned knowledge that all benefit when our mind, body, heart, and soul are in alignment.

CHAPTER 5

Making a Bigger Impact

Freeing the Canaries and Closing the Coal Mines
(for Good!)

> *And the day came when the risk to remain tight in a bud was more painful than the risk it took to blossom.*
>
> —ANAÏS NIN

> *When I dare to be powerful to use my strength in the service of my vision, then it becomes less and less important whether I am afraid.*
>
> —AUDRE LORDE

After I'd established a higher baseline for myself, I could not imagine guiding the "canaries in the coal mines"—the transformation agents and sensitive wise souls I work with—in the same way I had before. I slightly panicked, as just calling my tribe "canaries in coal mines" had in the past been very effective in empowering them. It was a major upgrade compared to being perceived, and often perceiving ourselves, as the black sheep and troublemakers in our families and circles. My practice was finally running smoothly. It had taken considerable blood, sweat, and tears to integrate my unconventional shamanic methods with conventional psychotherapeutic interventions and to openly share these in professional spaces. I was really enjoying the ease and magical flow of this plateau. What was being asked of me now?

MY DENIAL AND COMPLACENCY

It takes tremendous courage to summon and ask our guides and higher self if they agree whether or not our behavior, our systems, our policies, and our company cultures are aligned or if they are another iteration of the racist, offensive, and pervasive denial that we've inherited. The many shiny objects that seduce us these days have no mercy on our monkey minds. Depleted and foggy, we fall prey to denial and complacency that sound like this whenever more is asked of us:

- I can barely keep my head above the water. I really can't put anything else on my plate. I'm doing so much. This is someone else's mission.
- I'm emotionally overwhelmed and practicing setting healthy limits. I don't have the bandwidth and energy to help, and frankly I need to heal and help myself and my family first. We're always in some kind of crisis.
- I can't imagine being of any use. What can I possibly offer that will change social problems that are so ingrained and pervasive?
- I don't want to risk getting publicly attacked and humiliated. I don't have what it takes to deal with this aggressive nonsense. I need my daily peace and sanity.

That was me too. I was doing so much already. I didn't want to risk destabilizing the delicate balance that I'd finally mastered by fiddling with my formula. The truth is: we are all harmed by these excuses. The more we fret about them, the more we energize and materialize them. We gaslight ourselves by trying to talk, medicate, or numb our bodies and souls out of their true callings. We can keep avoiding these truths, but our symptoms will succeed in exposing our self-deception. It's hard to accept that we can't outsmart mystery and that it will always have the last word. Our symptoms are nature's way of attempting a coup and inspiring a paradigm shift in our daily routines: they are not a sign to fortify our resistance to change but a cue to stop and take stock.

THE REVOLUTIONARY REFRAME

We are often bearers of the "family's cross" because of our sensitive nature. That means that we end up struggling the most with psychological symptoms and emotional conflict that the rest of the family prefers to push underground. If we are not adequately supported when young, we're likely to become the "identified patient" in the family system and in many subsequent systems where we end up playing the same familiar roles. Parents, neighbors, relatives, and friends often don't get why we find it so important to confront and integrate painful memories and emotions that they have learned to dodge and tiptoe around. We see the problems and feel the pain that these unresolved issues cause, and we know that they won't disappear by themselves. Those who'd rather "let bygones be bygones" and prefer to "keep the peace" believe that we are making mountains out of molehills and creating problems that aren't there. They may view us as crybabies, weirdos, hypochondriacs, and rebels without a cause, or as crazy, troubled, demanding, overreactive, hypersensitive, and difficult to deal with, depending on how invested and forceful they are in keeping their own vulnerability and emotions off-limits and at bay. Even teachers, mental health providers, psychiatrists, and psychotherapists may pathologize and misdiagnose us rather than offer us validation, tools, and skills that empower us. Many helping professionals have been taught and trained, as I was, to look at presenting problems through an individualistic lens and downplay contextual, holistic, or transpersonal influences—such as being a sensitive soul trapped in an "unhealthy coal mine" and unable to share your true self. This oversight is unfortunate, because many of us—when able to reframe our inner sense of "black sheep" as "scapegoat"—realize that we've been unwittingly carrying our family's or ancestors' fears, unrealized dreams, confusion, and dis-ease and no longer need to. This change in perspective can create an instant reset and dramatic soul shift.

LOYAL TO A FAULT

These are the answers that I received in response to my earlier question on how to step up my game. Being devoted to the truth doesn't mean that we are obligated to bear our family's crosses or carry other people's karma and baggage. As one of my clients so poignantly said, *we can care without carrying* other people's issues and heavy loads. We will become more effective in our missions by no longer making knee-jerk sacrifices that harm our health and well-being. Like canaries, we have an unwavering zest for life. *Canaries keep on singing, even when caged and stuck in a dark coal mine.* There is an uncanny resemblance between their disposition and the disposition of the human canaries I guide, myself included. Our hardiness, resilience, and direct access to innate joy and truth definitely have advantages, but the disadvantages of this disposition are that it makes us more prone to inner climate denial and dissociation patterns. Our quick-to-ignite joy and compassion for others tend to drown out and diffuse personal warming signals, healthy boundaries, and self-protection. In times past, when toxic gases in the coal mines reached dangerous levels, the canaries stopped singing, got ill, and died. This signaled to the coal miners that they needed to exit the premises right away. Canaries supposedly lived short but "important and meaningful lives." Of course, only important and meaningful to those who consciously and intentionally used them for these purposes. They were greatly appreciated for making (being forced to make) this sacrifice, and although this is a step up from not being appreciated at all, we can do better, and we did do better. Today, modern carbon dioxide detectors have replaced these canaries, sparing their lives, and allowing them to enjoy their freedom in the wild instead of being cooped up and living their days in a cage in a dark coal mine.

OUTGROWING THE ULTIMATE COMPLIMENT

Is there enough wild nature left in us to want to live, uncaged, in a world free of coal mines (this question is for both the canaries and the miners)? Or have we become too domesticated, complacent, and inhibited to desire and imagine what that would be like? When my clients think of themselves as canaries called to heal symptoms that can shed light on humanity's problems, it heightens their sense of soul purpose and determination. They'd suspected all along that their suffering hadn't been in vain but had helped them to grow, come into their own, and make rewarding and meaningful contributions based on what they learned and shared. Helping others overcome similar challenges was at one time the ultimate compliment. I never anticipated that I'd ever feel this way but the idea of being a "canary in a coal mine"—within social systems and among people who are, willingly or unwittingly, exploiting us to avoid facing the natural consequences associated with their imbalanced and often exploitative behavior—now evokes a hard "No!" in me and clarity that this is far from a compliment or an honor. The time has come for us to outgrow our canary pride. I often hear from my clients—who are sensitive to accusations of victimhood—that they are not thinking any of these things or feeling any canary pride. On the contrary, they are sick and tired of being in so much pain.

Our conscious ego-mind could be thinking one thing and not be aware of what's happening at much deeper emotional, energetic, and physical levels. When these deeper parts have been shut off, and symptoms are the only truth-carrying parts that remain, they are unwilling to give up the messages and consciousness embedded in them unless we're willing to entertain root solutions. There is a way to stop this unnecessary pain and suffering. Just as the use of actual canaries has long been banned, the time has come for us, human canaries, to become an outdated concept. Wouldn't it be wonderful if we too could enjoy being free and wild? Instead of being harmed first to provide proof of dangerous practices, how about we become trusted informants? We're more than capable of effectively conveying, in clear language, what toxic social conditions, dynamics, and enterprises to avoid and why, without giving ourselves up as test subjects. We've got plenty of life experience that we can draw from.

TESTED BY TRUMP'S RALLY IN TULSA

Barely two weeks after the murder of George Floyd, Donald Trump announced that he planned to hold a rally, his first one since the pandemic broke out, on Juneteenth in Tulsa, of all places, the burgeoning Black Wall Street in 1921 where as many as three hundred Black people were killed by mobs of white people. Many considered this political move "almost blasphemous," "outrageous," "a slap in the face," and "insulting," given that Juneteenth (June 19) was a holiday commemorating the day enslaved people in the western portion of the Confederacy finally gained their freedom.[1] Russell Cobb, associate professor of Spanish and Latin American Studies at the University of Alberta, stated that "a Trump rally near a site of a race massacre during a global pandemic already sounded like a recipe for a dangerous social experiment."[2] Add to that the calculated timing, the heightened raw emotions of BLM protesters, and the message that this was sending: know your place, because history could easily repeat itself if BLM protesters were to partake in a "Black uprising."[3] A news article with a false allegation that a Black man had tried to rape a white woman, and a write-up entitled "To Lynch Negro Tonight," led to the Tulsa Race Massacre of 1921. The racial climate in June 2020 was similarly on edge and wouldn't require much provocation to result in violence. After significant protest, the Trump administration decided to move the rally to June 20. To my shock and dismay, there were some influential Black public figures who praised Trump for this decision. Burgess Owens insisted that "Tulsa is the right place, and the day after Juneteenth is the right time, for this rally. It's a celebration of the tenacity, work ethic, faith and entrepreneurial grit of an African-American community that has overcome both white racism and liberal paternalism to achieve economic independence. Let the rally begin."[4] Owens is a former Super Bowl champion with the Oakland Raiders, the US Representative (Republican) for Utah's Fourth Congressional District, and the author of *Liberalism: Or, How to Turn Good Men into Whiners, Weenies, and Wimps.* His book title cleared up my initial shock but not my dismay. The only light around this sinister event was that it was sparsely attended by fewer than seven thousand, because TikTok teens and K-pop stans registered for thousands of tickets and didn't show up,[5] making the boasting about the million-plus people supposedly attending sound even more ridiculous.

This unfathomably vile move majorly tripped me up. I could sense all the ancestors turning in their graves. Despite a burning desire to unleash all my feelings and thoughts about this situation, I tried equally hard to dim my inner fire and pass on the torch. It was much easier and less risky to sit back and let others who were eager to lead the way and show the rest of us their new anti-racist protocols, reading lists, daily, weekly, and monthly calendars, mission statements, petitions, reading lists, dialogue guidelines, and criteria for becoming a committed BLM anti-racist activist. They had teams of staff and support to get this all in place quickly and were doing a great job. Until they weren't. When similar patterns of white privilege and my own inner drama around this (criticizing from the sidelines instead of stepping up to the plate) started to play out, I took a hard look at how I was contributing to the dynamics. I reminded myself of one of the most important life lessons from Audre Lorde: Your silence will not protect you. How could I criticize the silent majority if I didn't speak up myself? I decided that hiding behind the scenes and holding back weren't going to be an option. Once I opened the floodgates, there was almost no stopping me. My soul had been waiting for this moment and was eager to revisit many topics that were so much more timely now than decades ago when I first researched and wrestled with them. Everything that I'd bottled up began to flow out of me and into this piece about Juneteenth and Trumpism.

JUNETEENTH VERSUS KETI KOTI

Happy Juneteenth. In Suriname, we call this holiday Keti Koti. Cutting of the chains. It has been celebrated since the abolition of slavery on July 1, 1863, but has been a national holiday since July 1, 1963. A statue of the runaway slave Kwakoe was erected that day in the center of Paramaribo to commemorate the hundred-year anniversary of the abolition of slavery. I think it's important to imagine what life could have been like for you and others if Juneteenth had been a national US holiday for sixty years.[6] What would it mean to be surrounded by statues, symbols, and monuments that celebrate this big day of freedom—instead of still arguing over Confederate symbols, flags, names of leaders, and statues that need to be removed from public and prominent spaces? Lines were getting drawn in the sand. On one side, a critical mass was acknowledging that white supremacy and institutionalized racism were alive and well within American society, and that it was high time for us to tackle them to the ground. On the opposite side, white backlash started to swell, amplified by its commander in chief. A few people unsubscribed from my list—fortunately, no nasty comments—most likely due to my taking a clear anti-racist stand, perceived as political (although I'm not the one conflating these). Or perhaps they left because I was still on the topic of racism, and they were ready to move on. The other extreme also happened. According to some of my online social entrepreneurial friends, businesses around them were collapsing for not taking a clear stand. They were being punished—many times by white followers—for not doing the "right thing." Harsh and impulsive, when no one had any clarity about what the "right thing" is or seemed to care. As long as we were doing something that made us feel better or added ammunition to the fight, all was good. That kind of cathartic explosion could unfortunately do more harm than good. It can feel these days as if we're navigating through a minefield, and any little thing—what you say or don't say, do or don't do—can blow up in your face. I know for sure that this is not transformational or helpful in the long run.

OVERNIGHT ANTI-RACIST "EXPERTS"

This kind of climate breeds overnight anti-racist "experts" who're leading the way and hitching their organization and business to the BLM movement to attract clients and gain support, even if they are total rookies on the subject. They're sometimes not even able to reference a single anti-racist book, podcast, or other resource, according to both a white client and a client of color who've been steeped in this work for years. On the flip side, you can feel all eyes on you if you're the only POC and are expected to take on the (often volunteer) role of diversity expert and share your perspectives on paper or in professional settings, on the spot (we can all learn from you and possibly run off with your best ideas without ever giving you credit …). Having teeth doesn't necessarily make you a dentist, and having your wisdom teeth pulled certainly doesn't qualify you to operate like an oral surgeon—implying that being a BIPOC doesn't make you an expert on the topic, anti-racist and anti-sexist educator Lasana Hotep explains.

Regardless, should you object to your volunteered role, you risk getting blamed for not being a team player but for being part of the problem. You can almost hear the accusations—"What is it that you people want?"—on the tip of someone's tongue. Perhaps it would have been blurted out if it weren't for the landmines.

THERE'S NO WINNING BECAUSE THE BAR IS SO LOW

How dare we not be grateful that we've finally got a critical mass to agree that losing Black lives due to police brutality is awful and needs to be stopped? Where is all this resentment, bitterness, apprehension, demand for more, and mistrust coming from? Why can't we all come together and unite for a change? Well ... isn't it a bit twisted and pathetic for a critical mass to finally agree that murder of Black Americans by excessive police force is wrong—in 2020? That this most basic human right is the big milestone to celebrate? And this milestone is by far not set in stone yet. We were starkly reminded of this by yet another cold-blooded police killing—of Rayshard Brooks—that occurred when protests sparked by the murders of George Floyd, Breonna Taylor, and Ahmaud Arbery had not even died down yet. How about equality in all areas of life? Health, financial security, professional success, representation, compensation, protection, and basic and sophisticated respect? *Are we ready to truly level the playing field and play fair? What stands in the way of our ability to share? Can we truly feel good about giving up some of our privileges, knee-jerk assumptions, and usual modes of operation—essentially, our usual sense of self—if that benefits a marginalized group?*

I've been doing a lot of reflecting on what it means to raise the racial equity bar for everyone, including myself. I've wondered what my reservations—in contrast to white leaders who have no qualms about yet again taking their comfortable place on top, whether new to a topic or not—about sharing my professional experiences and expertise in anti-racist discourse, research, and interventions for a good thirty years were all about. Some of these years involved compulsive rescuing; others involved very fulfilling work at a university counseling center and police department, facilitating multicultural immersion circles, workshops, and community-wide support of hate-crime prevention and interventions on race, ethnicity, religion, gender, sexual orientation, and all other relevant diversity-related topics. Undergrad and pre-doc interns, post-doc fellows, and I impacted thousands of students, staff, administrators, faculty, police, and community members, facilitating dialogue in residence halls, churches, classrooms, and conference rooms. We were first responders during intense times, like right after 9/11, but mostly focused on dismantling institutional and internalized racism day in, day out. We won several prestigious awards for this work, such as the Chancellor's Achievement Award and the Deanna Falge Award, a Staff Diversity and Affirmative Action Achievement Award. So it's not discomfort or a lack of confidence to shine or stand in my authority. It's something deeper that takes me back to my roots and my ancestors, and what inspired this work and journey to begin with.

It's not humility. It's about wisdom held in paradox, and nonpolarizing spiritual worldviews. Suriname has been called South America's hidden treasure by adventure travelers like Simon Romero in his *New York Times* article. He wrote, "Though I had been in the country only a few days, I felt as if I had traversed several continents and only now—drinking beer, shaking hands and striking up conversation with these men—was I getting a taste of Suriname's frontier."[7] He does an excellent job giving readers a taste of what it's like to live in a country that is ranked the second (along with Brazil and Belgium) most diverse in the world, following Benin, in a formal study: "The ranking was based around four overarching categories—cultural diversity, religious diversity, political diversity, and freedom for diversity—that incorporated such factors as the level of ethnic diversity; the number of immigrants; the number of languages spoken, religious beliefs and political parties; the level of religious freedom; LGBT rights and freedoms; and the level of personal freedom."[8]

RETRACING MY RACIALIZED AND RACIST ROOTS FOR DEEPER HEALING

I made my first pit stop at age twenty-seven in 1996, revisiting my headspace as a bushy-tailed third-year grad student in clinical psychology. I was specializing in multicultural psychology and had just written a scathing paper, "The Psychological Lynching of Multiracial People in the US." I sent it to Maria Root, PhD, leading researcher, writer, and national expert on the topic. It impressed her enough to agree to join my dissertation committee. My cross-national dissertation—researching historical race relations and the multiracial experiences of mixed people in the United States and Suriname—was quickly unfolding and taking me on an incredible journey. I'd decided that returning to my roots for stability and grounding was the only way I'd regain my mental health and soul authority. I'd explored all other options, and nothing was working. As a highly sensitive person of multiracial, multicultural, and multiethnic descent, I'd mastered swimming in and out of cultural streams and fish bowls throughout my childhood—intact and often celebrated. This was thanks to being born and raised in a culture where fluidly entering and exiting different social groups had become the mainstream and the norm (after up to six generations of primarily nonwhite racial mixing since the abolition of slavery in 1863, the descendants of white colonists made up only 1 percent of the population). I emigrated to the United States in 1983 at almost fourteen, and at the start of my dissertation research I had been here a good thirteen years. I was a quick learner and was ready to change strategy. I desperately needed to change strategy, and going back to my roots offered me the most promise. A sensitive and true canary, I had deeply internalized the gravity of white supremacy and race relations in the United States. The racist bullying and hatred had started within months after moving to Miami.

Six years later, my burning questions and insights had culminated in serious study. For years, I'd proceeded to either conduct my own research or contribute to several award-winning research projects at UC Davis, UC Berkeley, and the Pacific Graduate School of Psychology on race, ethnicity, gender, and class in relation to eating disorders, couples communication, emotional expression, suicide among Chinese Americans in San Francisco's Chinatown, bullying of Muslim children, and effective interventions with Black and Chicano SED (Severely Emotionally Disturbed) children in public schools. I'd counseled thousands of enlisted military of color at an Air Force Family Support Center, and had guided non-English-speaking and undocumented Chicano clients in East San Jose and low-income Black clients in East Palo Alto, areas known for lacking culturally sensitive mental health services. In my second year of grad school, I organized and led my school's Students of Color graduate group, and created eight student-run committees to reform our program's curriculum, attract students of color and reduce student attrition, hire faculty of color, do more community outreach, offer social support, improve communication, and more. I'd organized talks on race and race relations, put on a Color of Fear school-wide workshop, and founded a school newsletter, informing the school's board of directors, faculty, administrators, students, and president Allen Calvin about our challenges. He was responsive to my concerns, and was my biggest ally. He requested that copies of my newsletter be included in all the application packets that were sent out to new prospects. I was unstoppable and on a mission. But when I started to feel bugs crawl on my skin in bed at night and heard the ancestral drumming in my inner ear, I realized that even though all of my efforts and energy were making a difference, a big puzzle piece was missing.

ME AND MY SELF-CARE

As an academic, I'd learned that relying on my personal experiences and perspectives, and even using the pronoun "I," were taboo. It meant that we'd lost scientific objectivity. I'd been so entangled in this catch-22 trap that I couldn't see my way out of it. I was running in circles, doing all within my limited power to change a deeply ingrained system from the top down and from the outside in. I'd tried to change things from the inside out and from the bottom up, starting at the soul root level, as I'd learned from my ancestors, but felt repeatedly dismissed. I was perceived as a naive, idealistic, and young immigrant who just didn't get it. In America, only the tangible, physical, and material mattered, preferably in writing, policy, and law. It created a lot of self-doubt even though I knew darn well that I got the issues through and through. I got the complex racial dynamics that existed in my native Suriname *and* I got the complex historical and current race relations and inequities that existed in the United States. And even though I didn't get the intimately lived experience of every marginalized and racially oppressed person in the United States (which is not possible—not even people from our closest inner circle truly get our unique lived experience—it's their empathic abilities that you may be appreciating, and we all know what that feels like when they lack these), I had clear insight into the contextual and historical contributions of the racial mess we were in.

I also suspected that the historical contributions and solutions to systemic racism clarified by my dissertation research[9] in Suriname were so beyond the times and cultural zeitgeist that sharing them in 1998 would be even more provocative than now:

- The very low number of intact white families and married white women dramatically changed the hierarchical dynamics between Blacks and whites in a plantation colony that had a reputation of being one of the harshest in regard to its treatment of enslaved people. The growing power of escaped enslaved people who burned and terrorized plantations, and restored their culture and traditions by forming six separate tribes in the rainforest, was significant. They negotiated peace treaties after making Suriname an undesirable, treacherous region for future colonists.

- The integration of mixed children and freed Black women started in the mid- to late 1700s—recorded in church documents, baptisms, inheritance, land and property distributions, social events, government balls, and a legal marriage between a rich, educated free Black woman (daughter of a freed enslaved person, born in 1715) and a white colonist in 1767, two hundred years before antimiscegenation laws (prohibiting interracial marriage) were deemed unconstitutional by the US Supreme Court in 1967.

- There were no Jim Crow laws enforced after the abolition of slavery, no KKK or white supremacy groups, no brutal lynchings, hate-crimes, or vicious massacres of Blacks (close to four thousand total in the United States from 1882 to 1963); and there was more equal sharing of culture, music, language, religious values, and traditions that set the tone and stage for future immigrants and contract workers from China, Indonesia, and India who later joined this interdependent fabric and colorful and complex mix.

- Police presence, force, and brutality have consistently been very light and unfunded, and not used to keep Black people in line and subservient to racist law and order. There are no jails full of Black men and POC. But by no means a utopia, patterns of oppression appeared elsewhere. Military rule and violence peaked during sporadic periods of civil unrest and resistance (when my family left), following a multiethnic coup d'état in 1980 led by a military commander, Dési Bouterse, who ran the country from behind the scenes, changed the constitution, and was elected twice as president since then.[10] Unsuccessful in his divide-and-conquer politics in regard to the public, he was finally voted out in May 2020 after forty years of political corruption, plundering the national treasury, exploiting natural resources, drug trafficking, and being convicted of murder for giving orders to torture and execute fifteen multiethnic opposition leaders in 1982.

- Hierarchical values and cultural and religious superiority, most prominent within Hindustani and Chinese Surinamese groups, led to oppressive attitudes and behaviors within in-group members and between groups, portraying similar power plays involving privilege, stereotyping, and bigotry as in the United States. There was a greater focus on preserving cultural and religious purity than on preserving biological and racial purity, as is the case with white supremacy. My Chinese Hakka heritage familiarized me to the racist, elitist, patriarchal, and oppressive beliefs and hierarchical ranking that members within as well as outside of the in-group are subjected to.

- Even among other Caribbean nations, Suriname is heralded for being the most diverse and authentic in terms of the cultural expression of the unique ethnic groups that reside there. My dissertation data showed that this was not accidental: participants provided unprecedented research data by scoring *equally high* on horizontal individualism and horizontal collectivism scales and equally low on vertical scales. The United States scored the highest on scales measuring vertical individualism (most competitive, win-lose, either-or mentality, and the illusion of individual effort leading to fair rankings); and Japan, India, and China scored the highest on vertical collectivism (outright value ranking and worth based on birthright—caste, class, gender, prestige, status, racial purity, and roles within and between groups).

- The deep loss of culture and ethnic heritage among many white colonists and their descendants compared to their nonwhite Surinamese counterparts stood out. The same trend existed in the United States. The unresolved historical trauma and social oppression (religious crusades, public torture, feudalism, witch hunts, etc.) that led to this soul loss are embedded within Eurocentric either-or notions that pro-white = anti-nonwhite and other polarized notions of reality. This hierarchical pattern is woven into colonialism, imperialism, and the exploitation and domination of vulnerable people, their resources, and the natural world for one's own benefit, as if trying to band-aid or balm a deeply impoverished soul and inferiority complex. These tactics miss the point altogether and are ineffective. To heal an impoverished, hungry soul, it's important to first become aware of it. This is best done by stripping away addictions, privileges, and distractions, one by one, and embracing who emerges with curiosity and compassion.

FINAL ANALYSIS

Why is it that many people live in a chronic state of existential angst, fear (of poverty), and scarcity within one of the richest countries in the world? Right now, I'm not talking about the many BIPOC who actually live below the poverty line. I'm specifically addressing middle-class and upper-middle-class white families and BIPOC who either feel justified to protect their top-dog position, or do all that they can to obtain it, for an elusive sense of security that no one seems to harness. Some call it capitalism, but it's more complex than that. It's collective soul loss that has deep historical and cultural roots that require digging up and healing, because this one-upping and hierarchical mindset is what drives institutional racism, pecking-order anxiety, and white privilege. The ladder of success in American life is perceived to be fair by the groups and people who benefit the most from its setup. Rewards and privileges appear to be earned through honest-to-goodness effort, not through one's special status by birth, as is blatantly claimed in some hierarchically collectivistic cultures. This makes it difficult to acknowledge that privilege still operates in very similar ways, provided that for generations the start lines, resources, and obstacles along the way have been drastically different for different groups. The ones on top don't see the obstacles that they've been spared, and either truly don't get the problem, or feel relieved, entitled, and happy that they are on top and not on the bottom.

It seems nearly impossible to envision a whole different setup—with less compartmentalizing and more multicultural goodwill, spiritual abundance, and generosity—existing within Suriname, a third world country, because it challenges common overgeneralizations that the poorer the people, the more interracial conflict and competition will be stirred up. There are other confounding factors (e.g., vertical individualism) that cause this conflict and are in need of closer examination: Republicans, who envisioned that their trickle-down economic policies would distribute wealth across the board, were at least right about the trickle. For centuries, only a trickle of the wealth, material possessions, rights, privileges, and resources has gone to the descendants of ancestors who were worked to death to help build this country and make it what it is today. Imagine a different possibility than the trickle that maintains white supremacy and racial inequality: a coming together of diverse people, like in a beautiful orchestra, where each musician could play without reservation, was appreciated and fairly compensated, and never needed to worry about stepping on others' toes. On the contrary, the shining of each one would lead to victory celebrated by the whole. I honor my ancestors—West Africans from Ghana, Hakka Chinese from the Guangzhou district, Jewish Dutch originally from Portugal—and their Surinamese comrades who've learned to stay true to themselves and expand their understanding of their in-group. By no means perfect, they are still the best role models I've had in transcending the personal and venturing into transpersonal healing dimensions where we could both be fully ourselves, and trust that gifting this freedom to another would enhance our own joy and sense of wholeness. My Soul Authority model and my mastery in holding sacred and healing space for very diverse people have been inspired by all the blessings and wisdom that they've passed on to me.

CIRCULAR DOUGHNUT ECONOMICS

Wealth, status, and power don't cross over with us when we die, and can harm rather than help our beneficiaries. They can end up inheriting "privileges" based on misaligned values and entitled, oppressive premises that keep them shackled and make it harder to resist the allure of money, political power-tripping, mind games, and control within the material world. At this point in history, it's more important for us to recognize that we are all children of the same Earth Mother, and to learn to care for and attend to the basic needs and civil rights of family members who have been mistreated and are hurting the most—for starters. Not only is it the right thing to do; all of us sentient beings, including the planet, benefit when we function as one healthy, inter-connected whole. Kate Raworth, author of *Doughnut Economics: 7 Ways to Think Like a 21st Century Economist,* reveals in her revolutionary book why her circular model of economics is timely and optimally equipped to replace our old, harmful, and unrealistic notions of never-ending linear economic growth. She argues that:

> far from floating against a white background, the economy exists within the biosphere—that delicate living zone of Earth's land, waters, and atmosphere. And it continually draws in energy and matter from Earth's materials and living systems, while expelling

waste heat and matter back out into it. Everything that is produced—from clay bricks to Lego blocks, websites to construction sites, liver pâté to patio furniture, single cream to double glazing—depends upon this throughflow of energy and matter, from biomass and fossil fuels to metal ores and minerals. None of this is news. But if the economy is so evidently embedded in the biosphere, how has economics so blatantly ignored it?[11]

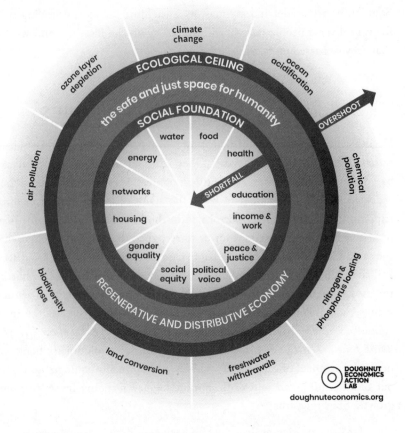

The Doughnut of Social and Planetary Boundaries (Raworth, 2017)

Raworth's holistic model is ego-ecosystem aligned on a macro-level in the sense that it discourages a shortfall of life's key essentials to human life (ego) and prohibits unacceptable overshooting behaviors that would harm the environment (egosystem). "Humanity's 21st century challenge is to meet the needs of all within the means of the planet. In other words, to ensure that no one falls short on life's essentials (from food and housing to healthcare and political voice), while ensuring that collectively we do not overshoot our pressure on Earth's life-supporting systems, on which we fundamentally depend—such as a stable climate, fertile soils, and a protective ozone layer. The Doughnut of social and planetary boundaries is a playfully serious approach to framing that challenge, and it acts as a compass for human progress this century."[12]

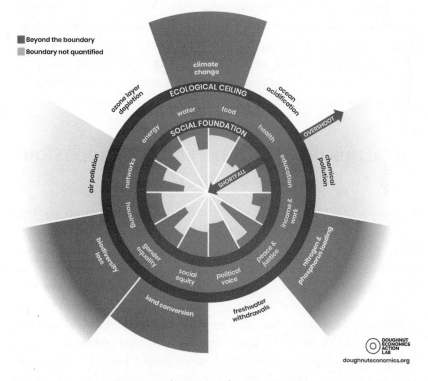

The Overshoot Doughnut (Raworth, 2017)

"The environmental ceiling consists of nine planetary boundaries, as set out by Rockstrom et al, beyond which lie unacceptable environmental degradation and potential tipping points in Earth systems. The twelve dimensions of the social foundation are derived from internationally agreed minimum social standards, as identified by the world's governments in the Sustainable Development Goals in 2015. Between social and planetary boundaries lies an environmentally safe and socially just space in which humanity can thrive."[13] Areas that are not in the red are not out of the woods. There just isn't enough officially measured data yet to include in the model.

Interestingly, there seems to be a direct correlation between our micro-level, ego-ecosystem misalignments and how these operate on a macro-level. Our inner climate denial has resulted in outer climate denial. We ignore and dismiss global warming signals in the same way we've learned to ignore personal warming signals. The shortfall and gaps in our social foundation have led to trauma experienced on the individual and nuclear-family level, leading to gaps in our psychological foundation and inner space—an implosion and collapse of our own energy and wholeness. Explosive, weird, and erratic climate patterns result when Earth attempts to reharmonize implosions and imbalances due to, for instance, icebergs melting. The same happens to our individual ecosystems that are out of alignment.

HEALING INHERITED IMPLOSION–EXPLOSION TRAUMA PATTERNS

Humans are more likely to engage in erratic and explosive behaviors when our ecosystems are experiencing a shortfall due to an implosion and problematic change in the temperature, circulation, and balance of vital life energy in our ecosystems due to unprocessed emotional or physical trauma or oppression. The walls that we, in the modern, industrial world, have built for protection from our own conscience and that of others (to squash the awful truths they could remind us of) have only made us sicker—in mind, body, heart, and soul. Our lower selves and inner critics have convinced us to twist and mold ourselves to avoid feeling vulnerable, messy, and out of control, but in doing so, we've become strangers to ourselves. Because of our hardened posturing and avoidant dirty pain patterns, we don't have much access to fertile, moist, composted soil and lack a vibrant, strong, and courageous root system for healthy growth.

This impoverished and fragile disposition has made it all too easy to get seduced into an implosion–explosion energy cycle where triggers reminding us of past wounding and unacceptable feelings—of shame, guilt, despair, hopelessness, low self-worth, and not being good enough—immediately spark explosive, aggressive reactions to inflate our deflated feelings and collapsed, imploded state. Our knee-jerk explosiveness includes blame, anger, hypervigilance, workaholism, overwhelm, scapegoating, attacks, exploitation, and attempts to manipulate and control others and the situation. We've learned to consider this explosiveness as the most viable and desirable remedy to our "bad feelings," and we confuse it with healthy self-assertiveness, speaking up, vitality, power, confidence, and success. How could we not? We don't have a lot of ancestors and elders left who can teach us how to do this the right and aligned way, because the majority of them and their legacies have been killed.

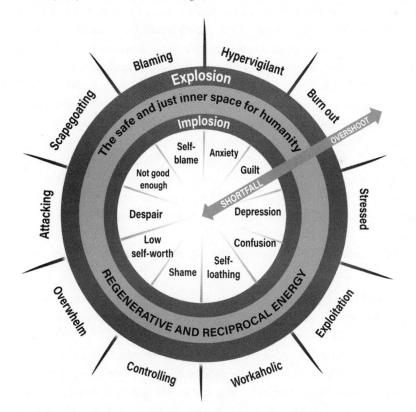

Implosion–Explosion Diagram (inspired by the Doughnut) (Van Tuyl, 2021)

THE PARALLELS BETWEEN SHORTFALL AND OVERSHOOT AND IMPLOSION AND EXPLOSION

If you examine the shortfall and overshooting aspects of Kate Raworth's Doughnut Economics diagram and my implosion and explosion ego-ecosystem diagram through a holistic lens and treat them each as a closed feedback loop, the parallels between them will make intuitive sense. Overshooting, just like our tendency to explode when imploded, doesn't exist in a vacuum. We are most likely to lash out, exploit, and overstep boundaries when we feel insecure, powerless, cheated, deprived, and soul impoverished. Even when material deficits or scarcity are no longer an issue, the psychic imprints that they leave behind can linger on for generations and cause our ego-minds to remain stuck in that trauma sensation. Our not-enoughness and scarcity mindset can distort how we perceive our material or social foundation and what we really have and need. It's easy for us to tirelessly try to satiate insatiable wants. Just as emotional eating really doesn't hit the spot, neither do these tactics. While hunting for more to fill our own pockets or impoverished souls, we don't make time or space to heal on a soul level. Hence, we perpetuate this emptiness and soul loss, making it harder to recognize or care about the severe shortfall of people in our backyard or around the globe—in terms of both their material and social foundation. Even when gilded in all the gold, money, power, and biotechnology to live forever, this will feel flat and empty, rather than privileged, the moment we take true spiritual stock. Not addressing the root psychological imbalances and/or shortfall of so many is one of the main reasons we are struggling with ego-ecological imbalances that pose serious threats to ourselves and our shared environment.

People suffering from a shortfall are easy prey for predators and are more likely to:

- Rely on overshooting work because they don't have any other options. They do this despite getting sick, abused, blamed, fined, punished, and vilified for their choices.
- Attract overshooting predators who are interested in making a quick buck and exploiting them and their resources for very little in return.
- Not know how, or have the resources, to take care of and protect themselves, their communities, and their environment from existing and new overshooting businesses that are harming them and the planet.

- Become exploiters and overshooters themselves, exploding and lashing out their imploded life energy to cope with vulnerable feelings, deep hurts, lack of foundational support, and uncertainties.

Our healing journey in learning to create a just and safe inner space for ourselves becomes most fulfilling and self-generating when we honor the parallel connections and needs of others for similar safe and just inner, as well as outer, spaces. True North living involves continuous exploration of and trust in our soul authority and multidimensional dynamic wholeness to find root solutions for long-standing and inherited social and earth justice problems.

TRAILBLAZING PATHS OF FREEDOM

Soul Authority supports consciousness pioneers from every community and industry to trailblaze a healthier, more honest way. It starts with examining our modern culture's relationship to power, productivity, and external approval at the expense of inner wisdom, emotional intelligence, intuition, and integrity—a.k.a. our superpowers. Anyone who's been victimized or oppressed, and has learned to implode life energy, can become a perpetrator and oppressor—someone who explodes their life energy and exploits the life energy of other people, sentient beings, or nature in harmful ways to displace their wounding onto a new target and attack it to feel inflated instead of deflated. In the same vein, anyone who relies on pervasive implosion–explosion dirty pain patterns can rebalance themselves, their choices, and the systems that they are a part of with the harmonizing energy of nature. I think of it as finding that sweet spot within yourself as you would with a guitar string, somewhere in between too loose and too tight. This is the safe and just inner space for humanity and what we will aim to cultivate with the help of Soul Authority tools and a protective sanctuary. None of us are immune to the many social pressures we face today that lean too heavily toward the "too tight," overworked, and stressed end. We are bound to feel depleted and deflated and risk collapsing because it's not humanly possible to keep up with the madness. Instead, we need to bravely reclaim our protesting humanity and rebellious, natural genius. Each one of us needs to do our own transformational work to liberate ourselves from the clutches of "more is better" and "not good enough"—the enticing whirlwinds and reinforcing hamster wheels that only blind and trap us.

65

PERMISSION TO PRACTICE
YOUR SUPERPOWERS

Clearing overwhelm, fear, and sabotaging patterns within your psyche and personal ecology will inevitably provide more mental space and emotional bandwidth to bring out and practice your superpowers. Especially when porous, sensitive, and prone to assuming too much responsibility, it is imperative to focus on our unmet potential and unique soul callings instead of on all the pain, sorrow, and work that still needs to get done. This way, instead of getting sidetracked and paralyzed, you'll feel excited and motivated to apply what you're learning to your personal and professional life, and to track the magic that you are attracting and manifesting in real time. The more consistent your practice, the greater your success in realizing your goals, fulfilling your personal dreams, and making a dent in your soul purpose endeavors, meaningful projects, and trailblazing work. You'll be amazed how much time, money, and energy you'll save every day when you no longer get lost in convoluted detours, fear, self-sabotage, and self-doubt. The shifts that you'll be making will help you to feel lighter, more in your authority, and more effective each new day. You will learn to alchemize all of the energy and weight that kept you down, and to steadily morph into your beautiful and efficient butterfly self after learning how to set up and secure your leakproof chrysalis.

CHAPTER 6

How to Use This Book and What to Expect

How to Become a Butterfly Instead of a Longer, Stronger Caterpillar

There is nothing in the caterpillar that tells you it's going to be a butterfly.

—BUCKMINSTER FULLER

We delight in the beauty of the butterfly but rarely admit the changes it has gone through to achieve that beauty.

—MAYA ANGELOU

It's always painful to set one's self against tradition, especially against the conventions and prejudices that hedge about womanhood.

—HELEN KELLER

Think of this book as your back pocket guide and best friend. Its main purpose is to offer you reassurance, fresh ideas, and simple, doable steps and intuitive techniques that will help you to embody your joyous whole self and to clear the most stubborn obstacles from your path. The ultimate goal is to demote your trauma-body from its default central role, and to anchor more fully in your truth-body to help you actualize your potent potential and soul callings. This is most effectively done by knowing how to navigate common bottleneck areas where most of us get stuck. All caterpillars go through a final major meltdown and messy phase where they become unidentifiable goop before they transform into a butterfly. Sensitive souls like us resist softening our heart and surrendering to this mysterious process when it matters most. This resistance is precisely what prevents us from transforming into the best, brightest, and happiest version of ourselves. When we approach this juncture, we fear embarking upon an unfamiliar path, we step on the brakes, and we hit a plateau. Even though we live close to water (tears, creative flow, emotion, intuition, and grief come naturally to us), we've learned to associate our compassion, adaptability, and vulnerability with being weak, defeated, broken, helpless, or hopeless. This was strategically orchestrated by those most threatened by our powerful presence and emotional defiance, and frankly, most afraid of their own feelings of vulnerability and truth bearing. The majority of us now mistrust our superpowers—our empathic sensitivity and emotional intensity—and avoid the signals that they send us.

HOW WE WERE PITTED AGAINST OURSELVES

There's nothing more embarrassing and shameful for a sensitive kid than turning into a blubbering puddle in front of others. Many of us can remember how much we hated these moments of utter dread. They were especially traumatic if mean kids or harsh adults made another cut into our raw hurt with their snide remarks, calling us a crybaby, or mocking us. Instead of relying on healthy anger to protect ourselves from mistreatment, we sidestepped self-advocacy and conflict as much as possible. We succumbed to pressures, left our bodies and pain, and directed our anger toward ourselves, hoping to improve the situation in a more peaceful, safe, or effective manner. This coping style worked to a degree, but created bigger problems. We may have successfully dodged jabs, jokes, mocking, or punches by avoiding or deescalating confrontation, but it taught us to become *our own worst enemy*. If you were directly or indirectly blamed for your emotional objections that were instigated by your parents' problems, for instance, it would have been impossible not to take this blame to heart. As a young child, you probably knew deep down that you couldn't possibly be the cause of your parents' headaches, high blood pressure, gray hairs, depression, divorce, alcoholism, violent outbursts, or suicide, but you needed to dismiss your inner wisdom to survive. You were forced to point your inner compass needle to danger (become primarily focused on avoiding pain) instead of toward your True North. Slowly but surely, your navigational heart compass became more hypervigilant than healthy, and eventually overrode your body's natural ecosystem that's guided by your truth-body. This is how your trauma-body, fear, and anxiety took the helm and started an inner war with your true nature.

PUNISHED FOR EXPOSING SHADOW PARTS

Wanting to connect with others from a place of authenticity, wholeness, and integrity that matched ours is what often got us in trouble. We either naively, spitefully, or fearfully provoked shadow parts that they may have kept underground their whole lives. Without deeper awareness of our soul authority, we are also prone to intentionally or unintentionally misuse our intuitive powers to fight back, and we stay entangled in relational conflict, assuming that beating others at their own problematic games is the only way we can be freed of their harmful influence. Instead, what this approach does is entrench us more into their ways. Even if we realize that we are being manipulated and reeled in and are somewhat effective at holding onto our clarity and boundaries, we may still need to play these warped social games to survive. Or we experience tremendous self-doubt and persecution fear (that sometimes even taps into past-life persecutions, which was the case with me) when we imagine pushing back and standing up for ourselves. Dissociation from our bodies, our preferred coping mechanism, is bound to cause problems. It makes us very susceptible to dirty pain tactics, especially since this is the mainstream and dominant way in which modern society deals with and perpetuates soul loss and trauma. These pervasive coping patterns need to be identified, tripped up, and realigned, because they do a lot of harm. You won't believe how many sensitive leaders hate themselves for having no control over their tears or feelings when triggered or reminded of old heartache. Sadly, not many realize that these very same triggers and feelings give them the best access to their inner treasures and power to alchemize clean pain.

THE ORIGINS OF THE NAME "SOUL AUTHORITY"

While working on this book and wondering what had inspired the name "Soul Authority," I remembered this painful altercation: "I see what's going on. You got authority issues," my clinical supervisor said under her breath not even a month after I'd been at my predoctoral internship site. She had a tendency to twist and pathologize my insights and objections when I resisted pathologizing my clients with demeaning interpretations and analyses that she was well versed in. In my eyes, she was abusing her authority and gaslighting me with false accusations about having authority issues whenever I challenged imbalances lurking under her expertise. Her spin on my version of the truth created much cognitive dissonance in me. Ironically, it also gave me increasingly more clarity and audacity, that *Nope, I ain't doing what she wants me to do—no matter how much she mocks me for coddling and having "social hours" with my clients instead of diving into their pathology and problems.* I was seeing my clients in their wholeness and had faith in their natural resilience and healing authority, and they were responding positively to my intuitive interventions. But not seeing eye to eye with my supervisor required me to prematurely end our annual arrangement. The year was 1999 and it was the first time in ten years that a drastic intervention (ending a supervisory relationship because of irreconcilable differences) was necessary at the training site I was at. Needless to say, every dagger of blame or animosity thrown at me—a rookie intern—had the potential to shred me into pieces.

UNWAVERING TRUST IN MY SOUL AUTHORITY

I wouldn't say it was confidence and faith in my clinical methods that saved me during this time (there were no experts I knew of who could vouch for or legitimize my unconventional ideas). It was knowing who I was at my core (thanks to all the data points I'd collected growing up in the rainforest) and knowing that living in alignment with this body wisdom was a nonnegotiable baseline requirement. Despite having invested a good five years already in my clinical training (and on the academic front, being one of the top students in my class), I told myself, *Let's see if this is where I truly belong. I'm willing to give this career up if I can't be my true self.* I gave myself permission to show my true colors, and thought, *Go ahead, bring it on, lady (and program). Let's hash it out here and now, and if I need to get a divorce from this field, better to know this sooner than later.* I haven't needed to, and my relationship with that one supervisor—a relational pattern of fierce limit-setting that you could say started with my mother—was a pivotal test in paving the way. It forced me to get straight to the root solution and foundation for future tests by being crystal clear that I won't sell my soul to anyone, anything, or any profession. I had unwavering faith that the universe would lead me to where I belonged even if that meant that everything I'd worked so hard for and valued would be taken from me (again). I'd already gone through that experience, and I knew that staying true to myself was the only way. I can see that some of the future tests were on some level even harder than this one, but each new one felt easier because of the Soul Authority foundational skills that allowed me to trust my embodied sense of harmony and to trust that this energetic wholeness would catalyze the wholeness in others.

RADICAL SELF-ACCEPTANCE

Reclaiming our soul authority requires dropping into our core self, embracing our mind, body, heart, and soul *as is,* and cultivating more trust than ever in our natural genius to harmoniously realign our energy, our emotions, and our body's healing wisdom. It will require quieting the trauma-body, not getting distracted by flare-ups of pain (for now), and continuing to practice our skills until we are able to see and appreciate our wholeness and our true nature in a totally new light. The results and benefits will be profound and worth striving for. Practicing radical self-acceptance and self-love with the help of Soul Authority tools will help you to:

- Re-member and experience yourself as a wondrous vessel of light, love, and life just by be-ing.
- Know in your cells and bones that you belong to a sacred web of life and that you are a beloved nature spirit that's an integral part and expression of the whole.
- Celebrate your natural genius by learning how to support the harmonious rhythms of the elements as they dance within and around you.
- Pull out your antennae receptors and translate subtle energies as well as intense emotions and grief into clarity, divine healing guidance, restored gifts, and empowering action.

WALKING YOUR SOUL'S LABYRINTH

I'll take you on a beautiful journey through hidden coves and passageways deep within your psyche. Before you know it, you'll be excavating jewel after jewel of personalized, custom-fit spiritual guidance and wisdom out of a buried treasure trove you never realized was there, waiting for you at the center of your soul's labyrinth and providing you the answers you most desire. I get that it may be hard to believe that this is possible. Remember that no caterpillar could ever have fathomed what the future had in store by looking in the mirror or examining the past. Becoming a butterfly *requires total trust* in your intuitive body awareness, and surrendering to guidance coming from deep within. Starting something new or starting over both excites and scares us. Just the thought of confronting and cleaning up the individual and collective human messes and systems we've inherited or have wrestled with our entire life overwhelms the majority of the sensitive souls and leaders I work with. Yet, it is possible to feel instant relief, calm, hope, and excitement after setting up and entering your sanctuary—no matter where you're from, what's going on in your life, or how deep you may be steeped in personal or societal hamster wheels of helplessness, despair, and anxiety. Entering your safe sanctuary activates your parasympathetic nervous system and insulates you in a protective womb-like chrysalis that's filled with soothing, gentle energy capable of harmonizing any kind of chaos. It also offers you the swiftest way out of the lose-lose double-bind that's now driven mostly by your own mental programming and gaslighting. I'm able to help many of my clients shift and enjoy profound freedom and fresh possibilities, often within their very first session. After getting a good sense of their dormant healing potential, they are eager to learn how to set up and enter this safe haven by themselves. I can't imagine any reason why this can't be the case for you.

INCREASING YOUR MENTAL FOCUS

For now, we will be entering your sanctuary in the same manner, to help train and strengthen your mental focus until you feel confident that you can activate and anchor your truth-body in the central throne of your being, at will. It may at first feel like learning a foreign language, but you will quickly realize that you're speaking your body's first language. You've been fluent in this language your whole life. We do not realize it because our bodies speak this intuitive, autonomic language outside of our awareness. It can fool the ego-mind into believing that it's primarily in charge and that its logical ways and words have more weight, when it's really just interfering. If the mind-body split is a few generations old, your ego-mind may not realize that it's exerting constant assimilation pressure on your body and causing you to experience inner conflict, pain, and dis-ease. It's almost as if our ego-mind is ice-skating over a frozen lake (the body) and prefers this arrangement to remain in control. When thawed and back online, your truth-body experiences a sense of homecoming when you dare to reclaim your wholeness and your throne in the center of your soul sanctuary. Suddenly, everything starts to come back alive and click into place internally. Your perspective on life also starts to shift, and perceived problems will feel less overwhelming, even before making any changes externally. I still remember how apprehensive Tabbi Singh, a professor of ancient history, was at first to try something unfamiliar. She was brilliant and very articulate, and had been in conventional therapy for years. Giving this up scared her the most because she had no idea who she was without her mind. I remember her vividly because of how much she ended up loving these meditations, almost instantly. This is what she said:

> Soul Authority sessions often left me feeling infused with strength—that my core elements were in equilibrium—something I never achieved easily with talk therapy alone, which seems to rely more heavily upon conscious recognition and effort to change one's behaviors, attitudes, and perceptions. Through hypnotherapy, I was able to come to terms with some behavioral patterns in a more productive way. Most rewarding, however, was an acute feeling of emotional and physical wholeness which I began to experience right away upon entering the sanctuary.

DEEP SENSE OF VALIDATION

My students and clients most often note feeling validated for what they've known deep down all along. They also experience a profound sense of hope and relief when they learn how simple and intuitive it is to retroactively nourish and restore themselves with supersoul foods. One of the key areas that these inner resources replenish is nature and ancestral deficit ruptures. Contrary to popular assumption, just reimmersing ourselves back into nature isn't the cure for nature deficit if we are not aligned and able to receive the renewable energy that nature offers. On the flip side, living in a city and in the modern world doesn't automatically mean that we are doomed. Our ego-ecosystem alignment is the deciding factor. Your body recognizes ego-ecosystem aligned ways of being and thinking as its true nature by instantly dropping and relaxing into it. You'll feel like a sponge when soaking this energy up, and if you've been parched, the replenishing can cause you to cry as soon as you reconnect to your true nature and sacred healing well. I love holding space for this sacred meeting, and basking in the healing aura my clients and students radiate when they experience this. Our true self is often hovering and not fully rooted in our body, because other voices and energies are monopolizing our inner space. This is the reason why dropping into the body could evoke visceral sensations akin to grief (more about this when we get to Earth and Water) and intense gratitude as you get reacquainted with these neglected parts. Seeing this transformation as beautiful, powerful, and necessary can help with the shame, helplessness, fear of emotional blubbering, and sense of inferiority that the trauma-body and mind have often learned to hate and to associate with this alchemical healing process. You may have experienced your true nature at times as radical self-acceptance and unconditional self-love, and may have referred to this powerful, wise, and compassionate part of yourself as your core self and wholeness. This is your soul authority in action; and the good news is that no one, no matter what they do, can destroy or take your natural genius—your body's built-in GPS—away from you. You may still feel lost at times, but with regular practice, you will develop confidence in your navigational skills and your ability to find your way home from anywhere.

NATURE'S CHECKS AND BALANCES

If lost in the woods with a compass, you would not blindly follow this compass if your physical environment indicated that you were going in circles, right? You would check to see what kind of magnetic interference, perhaps, was messing with your True North needle. If someone in your group insisted that their compass was more right than the sun, the mountains, and the current of the river, you would consider that person deluded or crazy and surely not someone you'd trust as a navigator and leader. Unfortunately, modern Western society is saturated with people like this, especially at the top, who are misleading us and cause us to second-guess our sense of truth and direction by dismissing sources of guidance that have withstood the tests of time. These ancient voices have become faint whispers that are getting drowned out by an overbearing and louder dominant majority who are taking destructive patterns to the next level with conspiracy theories and mind-control tactics that prey on isolated, lost, ungrounded, and fragmented souls. This Soul Authority system and the elemental guides function like nature's checks and balances and will restore trust and confidence in their guidance amid all the distractions, misguidance, and manipulative tactics that we are bombarded with these days.

ENERGETIC AND MAGNETIC INTERFERENCE

The energy of unhealed trauma is like an echo, keeping misaligned messages, unchallenged lessons, and role-modeling from parents, teachers, middle school friends, love interests, bosses, partners, friends, and ancestors alive within our bodies and minds. They are like the little magnets that can mess with the True North needles of the compasses of sensitive souls like us. Actually, they mess with everyone's True North needles. This is thankfully bothering us a lot more than most. We are presented with an important choice. We can either complacently go along with mainstream trends, or we can learn to trust that the pain and suffering that this disharmony causes us are an invitation for us to correct the imbalances and return to our true nature and health. Our whole lives, we've been rewarded with praise, grades, reviews, raises, money, promotions, privileges, compliments, belonging, and promises by teachers, bosses, co-workers, politicians, partners, parents, friends, and even our inner drill sergeant. We've gotten a lifetime of positive reinforcement for powering through our body's signals, our inner wisdom, and our better judgment. This set us up for powering over ourselves and others in the name of productivity, righteousness, or success, and made us more likely to adamantly defend what we do even when it harms us and oppresses others. We can't tell our own personal truth apart from a larger truth, and have no idea how on or off target we are in terms of our alignment with the greater good. It's hard to grasp that our own inner climate denial (of our emotions) and propensity to ignore personal warming signals (e.g., ongoing resentment, anger, rage) are perpetuating continuous and ever-expanding cycles of denial, defensiveness, and oppression.

These are some of the common "pellets" that often keep us trapped in the complex matrices and hamster wheels of modern life: achievement and success; retail therapy, false security blankets, and addictions (work, food, sex, substances, rage, video games, money, caretaking); covering up fear and uncertainty; drama that gets confused with vitality; scapegoating and punching bags used to release hurt, vulnerability, and frustrations; endless social media feeds; long to-do lists and little checks next to each item that give us a sense of control and accomplishment. Understanding that these are common ways in which the ego-mind gets double-binded and tricked into latching onto a chauvinistic, overgrown, or self-defeating caterpillar identity can offer a promising way out of this trap—but only if we are ready and willing to deflate an inflated ego-self and to reconnect the core self and fulfill root unmet needs.

YOUR SANCTUARY AS CHRYSALIS AND CAULDRON FOR ALCHEMIZING PAIN

Your unique sanctuary will not only provide you a safe refuge and respite from the onslaught of stimuli and demands that may overwhelm you on a daily basis. You will also learn how to creatively metabolize your pain, grieve loss, and turn past suffering into healing energy and insight for post-traumatic growth and the development of your soul purpose and leadership potential. Your powerful transformations will occur within a protective, womb-like soul sanctuary and chrysalis that's radically accepting of and able to contain and rebalance all parts of yourself. This is because it's regulated by your brilliant and expansive mind, which is much larger than your coconut brain. Within your elementally balanced sanctuary, you will enjoy heightened awareness and appreciation that your body resembles a mini-Earth and mysteriously functions like a private ecosystem that's both aligned with and held within the womb of Mother Nature. This conscious setup allows you to optimally honor your authentic self and brilliant light and wholeness. Instead of getting in your own way, you will become a powerful grounding rod and surge protector for short-circuiting emotions, a tree-like carbon/chaos-sink for overwhelm, and a catalyst for neutralizing and reintegrating the toxic polarizations and sharp shards that result from trauma. Soul healing requires learning to trust and align our ego-mind with the energy that runs through our ecosystem, and fiercely protecting our renatured integrity. Your powerfully aligned ego-ecosystem will in turn organically inspire and motivate others to regroup into a higher version of themselves and to update outdated social structures and systems accordingly. This is how we transform the world and trailblaze liberating paths for others from the inside out.

SOUL SANCTUARIES COME IN ALL SHAPES AND SIZES

Jenny Wong, a holistic educator and social entrepreneur, described herself as *very creative and sensitive.* She struggled with family-of-origin residual imprints and aggravations that would result in skin rashes at times. Entering her sanctuary was like entering a boundless playground for her soul. Many of my clients, like her, could not wait to dive in. Based on their inner journeys, you'd never guess that they were alchemizing pretty painful early trauma, significant abuse, and interpersonal conflicts. The fact that this kind of "fun" also effectively healed the issues at hand was both remarkable and affirmation that we weren't engaged in child's play. This is what she had to say:

> To experience such enriching voyages into myself and carrying it through in daily life has been one of the most unique, healing, and glorious dynamic practices that my spirit will hold onto through and through. This is just a fraction of the deep abyss filled with rich gleaming tokens that Loraine has equipped me with that sparkle throughout the day.

Below are reflections of how a soul sanctuary enhanced the lives of a few other practitioners. The teachings, protection, and support they received from their guides greatly varied. The results: they each got exactly what they needed.

> This is a totally unique set of practices, yet also universal. I really love the Soul Authority framework that Loraine has created. I've never seen anyone teach it in this way, but it's drawing on things anyone can tap into: nature, the elements, trees, animals. And each person brings their own understanding and wisdom to the practice, which is all celebrated and incorporated. In fact, each student is their own foundation for the practice, so it's a very creative process that comes from within, though guided by Loraine!
>
> —DANA STEWART, MSW, social worker
> and online course instructor

After a series of inquiries and investigations, I came to this realization: I give other people their space and sanctuaries, understanding and forgiveness on a universal level, but I do not give that to myself. I need to bring my sanctuary with me everywhere! And I need to expand it to the size that I need to feel safe because that's what I deserve, that's what everyone deserves, including me! Looking over at my frozen self on the ranch with Dante [her horse], a purple ring and bubble start to surround me and Dante together. No matter where I walk, this purple ring surrounds me as if it were some magic shield. I can hold on TIGHT to the tree in the center any time I need to.

—VALERIE VARGAS, EdD, special education teacher and artist

Cultivating a vibrant tree sanctuary with spirit guides and ancestors has helped me to navigate some significant life changes with clarity, grace, and peace, including a very tumultuous romantic relationship and difficult patterns with family members. I also got clearer on my soul authority, purpose, and understanding of power, thanks to my tree and animal guides. I feel even more in my integrity and in greater service to myself and the global community. I'm able to compost what no longer serves me. My sacred oak tree has grounded and nurtured me in a way that I couldn't have imagined, impacting how I see my connection to myself and others. I've been able to surrender to endings and open up to new relationship possibilities in delightful and surprising ways.

—ALYSSA NEWMAN, responsible minerals and community program manager, film producer and director, and board member of renewable energy and social justice nonprofits

Connecting to my tree guide in my sanctuary has now become a daily practice. Not only does it help ground me, but it reminds me of who I am and what my purpose is here on Earth. I use it in moments of uncertainty, to tackle anxiety, and even to drift into sleep. Even in the depths of a panic attack, finding myself in this sanctuary—with my tree and my guides—allows for a reset. Going into this sanctuary always helps me plug my energy back into a universal source.

—MIA DE LUCA, PhD, professor of
anthropology

CHAPTER 7

A Brief Overview and Orientation

Setting up a Soul Sanctuary within Mother Nature's Womb

There is a secret place. A radiant sanctuary. This magnificent refuge is inside you. Be brave and walk through the country of your own wild heart. Be gentle and know that you know nothing. Be still. Listen. Keep walking. No one else controls access to this perfect place. Give yourself your own unconditional permission to go there. Waste no time. Enter the center of your soul.

—ST. TERESA OF ÁVILA

The wilderness is an untamed, unpredictable place of solitude and searching. It is a place as dangerous as it is breathtaking, a place as sought after as it is feared. But it turns out to be the place of true belonging, and it's the bravest and most sacred place you will ever stand.... True belonging requires us to believe in and belong to ourselves so fully that we can find sacredness both in being a part of something and in standing alone when necessary.

—BRENÉ BROWN

One of the biggest challenges for humans is that we have lost the "nature" in our human nature.

—JULIA BUTTERFLY HILL

Soul authority empowers you as the sole author, alchemist, and agent of your life. This is both liberating and intimidating. Standing in our soul authority can be challenging for us sensitive souls because we tend to tune into the potential threat that our choices and needs could evoke in others before they've fully unfurled and formed in our mind. We can feel flooded by mixed emotions within seconds, and try to deliberate the pros and cons of each choice, to avoid conflict. Because there is no single choice that's all good or all bad (that won't hurt someone's feelings, however so slightly, or possibly trigger some kind of retaliatory, vicious response), our minds keep going and can't decide where to land. When our mind is unsettled, our body and energy also feel as if they are swirling around and will keep us ungrounded.

IN SEARCH OF A BULLETPROOF SAFE HAVEN

The logical mind resists settling in and relaxing, because there are no bullet-proof places left to safely settle into. We worry about this, overthink instead of feel our way out of this riddle, and get stuck in analysis paralysis, which causes us to doubt our reasoning and our sanity. Meanwhile, our cognitive mind functions just fine, and emotional overwhelm, fear, and self-doubt most likely get the better of us. This frustrates us to no end, because we can't control this unruly aspect of ourselves with our logical mind or strong will because the answers are buried in the spiritual and metaphysical realm—the most spooky and mysterious aspects of our existence that we've learned to fear and avoid like the plague. This has created the biggest conundrum and double-bind of all. It explains why many Westernized societies are currently in a spiritual crisis and are suffering from collective soul loss. We've become masters at rationalizing and justifying the psychological and physical toll that selling our soul (to either belong or succeed) has taken on us. Some of my sensitive clients remember feeling pressured to sever their connection to their heart and soul as early as kindergarten and grade school. I was one of them. I reluctantly molded myself to the ways of my mother, who'd attributed her success and accomplishments to how well she'd molded to Western and Eurocentric ways while getting her education abroad. She often boasted that I barely weighed six pounds when I was born. I slipped out with ease because she'd followed her doctor's advice to eat as little as possible, essentially starving herself and me. This is my version of the story now. Many of us were already negatively impacted and disempowered by patriarchal, oppressive forces while still in our mother's womb. My mother learned to give her socially conditioned inner critic—her egocentric self and colonized mind—free rein to waltz all over her with logic and reason, rather than pay attention to her heart and surrender to guidance from her body and inner mystic—her wise, soulcentric self and voice—and from other wise women and men. It's the reason many Westerners believe that they are born with this inner critic, not realizing that it's an inherited, culturally constructed myth to keep us complacent and small.

HIGHER-LEVEL THINKING

As Einstein noted, higher-level thinking and consciousness need to be activated and sustained to transform our outdated mindsets. This is what I discovered. It's much easier to renature ourselves and our thinking from the ground up than rewire ourselves with top-down knowledge and practices. It's really hard to pull up thought patterns by their roots, because our minds are so weedy and entangled. To get all the wee bits and pieces, we need to dive under the mind and venture into the energetic and emotional realms of our existence. It sounds scary, but isn't, if done well. Another reason to work from the bottom up: we can get sidetracked trying to mentally grasp complexity and paradox. Our logical mind is wired to polarize, and when it comes to grasping paradox, it often ends up bewildered and disoriented. Fortunately, we are able to grok paradox and holistic complexity with the help of concrete examples that our bodies—the aspect of ourselves most loyal to our true nature—are familiar with and have lived since birth. We can rekindle our interdependent relationship with ourselves as a biological organism and an extension of nature and Earth by tuning into our sacred animal self and body. A bottom-up, renaturing process will more readily disrupt the sabotaging mental patterns with embodied truths and complement a top-down, rewiring process with greater effectiveness. Think of the cells and organs within your body as both separate entities and as part of you. Or think about being pregnant and aware of your growing baby in your womb while simultaneously aware of your separate needs as a mother. We humans are like distinct organs that are a part of a larger body and whole. It may seem like our earlobe and pinky toe are worlds apart and don't really want to be bothered with whatever may be upsetting the other, but the blood that runs through both makes it foolish not to be concerned. What affects one will eventually affect the other. Similarly, the waterways and air that connect us all on Earth make it disconcerting for us to keep thinking that we will be granted a clean divorce from humans we don't like due to irreconcilable differences. Our boundaries are permeable to help us to commune and remain connected to a mysterious life force that is binding all of nature and life, including us, together into one. We react adversely when our porous boundaries are either too closed or too open, just as an organ would. If too many or too few particles pass through the barrier, or if the wrong particles or pathogens are passing through, we develop some kind of infection and fever in an attempt to expel the threat and regain balance and alignment. This is what I mean by our natural genius. Our bodies operate with protective, self-healing, and self-regulating ingenuity on all levels of our being, not just the physical, without our ego-minds directing this. As a matter of fact, a lot that the ego-mind tries to do is redundant and backfires. We are better off trusting this mysterious source of energy, love, and well-being instead of blocking and sabotaging it by getting in its way.

ENTERING YOUR SACRED GARDEN

We'll imagine entering your sacred garden and natural scape through the heart. A trail, a secret passageway, a flight of stairs, a keyhole, or a bridge are some examples of portals that have appeared in the meditations of clients as they imagine transitioning into their soul sanctuary. According to Taoist teachings, the heart is the seat of emotional consciousness:

> The Heavenly Heart is like the dwelling place, the Light in the master. Therefore when the Light circulates, the powers of the whole body arrange themselves before its throne, just as when a holy king has taken possession of the capital and has laid down the fundamental rules of order, all the states approach with tribute: or, just as when the master is quiet and calm, men servants and maids obey his orders of their own accord, and each does his work. Therefore you only have to make the Light circulate: that's the deepest and most wonderful secret.[1]

> —*The Secret of the Golden Flower*, translated by Richard Wilhelm

The objective is for this sanctuary to feel like a safe, womb-like inner space and protected greenhouse, ideal for sowing and growing new seeds and seedlings. Sometimes, our mental facilities are overdeveloped, and we can visualize entering our sanctuary but our bodies are not experiencing the crucial felt-shift you often do when you are taking a walk in the woods or other beautiful natural setting. Make sure your body and being are entering a peaceful soul sanctuary where your parasympathetic nervous system feels activated and most relaxed. We need to solicit cooperation from the ego-mind to set this up right, because sensitive wise souls like us tend to remain stuck in pain constrictions and, when directing attention inward, stumble into very layered and complex trauma that's poorly regulated by a fearful ego-mind. We can land in storms, blizzards, raging fires, scorching deserts, floods, or bloodbaths instead of in a calm, safe haven. This also tends to happen when closing our eyes and reconnecting to our bodies for just a brief moment while going about our days. Our conscious mind is unaware that this may have become our unconscious baseline, and the culprit of our daily overwhelm and need to constantly be on the go to escape our default crisis mode. Facing what ails us is the first step along our road of healing, but an overwhelming confrontation can tragically cause us to decide that this is not the right path for us.

Because we often have no idea why we are so easily triggered and flooded in some situations or by some people, we tend to blame them instead of see the triggers as messengers and mirrors of unhealed trauma. We unwittingly give in to strong pulls to do things we are not ready for: e.g., attempt to intuitively read, digest, and alchemize boatloads of unresolved pain. This is not a good idea until we have tested and know our capacity limits. We need to stretch, grow, and anchor deep enough to absorb the magnitude of these unmetabolized wounds and patterns.

This is why we begin your soul authority journey with a solid understanding of the architectural setup of your soul sanctuary and a few important safety guidelines and tips that will alert you to and divert you from common pitfalls. Consistency is key in solidifying your sanctuary enough (think of internalizing the loving, firm, and consistent parent you didn't have) so it will serve as a trusted safe haven, a grounding anchor, and eventually a catalyst and cauldron to alchemize uncomposted pain into fertile ground to cultivate your soul's purpose and liberation.

SOUL AUTHORITY'S MEDICINE WHEEL FORMATION

Our Soul Authority ego-ecosystem alignment is optimally held within a medicine wheel structure and is supported by the sacred four elements that have guided, protected, and empowered ancient earth-keepers and astrologers from every continent on the planet. They are held within the As Above, So Below, paradoxical, and holistic orientation to life, symbolized by the Sacred Ancestral Tree. The four sacred directions—North (Air), East (Fire), South (Earth), and West (Water)—are paired with the mind, spirit, body, and heart, and provide antidotes to the most common Western imbalances that I've encountered in my practice and that pertain to these core human dimensions. Our Sacred Heart Compass resides in the center where these aligned cardinal directions converge and reliably guide us toward True North. Each elemental guide around the wheel offers the ego-mind insight into ego-ecosystem misalignments as well as personalized guidance from elemental and nature guides regarding how to correct them. Embedded within this structure are the interwoven teachings of our Sacred Ancestral Tree as we move through the seasons, symbolizing our cyclical and spiral growth as our soul authority matures, flourishes, and provides protection, shade, nourishment, support, delight, and the breath of life for many other creatures. Our natural genius needs to kick into full gear to align and integrate these complex, moving systems into a harmonious, streamlined, and dynamic whole.

Here's a brief overview of the seven steps and objectives that I will guide you through in the next seven chapters.

Step 1. Sacred Ancestral Tree: To enhance our As Above, So Below, holistic orientation to life

Step 2. Air Guide: To enhance our mental focus and wisdom

Step 3. Fire Guide: To enhance our energetic boundaries and protection

Step 4. Earth Guide: To enhance our physical growth and grounding

Step 5. Water Guide: To enhance our emotional regulation and circulation

Step 6. Heart Compass Guide: To enhance our agency, self-trust, and sense of True North

Step 7. True North Living Guide: To enhance our visibility and impact

Step 1. As Above – So Below

Step 2.
Air – Wisdom
Mental
Face the truth
Spring
North

Step 5.
Water – Circulation
Emotional
Moon cycles
Winter
West

Step 6.
Heart
Compass

Step 3.
Fire – Protection
Energetic
Sun rises
Summer
East

Step 4.
Earth – Grounding
Physical
Has your back
Fall
South

Step 7. True North Living

Medicine Wheel Formation (Van Tuyl, 2021)

USING THE BODY'S 3-D STRUCTURAL SUPPORT

Our physical body favors symmetry and being in balance, and provides us with an optimal container and blueprint to set up our sanctuary. The ideal sitting position is on a chair with solid back support. After you have entered your inner garden sanctuary, you will be instructed to lean against the trunk of your tree. Being able to feel your back physically supported will deepen your ability to surrender and to shut off your overactive mind. You don't necessarily have to face North but if you are able to, it can enhance your connection with nature and in particular the sun and circadian and moon cycles, especially if you decide to do this meditation outside and are leaning against an actual tree. (Again, this is not necessary but definitely try it and compare notes if called to be outside. Most important is learning to renature your inner state so you always have access to your soul sanctuary, even when stuck in your office, a plane, a car, your home, or a busy city.)

Have your feet on the ground, one hand on your heart, and the other hand on your belly button to activate your power center. Imagine an invisible umbilical cord connecting you to Mother Earth's womb, and imagine this womb completely engulfing your sanctuary and constantly nourishing and detoxing you and your entire ecosystem and soul sanctuary. You are paradoxically in your sanctuary, and your sanctuary is in you. If it's confusing to grok this at first, consider it part of the practice in conceiving paradox. Once you get the hang of this, you'll find this meditation to be very powerful. It can extract imbalanced energies that were passed down from womb to womb, replenish depleted parts of your energetic body, and create a bit more space between your very young preverbal self and your birth mother. As you enter your sanctuary through your heart center, tap on your sternum to wake up your heart. Feel yourself dropping into your body and coming more alive with each tap. Notice the taps evenly distributing your energy, like a drop of food coloring in a glass of water that is dispersing into every direction almost instantly. If you've been caught up in worry and ruminations, you'll feel top-heavy and may fret about doing these steps right. Instead of energizing your brain more, pull the energy into the lower parts of your body by focusing on your feet on the ground and feeling your bottom firmly on the chair. Let Earth's gravity pull your energy down. Breathe into areas of tension, and give out a big sigh of release with each exhale, dropping your shoulders and your energy down with each exhale.

Imagine feeling as heavy as a sack of rice that's sitting comfortably in your pelvis between your hip bones. If there are concentrated pain points or parts screaming for your attention, consciously soothe and dilute this energy with the help of your tree guide serving as a grounding rod. You can also imagine ironing out all the emotionally charged wrinkles within your energy field with a steaming iron that's not too hot or too cool. You want your field to feel like a silky, smooth sheet that's covering your whole body. You will do the opposite later: bring pain points and energetic tension to the forefront to examine under a microscope, but only after you've cultivated a steady, compassionate inner climate. Mastering this skill will allow you to safely transform buried pain, honor unmet needs that are held within your trauma-body, and embody and sustain soul authority over the purified energy of your truth-body for increasingly longer periods. As you navigate through the layers of yourself and the circles of influence that have shaped (and constricted) your identity, starting with your family of origin, demographic groups (i.e., race, gender, class, sexual orientation), friendships, and so on, you will learn to alchemize oppressive karmic (dirty pain) patterns from the inside out with liberating dharmic (clean pain) patterns, and to ripple healing consciousness back into these same circles of influence.

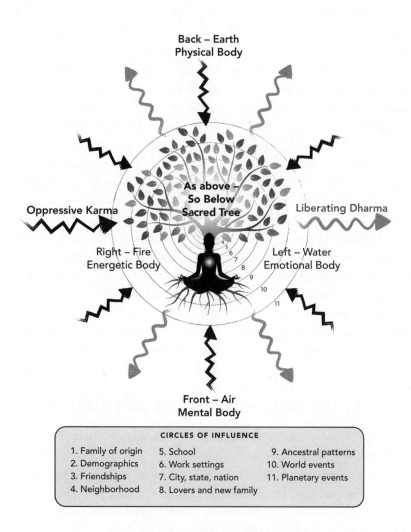

Soul Sanctuary Diagram (Van Tuyl, 2021)

YOU ARE A COMPASSIONATE NATURE SPIRIT

Most core shamanic journey teachers instruct students to imagine entering their inner scapes through the lower world—e.g., through a hole in the ground, a root system, a hollow trunk, or a body of water—or entering through the upper world—e.g., from the top of a mountain, a ladder extending down from the clouds, or the back of a bird. It's not typical to enter "nonordinary reality" through the middle world, because you can encounter a mixture of entities and spirits in the middle world, just as you do in real life, whereas the upper and lower worlds are inhabited by compassionate beings only. There is a consensus among most shamanic practitioners that nature guides in the middle world are the most trustworthy and compassionate. We will start in the middle world and learn to ground there right away, because we are, at our core, compassionate nature beings. If we deal directly from the get-go with whoever and whatever stands in our way or objects to this claim, we reduce a lot of manipulative run-around and are better able to "fast-track" our transformation, according to one of my students. The ego-mind needs practice and encouragement to surrender and to choose this higher-self-aligned path (again and again). Being engulfed in the womb of Mother Nature provides us the structure and holding support we need to accomplish this feat, instead of dodging this scary step with avoidance tactics. Being given the rare opportunity to question and reflect with brazen honesty what the ego-mind truly wants and what hand it would play if it had access to a full deck of cards is super helpful in breaking this stubborn dirty pain pattern. For many, while in the middle world it's very freeing and reassuring to part-ner with allies and guides within an elementally balanced sanctuary that resides within ourselves that we are able to access anywhere and anytime.

YOUR TRUTH-BODY AND AUTHORITY

The most important skill to get under your belt is learning to activate and amplify your parasympathetic nervous system and natural genius at will. Because your physical body naturally heals and regulates your complex ecosystem without your direct command, it's more a matter of clearing ego-mind preoccupations that interfere with and dilute your awareness of the healing power and authority of your truth-body. Most of us take our bodies for granted until we get sick. It then slowly sinks in how little we know about the home and sanctuary of our soul, and how often we've blindly given our power away to experts, authority figures, mental health practitioners, and doctors who tend to overpathologize and overmedicate our sane symptoms, medical mysteries, and soul's efforts that are trying to communicate to us. On the flip side, holistic healers and well-meaning pioneers in alternative health and esoteric practices often tell us to trust our bodies and that we know ourselves better than any expert or doctor, and that we are ultimately the authority of our bodies and lives. Although this is definitely a step up from placing automatic blind faith in the experts, blindly trusting ourselves could also get us in trouble, just because there are so many complex dramas, epic battles, myths, and narratives that are constantly getting played out inside of us. Especially if we are sensitive and empathic, all kinds of voices and energies can hijack our minds and occupy our bodies outside of our awareness. It takes years of rigorous study to get a basic grasp of the physiological, biological, meridian, and mechanical structures and workings of our miraculous bodies, let alone what constitutes a healthy versus unhealthy range of human variation in regard to dis-ease. To top this complexity, physical components and symptoms that seem fixed are actually always in flux because of the energetic factors I mentioned above. I can't tell you how many medical mysteries have naturally dissolved after my clients decoded important messages with the help of their guides (after seeing countless experts in allopathic medicine and holistic healing with less dramatic results). Opening up hidden channels of communication within our pain-body can be very eye-opening and can help us develop self-trust as well as trust in medical and healing experts in a systematic and organized way. The best way to cultivate this kind of clear and direct communication with all involved parties, including our bodymind, is by establishing energetic boundaries with the help of a soul sanctuary.

PITFALLS: SETTING LIMITS WITH THE TRAUMA-BODY

Let's address the most common pitfalls to avoid when you set up your sanctuary. It may feel strange to think of needing to set limits with parts of your trauma-body that may constantly be sabotaging you (e.g., your imploding default inner critic and your exploding self-redeeming warrior), but as you learn to consciously protect what's at risk and to make sure to align your sense of truth with a larger truth—with nature and the elements serving as the most reliable system of checks and balances for your Sacred Heart Compass—you will eventually grow big and strong enough to quiet and heal the voices that fuel these powerful impulses and cycles. Our bodies and hearts short-circuit when overwhelmed by trauma, intense pain, and emotion. It causes our soul to shoot out of the body, and your ego-mind may get invested in keeping things this way. The ego-mind forms undermining narratives and core beliefs that justify and solidify these constricted patterns. The misaligned ways of holding, avoiding, and exploding undigested emotions end up forming your trauma-body and karmic, rather than dharmic, path. Remember that your ego-mind has been conditioned and colonized for centuries to operate in ways that are unnatural and that contradict your body's wisdom. Even if you have intentionally chosen to be on board with this misaligned program, convinced that it will get you ahead in life, your body knows the truth. It will create a full-blown false self—the trauma-body—to appease your dominating ego-mind and to manage the dissonance. Many of us are not deliberately choosing misaligned ways of being, but have been deceived by a very convincing trick of the mind. It's very confusing when our powerful felt-experience of our truth-body has been much more fleeting over the course of our lives compared to the constant, overbearing presence of our default trauma-body (that, since birth, has been occupied by inherited trauma and undigested intergenerational ways of dealing with pain). If you are mind-boggled by the fact that your truest self is not the self you've known your whole life, you are on the right track. It will make more sense over time with practice and comparative data.

FEAR OF INTENSE EMOTION AND REJECTION

Our trauma-body ends up dominating and occupying our inner space with a high baseline fear of clean pain and other intense emotions. Instead of digesting and purging out what doesn't sit well with our systems—a process we can't stop on the physical level but can on the emotional one—we hold the ick in to avoid looking gross or having to deal with the mess. We can't metabolize all when mistreated, because we can't reintegrate and heal what isn't ours. Some of the reasons for upholding these dirty pain patterns have been passed down from womb to womb and from broken heart to broken heart, making it really difficult to recognize the original trauma that generated the misalignment. We confuse core beliefs and family values with absolute and universal truths, and we disconnect from our own regulating emotions and energy, except for the overwhelming fear of rejection that we anticipate when challenging the family's status quo. This makes intuitive sense. When empty and lacking soul authority, we feel extremely vulnerable and depend even more on our social groups for belonging and survival. At a certain point, we can lose complete sight of the truth and any sense of what could be off. It's like inheriting a house with blown fuses and not realizing that you have been operating at half power your whole life. Or that there is a fuse box where you could reset blown circuits. Even if you did sense that something was wrong, your family may have given you the evil eye and a clear sense that it's not okay to challenge their preferred modes of operating. It's better to learn to live with whatever is wrong than to dig up problems that no one wants to confront. This is how a dirty, ancestral pattern of denial can end up dominating the family scene for generations. A healthier way to relate to your true nature is to think of it as the weather and climate, always in flux and closely impacted by all that's happening around you. When we reset and reconnect with the underlying healing power and rhythm that's integral to who we are, it will not only anchor us in the deep now and give us access to infinite possibilities, it will also backlight our day-to-day patterns. Anchoring in this vast field of love will help us to feel safe enough to eventually fall apart and to break down whatever we are holding onto too tightly. This gives us the chance to reconnect, reharmonize, and reintegrate at a higher level of spiritual order after clearing all the superficial kinks in our ego-ecosystem alignment that no longer serve us. If we are lucky enough, our loved ones will come around and recognize that our devotion to our wholeness and soul authority synchronistically supports theirs.

IN CHARGE OF THE GREENHOUSE GAUGES

True North guidance from your heart, body, and mind is most trustworthy when it's grounded in your own personal and unique greenhouse that is as predictable, soothing, and gentle as the stillness that calms us in nature. Within your soul sanctuary greenhouse, you are in charge of all the gauges, controls, barometers, and thermostats for optimal wind, heat, moisture, pressure, condensation, and fertilizer so that delicate seeds and seedlings can sprout and grow. Harsh climate conditions caused by deprivation or excess of any one of the elements—e.g., extreme heat, frost, flooding, lack of water—even if just for a day, can cause the seedlings to die. A harsh inner climate is akin to self-loathing, self-berating, and lack of self-compassion. This is not a natural state and is the reason why it's difficult to grow new and healthier habits until this form of self-destructiveness and criticism is no longer a knee-jerk response when triggered. Once these skills are mastered, your sanctuary will serve as a sterile ICU (inner-critic uprooting) triage for deeper healing and psychic surgery that transforms pain into purpose. This will be guided by the harmonizing elements, spirit animals, and wise ancestors you will learn to connect with after mastering round one of your sanctuary setup.

Most of us have needed to do a good number of stabs in the dark in dealing with life. If that's you, your ego-mind probably has gotten significantly attached to its ways. You can imagine the potential risks and harm that can be caused by self-defeating thoughts, assumptions, behaviors, and distorted or limiting worldviews that are used to running amok. We can't attempt more sophisticated and intuitive interventions before setting up your sanctuary right because this is the kind of ego-mind control that is healthy to have but that we sadly lack. We want to honor how far your ego-mind has taken you, and also gently explain that unless you want to become a longer and stronger caterpillar, you now need to switch gears, access a whole new layer of body wisdom, and embark on an adventure that may feel like the complete opposite of what was so effective in the past. The step-by-step guidance that I will be offering you in the meditation section of each of the following chapters follows an intentional and intuitive sequence that will soon feel like second nature. Once your sanctuary is more robust, you will be able to examine and neutralize more unruly weather and climate patterns with ease and be able to clear dis-ease in natural and regenerative ways.

GUIDANCE FOR EXPERIENCED MEDITATORS

The Soul Authority ego-eco alignment system has been influenced by the following meditation disciplines and orientations. Its framework allows you to integrate these separate components into a harmonious whole as well as to troubleshoot and deepen your practice should you run into obstacles.

- Samatha meditation: activates your inner stillness, self-compassion, relaxation response, and parasympathetic nervous system when entering a safe haven—your soul sanctuary—and learning how to fiercely protect it and take full responsibility for it.
- Transcendental meditation: allows you to access and hold more sacred space in your bodymind than usual, and introduces the ego-mind to the freeing principles of the deep now, equanimity, and clear consciousness

beyond your familiar sense of self and reality, which is mostly informed by the pain-body.

- Yoga meditation: cultivates greater unification and alignment between mind-body-spirit with the help of the breath and your body awareness, which helps to isolate and reveal your natural inner state of peace.

- One-pointed focus: focuses the ego-mind on nature and the healing powers of the elements. By releasing its grip on fear, the usual scripts, thoughts, and stories can more easily float by like clouds or sailboats, and your expanded, loving self will, by default, enjoy more breathing room.

- Mindfulness meditation: develops your nonjudgmental awareness, present-moment perception, and keener observation skills. As a result, false narratives and old stories have less space to occupy within your sanctuary, and your whole soul regularly gets seen and energized.

- Nature bathing: by bathing in the pristine energy of nature and the woods, you are able to cleanse yourself of modern-day toxins and norms that are misaligned with your true nature. Because nature deficit affects your inner wiring, deep healing requires renaturing of the ego-mind from the ground up, and physical reimmersion in nature is often not enough.

- Vipassana meditation: dissolves and transforms suffering, mental delusions, imbalances, and disconnection through clear self-observation, intuitive insight, direct experience, and felt-sensation of what is aligned and what isn't, and uses this guidance to reconnect split parts to the whole.

- Shamanic journeying: opens you up to receive guidance from the elements; nature and guardian spirits; and animal, archetypal, angelic, ancestral, and ascended masters, teachers, and helpers to deepen the connection between parts, bodies, and dimensions within the self, often creating heroic and mythical stories and parables that are universally inspirational. Because we build the sanctuary in the middle world (where a mixture of beings reside), it's best and safest to first cultivate one-pointed focus and learn to sustain your ego-eco alignment before invoking your own dream team of guides.

- Metta loving-kindness meditation: aims to heal and empower you first, and then, like a sacred well, expands and ripples your wellness and healing waters outward to all of life: all sentient beings (even your enemies), all species, the planet, and the Universe.

CHAPTER 8

Step 1: Sacred Ancestral Tree

Wondering Why You Feel Overwhelmed and What "Ancestral Deficit" and "Nature Deficit" Have to Do with It?

Objective of the Sacred Ancestral Tree Guide and As Above, So Below Teachings: To reconnect our disconnected, polarized ego-mind to holistic, nature-centered guidance and equanimity that mirror spiritual principles of wholeness. By aligning our modern mind with the paradoxical mysteries of life, this Sacred Ancestral Tree guide offers us an all-encompassing container and ancient ancestral guide that will help us to more fully digest, compost, accept, and benefit from trials and triumphs, hurting and healing, grief and growth, trauma and recovery, death and rebirth, and the seasonal, circular, and spiral growth cycles of nature embedded within our personal ecosystems. This inclusive mindset serves as a buffer and protects us from the reductionistic impact of rigid, linear, judgmental, rational, and dualistic worldviews that limit modern-day societies and human consciousness.

TOPICS:

How to detect and correct inner climate denial, ego-ecosystem misalignments, and rigid, good–bad thinking that slowly squash our soul

> *No one comes from the earth like grass. We come like trees. We all have roots.*
>
> —MAYA ANGELOU

The power of the seed, like Heaven and Earth, is subject to mortality, but the primordial spirit is beyond the polar differences.

—LAO TZU

[The Secret of the Golden Flower] is built on the premise that cosmos and man in the last analysis obey common laws; that man is a cosmos in miniature and is not divided from the great cosmos by any fixed limits. The same laws rule for the one as for the other, and from the one a way leads into the other. The psyche and the cosmos are related to each other like the inner and outer worlds. Therefore man participates by nature in all cosmic events.

—*THE SECRET OF THE GOLDEN FLOWER,*
TRANSLATED BY RICHARD WILHELM

AS ABOVE, SO BELOW AND THE ELEMENTS

The hermetic maxim As Above, So Below refers to this paradoxical concept of the micro being the representation of the macro and vice versa. It reminds me of the idea of not being a drop in the ocean but the ocean in a drop, as Rumi once said. Or each of us being a mini-universe and as mysterious and unexplored as the vast universe that engulfs us. Our Westernized and colonized ego-mind is severely threatened by this level of complexity, multidimensionality, mystery, and intuitive insight. It challenges our ego-mind's main mission: to keep us physically safe and pain-free. The soul is so all-encompassing and powerful, the ego fears that it will entice us to dismiss our alarm signals by either bypassing them or transcending them—because we've had to do this to keep going, and we still have a tendency to do this. We tend to skip over the many shades of gray and the nuances that our ego-mind and soul could consider besides these two psychological go-to's: denial and dissociation on one end of the extreme (shutting down emotional wisdom) and despair and desperation on the other (walking around with frayed nerves and awareness). Most of us were not taught to reflect much on the different layers of ourselves—mental, energetic, physical, and emotional—and how important it is to keep them distinct but paradoxically in balance and harmony, just like the elements in nature. Many ancient mystics and astrologers around the world—Celtic, Chinese, African, Native American, and Indigenous tribes—honored how these life-giving elements,

Air, Fire, Earth, and Water, corresponded with the sacred and mysterious laws of nature, the seasons, the planets, and different aspects of ourselves. Setting up a sanctuary helps us to discern, and align our energy and body vessel with, paradoxical mystery and As Above, So Below principles. A double-minded practice helps us to become more intimately acquainted with the holistic, yin–yang relationship between primordial forces in life, which is the key antidote to implosion–explosion cycles. Opposites begin to appear less mutually exclusive, and we start to notice their interdependence. We realize that they actually support one another, alchemize change, and even give birth to one another when they reach the extreme end of these artificially polarized dimensions:

- Personal and global
- Us and them
- Human and nature
- Sacred and secular
- Small self and big self
- Self and no self
- Ego and soul
- Future and past
- Directive and receptive
- Rising and falling
- Good and bad
- Day and night
- Right and wrong
- Light and shadow
- Pain and pleasure

- Action and stillness
- Success and failure
- Life and death
- Wet and dry
- Expanding and contracting
- Exploding and imploding
- Wholeness and brokenness
- Truth and denial
- Material and spiritual
- Body and mind
- Seen and unseen
- Masculine and feminine
- Now and later
- Thought and feeling

… and many other polarities

Some examples of this are quarantining and masking ourselves to protect others, or setting firm boundaries around our optimal self-care to benefit the group. We may also live more authentically the closer we get to our deaths, and may discover our greatest gifts in the depths of our greatest loss and despair. You also hear of leaders who experienced their greatest downfall when at their peak or their greatest successes because of what they learned during their darkest days. You may discover that the most rational people are actually the most emotionally charged and stuck, and that the most emotional people tend to have the most rigid beliefs.

EMBODYING THE PARADOXICAL NATURE OF REALITY

Our linear and concrete ways of viewing the world are more culture-bound than we realize. Imagine growing up in a rainforest village, and from the moment you are born, gathering around the sacred kankantri, a giant silk cotton tree that can have a base that's 40–50 feet wide and can grow up to 150–200 feet tall. It's a living cathedral and altar that your parents and grandparents are paying their respects to, and that your ancestors revered long before you were born. It's intuitively clear that your descendants will gather by this same tree long after you die. Your mind is from the get-go supported and primed to think in expansive terms. You are a small piece of a beautiful, intricate collage. You matter. You are sustained by magic. The sun feeds this immense tree through its leaves, and the soil feeds it through its roots. You somehow get that you're similarly kept alive by sun and soil. You are just one degree removed from your food, which is an equal opportunity provider and couldn't care less what you look like, who you love, or what language you speak. You are viscerally and palpably invested in all there is to learn about these food sources—how to sustain them, how to catch them, how to plant them, and how to find them—to enhance your chances of survival. You can do this without language, as Kajë, one of the most skilled boatsmen and fishermen of a Saramaccan village deep in the rainforest of Suriname, demonstrated. He was deaf and mute, but extraordinarily astute and one of the most valued members of the village.

THE LOGICAL MIND AND ITS PLACE IN THE NATURAL WORLD

Cognitive learning and book learning have their place, but they enhance your success only in specific trades that do not matter as much in the rainforest as they do in industrialized societies. Practical skills, knowledge, and intuitive wisdom matter much more in a society where living in a cooperative and harmonious relationship with nature and one another is directly linked to your survival. Although it's great to have language and words to foster these, it's not necessary. The mind, body, heart, and soul are able to hold a lot of energy and complex information that can be pointed out or practiced without words. There is so much more to learn and absorb from nature when our minds are not filled with data and existential anxiety about grades, which far too many kids before the age of ten learn to link to their future success and chances of survival. You learn in the forest that you are a sentient being, a nature spirit just like any of the other trillions of life forms on the planet. And that despite our unique blueprints, we're designed to live in harmony with one another and to exist at the mercy of a mysterious system of checks and balances that favors complexity, beauty, spirals, cooperation, and abundant life over homogeneity, dominance, and destruction. This fervor for life and diversity is apparent in the rainforest, the desert, the ocean, and many other climates and life forms. It is certainly present in our cells and our genetic makeup as human beings, one of the most complex species alive on the planet. Sadly, we lost our ways, and our mind has been reduced to a fraction of its size and potential.

HUMAN DOMINATION OF NATURE

Somewhere along the way, our frontal lobes resisted surrendering to this magnificent and mysterious life force that can also be brutal and overpowering. We improved our chances for physical survival through clever discoveries, and we fooled ourselves into thinking that we were beating nature and this ancient system. We gained an advantage over others by choosing competition over cooperation but did so at the expense of our collective well-being and souls. Since then, millions of present-day humans have bought into this myth. Over the generations, we have almost completely split our minds from our bodies and souls, and are convinced that we can outsmart wisdom and mystery. Starting in kindergarten and grade school, we learn to override signs and signals from our bodies, hearts, and souls that indicate that something is awry. We keep molding ourselves, our energy, and our emotions into some prepackaged form and imagine that shutting down or slicing off parts of our colorful complexity to fit into a neat box will improve our chances of success and survival. Even if we go about our days with our heads in the sand, our shortsighted and shallow mindsets luckily take us only so far.

Our bodies can't help but protest with symptoms of dis-ease. Tension tends to break out into all kinds of stress-related physical ailments and interpersonal conflict. It also manifests into stubborn mental dis-orders, ranging from depression and anxiety to more severe issues, such as bipolar disorder, psychosis, delusions (conspiracies), schizophrenia, and personality disorders (PDs), such as borderline PD, narcissism, paranoia, and antisocial PD with psychopathic and sociopathic deviances. Seeing our symptoms as sane and in service of Source can boost our confidence that our hearts, bodies, minds, and souls are still more devoted to the ways of mystery. Our innate wholeness provides undeniable clues to whether or not we're aligned with our higher self by making us sick when we aren't. Our symptoms provide evidence that no matter how well we talk ourselves into believing what we'd rather believe, our bodies will let us know if we're in disagreement and experiencing dis-ease. The question is: will we finally listen, or will we look for more effective ways to hush the symptoms and dismiss the messages? Especially in the industrialized world, our ego-defenses and personality tics are so all-consuming that just the thought of loosening their grip can cause us to spin into a self-destructive, imploding cycle. We need to get okay with just observing this through our soulcentric lenses and not being pulled in.

MOTHER EARTH AND THE ANCESTORS HAVE OUR BACKS

Our exploitative disposition and disconnected sense of self is a sign of not only "nature deficit" but also "ancestral deficit." Overwhelm, fear, and self-doubt are what we feel in our hearts and bodies when we forget that Earth and our ancestors have our backs. These blocks are the by-product of our isolated, colonized mindsets, and our loss of connection to guidance that's bigger and far more mysterious than the concrete reality we abide by. We've really made a mess of things the past few hundred to thousands of years. There are very few societies left on Earth that still live as intimately with nature as my Maroon guides, consciously protecting their ancient, self-sufficient ways and villages deep in the rainforests of Suriname from harmful energy. In the modern world, there are few intact social groups left (except for the ones formed by lone wolves, courageous truth-seekers, and marginalized consciousness pioneers creating a new center and a new world order) that feel truly safe to belong to. It's important to connect to our ancient ancestors who once lived in close harmony with nature and the Earth, even if this was hundreds or thousands of years ago. "When we humans lose our roots, we too begin to wither—losing our balance, our health and our spiritual foundation. I call this Ancestor Deficit Disorder—the new ADD. And I believe it is a spiritual epidemic,"[1] says Steven Crandell, the director of content and communities at Spiritual Directors International. During the first meeting with my advanced ancestral group, I pulled an ancestral tree card from a tarot deck after asking for a guide to oversee and protect the work we would be doing. The guidance that came through in the next three months aimed to deepen our trust in ancestors and humans who lived in physical form and harmony according to As Above, So Below principles until this trust was comparable to the trust we have in nature and the trees, our oldest ancestors.

EMBODYING ANCESTRAL AND CULTURAL WISDOM

My dissertation research findings helped me to feel less alone and to be able to forge forward along my unconventional path, which resulted in the creation of Soul Authority's holistic and paradoxical framework later down the line. My Maroon guides and my great-grandmother ancestral guide told me not to take my rare experience of true belonging and authenticity for granted. Even if clients didn't have this experience, I've witnessed time and again that some deeply ache for this and are able to grok and grieve this loss. It releases them of the burden of no longer carrying their ancestors' unresolved pain of being denied this birthright. They are also greatly helped when able to access the guidance of ancient ancestors who are highly invested in the actualization of their soul purpose. If we don't go this deep, lost ghosts will keep on reliving their traumas and unresolved issues through us and through leaders who have much more power in this day and age to do grave harm to many. We are clearly getting crushed under the weight of their unfinished business and need to do something about this before it's too late. Clearing ancestral lines relieves the next generation of all this heavy baggage, and helps them to connect to their guides and truth more readily so that they are less vulnerable to mind control and future demagogues.

Reconnecting to our true nature and to healthy ancestors will help us to access more courage and inner strength to stand up for ourselves. We will also receive reassurance from them that our bold soul authority is paying off and is causing important shifts. Experiencing ourselves in a soothing, protected soul sanctuary within the womb of Mother Nature and supported by ancient and wise ancestors from each bloodline is one of the most powerful ways to reset ourselves. It heals collective shame about being human and connects us to ancestral lineages that we are proud of and want to rebirth back into existence. When we meditate, aligned ancestral connections can instantly backlight our stuck patterns and emotional hang-ups, and inspire us to heal and to transform what is ready to shift. It's like accessing a recovered social blueprint of a healthy and interconnected community that offers us much-needed wisdom and guidance to renature our denatured minds, one person, one family, one community, and one ecosystem at a time.

YOU CAN KILL ME, BUT I WON'T DIE

To expand my imagination and boldness, my ancestors offered me this mantra they may have said to themselves: "You can kill me, but I won't die." It was a spin on "You can run, but you can't hide." It has the reverse message. I will discover my true power and true self only when I stop running. We need to anchor in the power, permanence, and peace of the deep now and stay put, no matter what. Present-moment stillness and eternal love are the only constant and guarantee in life, and prevent us from energizing and materializing our worst fears. My ancestors conveyed that they are pleased that we are raising the bar around our self-care and body protection. None of this was an option in their lifetimes. That said, they want us to dig deeper, to ground in our true nature, and to continue to speak up against injustice, inequality, and civil rights violations, because they got our backs and we will prevail. Many shades of gray between the lose-lose extremes of the double-bind—which places denial and dissociation on one end and despair and desperation on the other—will become apparent when we are no longer stuck in it. There is more space to ask ourselves hard and honest questions and to envision solutions in this sacred space of stillness, like *What do we need to do differently to remain conscious and real? How and what can we learn from our past mistakes? How can we come together as one human family and orchestrate more effective solutions in an organized and steady fashion?*

Remember that being double-minded means being able to put yourself in other people's shoes while remaining slightly more aware of yourself. You are practicing dual consciousness, something that members of minority and marginalized groups have done their whole lives. This is how to fine-tune this skill. Having one foot in the deep now—our connection to profound peace and limitless wisdom—and the other in the deep mess allows the truth of the pain to be buffered by your untouchable wholeness so you can drop into your body wisdom with less reactivity. Those of us not subjected to daily racial violence, logistical obstructions, and systemic oppression have far more bandwidth and power to heat up our alchemizing cauldrons and make the changes we want to see in the world and in ourselves. We need to harness the resources and the responsibility we have to empower ourselves and heal the social, climate, and racial injustices that are harming everyone. We each need to speak up and make our vision count at home, at work, and in our communities.

This will require using our superpowers and soul authority to:

- Assess what's really going on in a given situation.
- Realign and renature interpersonal processes and social systems in ways that support and liberate us as well as others and the planet.
- Reduce carbon emissions through use of electric vehicles, solar and other renewable energy, and efficient appliances.
- Vote with our wallets as much as with our ballots in choosing our leaders.

REESTABLISHING TRUST IN OUR HUMAN RESILIENCE

We've ignored a lot of personal warming and global warming signals over the generations to have gotten where we are now. We need to restore trust in our own immune systems, especially when it comes to our emotional and psychological defenses and patterns. They're a bit out of whack, to say the least. We each need to repair our empathic and intuitive connections to ourselves and take inventory of how systemic oppression, exploitation, social injustices, or perpetual imbalanced behavior have impacted our knee-jerk perceptions, assumptions, and behaviors over the generations. Practicing a win-win double-mind will also allow us, while deeply rooted in the present and insulated in our truth-body, to transform harmful trauma imprints from the past into creative fuel. This practice and energetic setup will serve as a template when relating to others and will inspire them to reintegrate themselves before you've even said a word. We help and heal ourselves by helping and healing others. We help and heal others by helping and healing ourselves. It's not just our faith in leaders that's in jeopardy. Our faith in fellow citizens who do not share our priorities and basic sense of reality is also sparse, especially for sensitive people. Exercising boundaries was often our least preferred way of protecting ourselves, because it often led to negative repercussions and punishment. But when we were able to do it successfully, it was often the most effective way to stand in our power and inspire change. Try to remember what that felt like. It will now be much easier to set boundaries when insulated in your protective sanctuary and not so emotionally charged, thanks to your grounding central tree. It allows us to lead others from a place of integrity as long as we believe in the importance of what we have to offer, stick to our missions, and are present enough to make the most strategic and sound decisions based on today's dangers and demons. Soul Authority strategies will support you all the way with this important objective.

BEING PRESENT WITH ALL THAT IS

It's time for our minds to connect to deep body wisdom and to restore trust in our luminous and mysterious selves. A meditation or grounding practice improves our ability to be more present with clear, raw, and colorful emotion without any kind of story line or knee-jerk tendency to squash it or shut it down. It's important to stretch and strengthen your inner vessel enough so you can hold more energy and intensity without short-circuiting. It not only stops the swinging between overwhelm (short-circuiting) on one end of the extreme, and fear (paralysis) on the other; it's also a powerful antidote to self-doubt, which is, ironically, a trustworthy signal telling us when we are not solid, expansive, or clear enough to proceed. The easiest way to drop back into our bodies without getting stuck in overwhelm or fear is through your double-minded practice, where one part of your mind will remain attuned to your private ecosystem (in your safe and protected sanctuary) and another part of your mind will paradoxically attune to the whole (kind of like being attuned to your stomach—hungry—or your bladder—full—as well as your body as a whole).

REFLECTIONS FROM PRACTITIONERS ON WORKING WITH A TREE GUIDE

My sanctuary allows me to connect to my inner wisdom and trust my intuition. My sacred tree helps me to stay grounded and rooted while also connected to the ethereal and cosmos. This has helped me to take in lessons from nature about cycles, resilience, and equanimity. Most importantly, it has given me the courage and conviction to change career paths and follow my calling. As a social justice advocate and mental health counselor, fighting against social inequities and supporting people in healing is incredibly meaningful, but it can be challenging at times. Loraine's Soul Authority model helps me stay grounded and centered with strong boundaries so I can be more effective and also take care of myself.

—Jessica Vechakul, PhD, mechanical engineering, LMFT, psychotherapist and spiritual counselor

I've always found myself gravitating toward the forestry and natural nooks that could be found in any given city. This has always been a solace endeavor, evoking a sort of flooding serenity and connectivity. Still, with every deep-rooted moment came a sense of imbalance when transitioning back into the busy life I lead. This is why for me, connecting with my tree guide has meant holding space for that balance and nourishment within myself wherever I may go. I see the rings within the tree that mark the different ways in which I've grown throughout my own life as well as within a greater ancient context of relationships. Now, I am better able to stay attuned with the wisdom and connectivity that has always allured me to the natural world as I navigate not-so-holistic environments.

—Mirah Mirzazadeh, child welfare and early development major/minor

RECITE AND RECORD

Now let's get to it! I'm so excited for you to explore your sanctuary and gather your own experiences. Remember, they will be as different as your fingerprints, all miraculous and all somewhat universal and recognizable as soul blueprints. All in divine time, as my guides like to say, so don't leap forward, trying to be somewhere else. Drop in deeper, and expand out to integrate more of you. This is what allows us to "move on," "clear blocks," and "get unstuck," if this happens to be your concern. I recommend reciting and recording this script, word for word, to play back to yourself and listen to with your eyes closed in your seated position. This will allow your ego-mind to drop into your body and offer you exactly what you need to get the most of this guided meditation and first orientation into your sanctuary. Some things to consider: Read at a slower than usual pace, breathe calmly and evenly, use inflection, and imagine yourself in the scene taking in as much as you can through your five senses. Put your psychic and additional senses (sixth, seventh, eighth, and so on) on hold for now until your trust in this underlying layer feels as unwavering as the sun rising each morning.

Meditation Script for Your Sacred Ancestral Tree

Imagine a place on the planet where you have actually been or that you know exists where each of the four elements are present. You sense, feel, hear, or see a gentle, refreshing breeze, warm sunrays, strong, grounding mountains, boulders and trees, and flowing, soothing bodies of water that are nearby. All of these elements are gently dancing with one another (Air—front, Fire—right, Earth—back, and Water—left) and creating a mild and pleasant greenhouse climate all around you. You are drawn to it because it's so easy for your parasympathetic nervous system to come alive and for your own true nature to resonate with the soothing and self-healing power of this place.

Feel this place vibrate in your heart center and as you step into it, notice how it expands out until these sensations engulf each and every cell of your body. Your breath is like that breeze, your heart and body's temperature like those sunrays, your bones and body like the mountains, and your blood, sweat, and tears like the waterways in your sanctuary. Note and acknowledge the role of your elemental guides in fortifying your inner sense of harmony and your body's natural genius in calmly, but firmly, reestablishing balance should any one of these elements feel a bit out of whack.

Side note (don't record): If you are for whatever reason not able to gain control of your greenhouse gauges and sustain a mild climate in your sanctuary, it would be completely fine to come out of the meditation, especially if you feel unsafe, your symptoms and discomfort are getting more activated, or you are getting bombarded by disturbing imagery or sensations. Our bodies are different every day. Lack of sleep, hangovers, substances, illness, extreme worry, loss, recent crisis or trauma, big life transitions, and so on can make it difficult to ground and to hold sacred space for yourself. No worries if this is where you are at. Learn to honor these natural fluctuations, and be concerned if you no longer detect them. You may need to decharge the intensity of this energy by talking to a loved one or therapist, or do some journaling, exercise, or art, and attempt this again.

Next, look for a central tree in the middle of your sanctuary. If there's more than one, take a moment to decide which one is tugging the most at your heartstrings. Look for a tree that's mature, sturdy, and ideally suited to serve as your Sacred Ancestral Tree guide. This could be a tree that's very familiar to you. Perhaps one that was in your backyard, in a park, or at a favorite vacation or retreat spot that you often played around, loved, or climbed as a child. Approach the tree and try to make a connection. This could be done telepathically, through touch, or through indirect signs of communication. Ask the tree if it's your Sacred Ancestral Tree guide to help ground, center, and own your soul authority's throne. Wait until you get a clear indication that this is the case before proceeding. If it's not your central tree guide, ask for guidance where you might be able to find this tree.

Once you've found your tree, sit at the base and lean your back against the trunk. Feel its sturdy support light up your spine, letting you know that the tree has your back and is strengthening your courage and backbone. Rest your head against the trunk of the tree. Open your crown chakra above your head to receive inspiration and guidance from the sky, and open your base chakra to ground and root nourishment from the earth into your body and sanctuary. Feel your upper body align with the upper part of the tree. Your arms, hands, fingers, fingertips, and the antennae above your crown are like the branches and leaves of your tree, reaching upward and outward toward the warmth of the sun, the star ancestors, and beyond, soaking up and absorbing energy, light, and wisdom without any reservations or inhibitions.

Pull all of this energy, light, and wisdom into your body through your chakra channel, and drop into the lower part of your body, your legs, feet, and toes. Feel your roots extend from the base of your spine and your feet, reaching downward and outward into the dark, cool soil toward the center of the Earth, the heart of Gaia, and beyond, holding steady and absorbing, without any inhibitions or reservations, all the nourishment, wisdom, and guidance from the minerals, elements, plants, animals, and ancestors, and all who came before us and enriched the Earth with their presence and composted wisdom.

Notice the powerful intermingling of these two opposite sources of energy in your body, representing the above and below, light and dark, seen and unseen, spirit and matter, masculine and feminine, future and past, pleasure and pain, good and bad, success and failure, day and night, and so many opposites we tend to split and polarize in life. Experience their harmonious and joyous coming together within your truth-body in support of one singular agenda: sustaining your life and wholeness and connecting you to a larger, infinite reality where they are relating and have always related to one another as nature designed, peacefully, respectfully, generously, and cooperatively, like a dynamic yin–yang symbol that's constantly in kaleidoscopic motion.

Notice how this mysterious energy coming from these two life-giving giants has always been there and has never abandoned you, not even for a second. It manifests and fuels your tree, helping it to grow tall, in a line, and wide, in rings, circles, and seasons of apparent decline and death only to sprout back each year with more leaves and more vigor, vitality, inner strength, and roots, appearing perfectly still on the outside, while very active on the inside, following an organic but predictable, spiral path of maturation and refinement from seed to sapling to mature mother tree, bearing flowers, fruit, shade, and many other benefits that support a multitude of other life forms, season after season.

Have your ego-mind take in the magnificence of your soul and this part of yourself that has existed throughout time, not only in the bodies of your ancient tree ancestors but also in a long line of prehuman and human ancestors who lived in close and symbiotic relationship with nature. Notice how recent disruptions and disconnection from nature within more recent generations have disoriented you and caused you to overidentify with external trauma that clearly hasn't broken or killed you. You are still here, alive and kicking. It's therefore best to do what your tree does and shift all that doesn't belong inside of your pristine and fine energy field onto your bark and not let it obstruct the flow of life running through your tree trunk (which especially experienced meditators may sense is aligned with your chakra channel). You will learn how to shed the bark in time or your tree will naturally do it, as long as you stay focused on moving out what doesn't belong inside of you.

Hold this template of your truth-body in place and, with the help of your ancient and oldest unbroken lineage of vibrant and wise ancestors, flush the troubled and pained ancestors who are stuck in the gaps with light and love, and show them their own sanctuary templates that they can step into and occupy at any time. Then lean against the trunk of your tree and enjoy the unbroken line of light and energy circulating from your heart to the hearts of your healthy and supportive ancestors and back, giving you the courage to rebirth this renatured way of life back into modern society.

Allow each of these insights and teachings from your Sacred Ancestral Tree guide to sink in and take root in the depths of your consciousness and the cells and bones of your body. Know that this is your most updated and upgraded self and that you will notice shifts within yourself and in all your relationships with others for the next days, weeks, months, and years to come. Slowly retrace your steps and find your way back into the room or setting that you're in. Notice the chair that you're sitting in, stretch a bit, and bring your mind and attention fully back into the here and now. Notice your surroundings, wiggle into your body, bring all of your energy and attention back to the space you are in, and open your eyes slowly.

Alchemy Action Steps: Realign your ego-mind with your soul's ecosystem and grand design.

Explore the following suggestions to deepen your connection with your Sacred Ancestral Tree and feel free to add your own ideas to the list:

- Go on a hike in the natural world or take a stroll through a park. Go barefoot if you can. Pay very close attention to the elements and their role in sustaining all the plants and living beings around you, including you.

- Visit with a tree. Notice its bark, its roots, and its branches and leaves. Lean against it, listen to the tree meditation once more, and see if the tactile stimulation and physical closeness deepen your learning. Collect empirical evidence of some of the teachings and insights that you received from your Sacred Ancestral Tree.

- Set up an altar with a tree image, drawing, or totem in the middle. Place each of the elements (actual or symbols) in this order around the tree: a feather (North—Air), candle (East—Fire), dirt (South—Earth), and bowl (West—Water). Be receptive to guidance and insights from each of these elemental teachers as you handle them and cultivate a relationship with them. Connect with them on a daily basis and ask them to illuminate misaligned patterns in your blindspot.

- Place pictures of ancestors in need of healing or who've guided you on your altar. If you get the sense that they are too dependent on you to metabolize and alleviate their suffering, remind them to connect to their own Sacred Ancestral Tree and soul sanctuary, and to follow your example and what you will be learning.

CHAPTER 9

Step 2: Air

Need Clear Direction, Creative Inspiration, and Fresh Ideas but Unable to Blow Steam and Purify a Thick Smokescreen of Mental Fog and Smog?

Objective of the Air Guide and Wisdom Teachings: To expand our mental abilities and cognitive access to the big picture, the long view, and our highest truth. Through mindful breathing, the Air Wisdom guide provides creative inspiration, out-of-the-box solutions, nonjudgmental spaciousness, spiritual insight, and fresh ideas. A clear view dissolves false narratives and limiting stories about ourselves, others, problems, and reality. It also provides us a road map of the journey ahead and the opportunity to embark on it with intention rather than reactivity.

TOPICS:

Why losing your mind could help you to find your soul

Accessing the spiritual order under mental dis-order

And into the forest I go, to lose my mind and find my soul.

—JOHN MUIR

The soul always knows what to do to heal itself. The challenge is to silence the mind.

—CAROLINE MYSS

*We've been trying to outsmart mystery and nature and force-fit it
all into a tiny box that's under our total control. What we need to do
instead is renature our denatured minds and learn to control our controlling tendencies.*

—LORAINE VAN TUYL

I vividly remember the very first shamanic journey I ever did. I was a first-
year student in grad school. A student from ITP, the Institute of Transpersonal
Psychology, right next door to us needed practice and led a group of us on a
shamanic journey. Within seconds of drumming, I'd landed in the jungles of
Suriname, and started my journey into the lower world, deep into the earth. An
adorable squirrel monkey showed up. They are very common in Suriname—I
had one as a pet but he was stolen within two days. My monkey guide took me
down a maze of tunnels into the earth. There were human bones everywhere,
embedded within the layers of earth. I instantly received the message that my
monkey guide was one of the three wise monkeys that "see no evil, speak no
evil, hear no evil." I'd gotten lost in the layers of denial—or was it willful dis-
missal?—about slavery, the thousands of African lives that had been tortured
and killed on plantations, and ongoing racism. I wasn't ready yet to make all the
connections but was getting mentally prepared for the reunion with my great-
grandmother two years later.

HUMAN INNER CLIMATE DENIAL

Fast-forward twenty-five years. An eerie, *Dune*-like apocalyptic smoky sky
hung over our house and cast a frightening, fiery orange glow of alarm all
over San Francisco on September 9, 2020. Out-of-control wildfires along the
entire west coast of the United States had turned our sunny, health-conscious
state into a terrifying inferno and hazard zone for weeks on end. The dread
of increasingly more frequent and devastating climate disasters is looming
larger and engulfing us more each day. This is nothing new in many areas
around the world where climate injustices and crises—ranging from wildfires,
floods, poor air, and toxic water to more intense hurricanes, arctic winters, and
storms—have taken their toll on families and communities for years. On this
particular doomsday, it felt as if we, at the top level of the *Titanic,* were getting clear signs and alarm signals that our mother ship was sinking. I doubt

that the gravity of the situation was really sinking in as much as it needed to. Were those of us in privileged positions now more inclined to do something about our situation? It felt like another memorable three wise monkeys moment. It caused me to question where we lost our wisdom along the way and how to get it back.

SPIRITUAL ORDER UNDER THE MENTAL DIS-ORDER

Pain and dis-ease provide us the impetus to change our ways and restore our health and balance. Have we spun too far away from our center to retrace our steps? I knew I was experiencing lots of symptoms, both physical and emotional, and I felt buried under layers of mutated dirty pain that made it difficult to discern up from down and left from right, let alone identify the root cause of what led us to the highest levels of harm and purple ratings, in regard to both our air quality and our COVID-19 risk level during this perfect storm—the culmination of significant human contribution. If I were to describe my sane symptoms on this particularly insane day, I'd say that I felt anxiously suspended in time and space between George Floyd's murder and the November elections, surrounded by raging wildfires, stuck inside with air purifiers working 24/7 and deprived of my daily earthly anchors, feeling neither here nor there, but definitely aware of being smack in the middle of a global pandemic that was strangely both suffocating and causing me to hold my breath behind a mask that was simultaneously protecting me from the coronavirus and harmful smoke particles. It really doesn't get more insane than this.

Perhaps the truth of our dire straits is not sinking in because we are wasting precious time on deciphering our complicated syndromes, which could honestly keep us in analysis paralysis for lifetimes. We are invested in practical, quick-fix solutions to make our complex modern lives less complex and give us more breathing room to get ahead, but this unfortunately never happens. As much as I loved meeting my clients in person, I, and I believe many others, have given up our physical spaces and offices because of the convenience of virtual meetings. We are grieving the transition from in-person to virtual meetings but are at the same time getting accustomed to and enjoying the ease and minimal effort in getting to work. Is this how we have gradually denatured ourselves over the generations? I can imagine the next generation, not knowing any better, and adopting this more advanced but denatured existence. Will we, humans, over an extended time become uber efficient and productive, but also more sedentary, dystopic, unconscious, and disconnected, as portrayed in animated movies, like Pixar's brilliant *WALL·E,* and completely forget one day all that we've taken for granted and lost? How about we wise up, save ourselves unnecessary suffering, and trust our soul's higher knowing and bottom line: our self-serving ways are killing us and countless forms of life on the planet.

How did we get too smart and stubborn for our own good? We are moving so fast and are so enthralled by the instant rewards of our fancy inventions that we don't have the time or incentive to drop in and reflect on the long view and our highest good to check if we are still aligned. Our nearest relatives, primates, may shed light on what happened somewhere along our human evolution. Some primate species have gotten so smart, they're starting to show exploitative and ruthless behaviors that we once thought were only characteristic of humans. Tool-wielding long-tailed macaques on a remote island in Thailand have learned to forage and to crack shellfish open using a rock. They are the only other species, beside humans, who have learned to overharvest a food source to the point of near extinction.[1] A similar species of little rascals are using their smarts to bully and take advantage of squirrels in southern India. The squirrels have a much better nose for detecting ripe jackfruit. Once they do, the monkeys shoo them away and steal their fruit. Even when their bellies are full, the monkeys continue to harass the squirrels and prevent them from eating other fruit hanging on trees in abundance.[2] There are many species on the planet—plants, insects, birds, fish, and mammals—who develop cooperative relationships with one another, within and across species. Do these primates have a sadistic gene that feels tickled when hogging all the food, food they can't even consume, and having others cater to their needs without any sign of recognition or reward? The drill, a little-studied Old World monkey, looks like a baboon and lives in a small area in West Africa. They are highly social, and live in multi-male and multi-female groups of about twenty individuals, with one male who dominates breeding choices. At least on one occasion, this alpha male ousted an elderly, toothless male out of the group to live and struggle on his own. The only way he was able to eat was by scavenging for food, because of his missing canines.[3] What burden or threat did he pose to the alpha male? None that I can think of other than looking like a loser. The extreme ostracization of this vulnerable group member—making him fend for himself, alone—seems even more ruthless because these primates have a keen understanding of the survival and emotional benefits of a social group. Apparently, knowing this doesn't necessarily translate into empathizing with or caring one iota about the fate of the ousted member.

IS THIS DARWINISM?

Does survival of the fittest mean that nature will always favor the most selfish and the strongest and bossiest alpha members of a group? When I look at the behavior of our primate relatives, it appears that pro-social urges and consciousness can't keep up with our smarts and don't stand a chance compared to hunger, power-tripping, and greed. If the macaques were made conscious that their overindulgence on oysters would mean no more one day, would they stop eating them in excess? Trust that the other guy or gal wasn't secretly harvesting more than their allotted share? What benefit would this restraint offer them? I doubt that this foresight would be enough to change their behavior. I wish I could ask a silverback gorilla, who could probably kill a youngster with just one slap, what he gets out of self-restraint. Silverbacks, the alpha males in gorilla social groups, have the patience and gentleness of a saint even when they are relentlessly used as jungle gyms and trampolines by their tireless offspring.[4] Is it just instinct or do we have the potential to consider the needs of others and balance these with our own in a double-minded manner, as silverbacks, chimpanzees (who'd bravely risk their lives to protect offspring),[5] and many primate mothers are able to do? Growing up in a teeming-with-life tropical climate—mosquitoes, grass lice, sand lice, flesh-eating bacteria, rats, snakes, etc.—taught me that Mother Earth is not to be messed with when dishing out natural consequences. She is generous, fierce, and ruthless, unwavering in upholding a system of checks and balances that especially helped derailing ego-minds get back in line. For instance, the long-tailed macaques on the remote island in Thailand will soon need to find a new food source. Their oyster foraging technology may get forgotten entirely, and oysters may get the chance to recover, or not. The fact that the macaques are confined to a limited space, and have not yet figured out how to scale and spread their exploitative tendencies with more sophisticated discoveries and modern technology—a boat, an airplane, a computer, and the internet—across the planet is a relief and a benefit for the greater good. They will be forced to change their ways or may even become extinct themselves if they don't learn the importance of sustainable foraging. Our human advancements in technology are deluding us to think that we are smarter than these macaques and are a few steps ahead of mystery and nature. The truth is we're tragically depriving ourselves of the greatest gift of life by continuously chasing shiny metal objects and stringing them together in sophisticated arrangements. Sadly, they will never come close to the wonders and restorative life-giving powers of nature, Mother Earth, and our bodies.

THE BIGGEST LITTLE FARM

John and Molly Chester are bold dreamers and one day—nudged by their pooch, who had trouble adjusting to living in a cramped apartment—decided to upend their lives and purchase a two-hundred-acre, abandoned farm in Moorpark, California. They hoped to restore it into an organic farm and could not be swayed otherwise, even though their vision seemed ludicrous to many. Perseverance and trust in the innate wisdom and harmony of nature are what pulled this hardy couple through when they reached their edge, over and over again, and discovered deeper reservoirs of tolerance for hardship, setbacks, and natural disasters. At first, just getting a shovel through the parched, barren dirt seemed impossible, but with the help of worms and organic matter, they were able to revive the soil and start planting, bit by bit. They were often just inches away from throwing in the towel when, just in the nick of time, a new animal or insect species made a natural solution possible. Pest problems or major issues that seemed insurmountable just days before—ranging from snails, swarms of bugs, snakes, and coyotes eating fruit, eggs, and chicken—were resolved when practicing equanimity. This created spaciousness and solid emotional grounding to make aligned interventions inspired by nature—geese, owls, and other creatures coming to the rescue—instead of stepping in with premature solutions and misaligned fix-its—e.g., shooting the coyotes—that their frustrated ego-minds were tempting them with.

In what may have seemed like a grueling eight years of extreme ups and downs—a pendulum that was given permission to swing as far left and as far right as needed amid the threat of wildfires and flash floods—things eventually settled down, and the formerly abandoned farm is now a gorgeous and luscious, fully functional organic farm with a biodiverse habitat and a wide variety of flora and fauna. The many animals and plants (now more than one hundred vegetable and seventy-five fruit varieties) at the Biggest Little Farm[6]—Apricot Lane Farms—have restored its equilibrium and delicate balance with indisputable, well-documented data; this proves that it's not too late to harmonize our arid human nature and ecosystems as long as we practice similar perseverance and trust in the process. The mysterious and powerful interconnections between all forms of life is not a fairy tale and feel-good fantasy. It's well and alive, and provides inspiring evidence that we can renature our minds and lives in similar ways as long as we surrender to nature and act upon the guidance we are receiving. Making mental space for this disintegrating and reharmonizing process is the best way to prime the mind for soul authority.

A SOULCENTRIC LIFE: MORE FREE THAN YOU'LL EVER BE

As a child, the truth helped me to feel awake, strong, and protected. I searched high and low until I found it. I vividly remember reading about an enslaved man who taunted his enslaver while being tortured to death. One of the last things the enslaved man said to his enslaver was "I'm more free than you will ever be." I wouldn't be able to tell you how I knew the difference between what was real and what was fake, what was true and what was untrue. I just knew in my bones that what the enslaved man said sounded true and powerful, and that he'd checkmated his enslaver, who was so sure that he had the upper hand. All I wanted was someone to validate that a soulcentric life was the better choice, and when considering the two horrific human conditions I was reading about—one of the many hypothetical mental games I liked to play—I decided that I'd rather be the enslaved man than the enslaver. I must have been around eight and was already interested in death and very intense and dark books, like Elie Wiesel's *Night*.[7] They stretched my mind and spiritual muscles to an expanded size that my body must have lived in before, because the spiritual epiphanies in them made me feel at peace and powerful. I intuitively got that those who didn't live a soulcentric life were taking their misery out on others, and I needed to understand how they'd contracted this terrible sickness of the soul, to protect myself and my family from it. Although the enslaved man was more free than his enslaver, the ones who were truly free were the Maroons in the jungle, living according to the laws of nature. I didn't get why living in peace like this was so difficult to honor, and how humans in most of the world got sucked into doing such inhumane things, believing that it made them superior.

HEALING WHITE SUPREMACY AT THE ROOT

It's been heartening to work with young, unstoppable trailblazers who are just as relentless as I was in getting to the bottom of the truth by confronting soul pain passed down through the generations. Many BIPOC have traced trauma in their lineage to colonization, slavery, white supremacy, and patriarchy. White clients have helped me to gain more clarity about what's driving this oppressive white power, privilege, and supremacy: fear and pain of losing their (false, but only known) "white cultural identity," terror and utter helplessness in grieving older and deeper cultural losses, and difficulty accessing social, political, and economic oppression and religiously sanctioned torture that occurred centuries ago in Europe. It explains why "higher taxes" (even when exempt from needing to pay them) and certain buzzwords trigger immediate associations of political oppression, leading to the rejection of government-sanctioned public goods and services that they themselves need and would benefit from, such as education, health care, retirement, and so on. Many would rather forgo these benefits if these resources threaten to close the gap between them and their scapegoat. Their misguided attempts to escape and to exorcise the demons (through racist scapegoating: hate speech, bigotry, and violence) that are still plaguing them may feel effective; but much of the unresolved pain, violence, misery, and internalized oppression within these groups actually ends up devolving into a white power "culture." Unfortunately, this culture often functions more like a social pact, fraught with dirty pain habits and denial of one's true nature, ethnic heritage, and feelings of inferiority. The lower self dominates over others and any sense of integrity to temporarily "feel better," but this prevents the person from ever "getting better" and repairing soul splits at the root levels.

HAUNTED BY THE WAYS OF THE OLD WORLD

Most white people in the United States don't realize that many of their ancestors were serfs and peasants, and were treated almost as poorly as enslaved people within the oppressive feudal system of the Middle Ages. As indentured servants, they didn't own the land they worked on and were pledged to their feudal lord for life. Unlike enslaved people, they could not be bought or sold, but in some places, like Russia and England, they could be traded like enslaved people, could be sold with the land, could be tortured and abused with no rights over their own bodies, and could marry only with their lord's permission.[8] They worked long days, six days a week, and sometimes did not have enough food to survive. Most were dead before they reached forty years of age.[9] The dirty pain patterns and the kind of self-system that were passed down through the generations resemble the structural layout of the medieval castles, manors, and fiefs of the Middle Ages, a setup designed to protect the grave inequities and the power of the royal blue bloods and monarchs that were supposedly granted through divine right. Those who inherited this self-system, regardless of actual ranks, likely feel under constant threat, eager to defend unearned and religiously endorsed entitlements and privileges, and intolerant of self-reflection and vulnerability. Challenging what influenced their thinking and intergenerational trauma is often completely off-limits. Because the "perks" of white privilege and supremacy are not paying off as much as they used to—and are causing increasingly more negative social repercussions—bursts of extinction energy and more desperate and violent attempts to cling onto these destructive and deluded ideologies are being released and employed. Consciousness, financial security, psychological and professional growth, and upward mobility are confused with elitism, and seen as the enemy, spiking the walls with more impenetrable defensiveness. This is how many remain stuck in caterpillarhood.

It's not too late to let go of these familiar, but false stories and dig deeper until you get to a level within yourself that feels a bit mushy and foreign. This is the part of yourself to examine within your safe sanctuary. A sanctuary chrysalis that's fully occupied with your primal energy and guided by your truth-body will naturally reveal the cracks, blindspots, imbalances, ego-ecosystem misalignments, energy leaks, and porous boundaries in need of repair. Each of the elements will fill in and harmonize these imbalances in our ecosystem just like

Earth naturally does. All that the ego-mind needs to do now is make space, back up, and surrender to this renaturing transformation and metamorphosis into a higher form—your butterfly self.

REFLECTIONS FROM PRACTITIONERS ON WORKING WITH THE AIR ELEMENT

Air bestows license to explore ideas that would otherwise be deemed outlandish. When channeling the air element, my thoughts are carefree and whimsical, yet steadily guided by some unknown force—just like the wind as we know it. It transports and encourages me to conduct an investigation from every possible angle without fear of retribution. Without fear of arriving at a "wrong" conclusion, air imbues wisdom and experience. I can enact countless scenarios with air until I find a solution. I can navigate stressors at work with grace, wisdom, and professionalism. Similarly, family predicaments become a mere quandary worth dissecting. With every tangled, convoluted problem I am given, air displays new doors and opportunities that I otherwise would have missed. Imaginative solutions are only limited by fictitious rules that forbid exploration. Air has no understanding of "forbidden" and thus encourages and supports any concept I care to study.

—Valerie Vargas, EdD, special education
teacher and artist

Soul Authority sessions allowed me to access a deeper truth within myself that I have known all along but have had difficulty bringing to my conscious awareness. With this awareness, I am opening up to different parts of myself that have needed love and attention for a long, long time.

—Grace Mitchell, MFT, psychotherapist

Meditation Script for Air

Imagine sitting at the base of your Sacred Ancestral Tree in your inner sanctuary and leaning your back against the trunk. Feel its sturdy support light up your spine, letting you know that the tree has your back and is strengthening your courage and backbone. Rest your head against the trunk of the tree. Open your crown chakra above your head to receive inspiration and guidance from the sky, and open your base chakra to ground and root nourishment from the earth into your body and sanctuary.

> *Note: Ground yourself first with the full Sacred Ancestral Tree meditation script if you don't feel relaxed and resourced enough to go deeper in your meditation with the Air element and with any of the subsequent elements in the steps that follow.*

Notice your deep and intimate relationship with air, the invisible and most mysterious of the four elements. Each one of the elements has a constructive and destructive aspect to humans: Air—respiration and storms; Fire—heat and wildfires; Earth—food and earthquakes; Water—hydration and floods. Air is the most critical of these four in keeping us alive. Most living things perish within minutes without oxygen. Still, it's the easiest one to take for granted because it requires us opening our third eye, our sixth chakra, to "see" its important role and impact. Air connects us to all living things through our interdependence with this sacred life force: the breath of life. Your lungs and respiration are like the atmosphere and airstreams, capturing, recycling, and exchanging gases, oxygen, and carbon dioxide within your body's ecosystem. Breathe together with your tree, inhaling oxygen and exhaling carbon dioxide, and imagine your tree inhaling carbon dioxide and exhaling oxygen. Reflect for a moment on how beautiful your symbiotic relationship is, each providing this essential breath of life to the other.

If the Earth's crust formed one hour (instead of 4.5 billion years) ago, the amount of time that humans have been around would be less than a minute.[10] The tree is one of your oldest, earth-bound ancestors (appearing about six to seven minutes ago using this time clock), alchemizing and embodying the magical energies of the above and the below and the life-giving support of each of the elements—sun-Fire, Earth, Air, and Water—turning it into food and making the planet habitable for all living things. We wouldn't be here without trees. Take a moment to notice the flow of air in your sanctuary and that gentle breeze of air softly caressing the skin on your face. What does it smell like? What does it sound like? Perhaps you're able to smell the scent of plant allies such as peppermint, lavender, rosemary, sage, or palo santo wood. Or hear the rustling of leaves above your head. Allow this fresh air to clear your mind and help you face your highest truth, the big picture, and the long view. Open your mind to new visions and ideas, and breathe in more spaciousness into the familiar, but most likely false and limited, narratives and stories about yourself and the world.

See them unwind and realign into a self-concept and worldview that your heart longs for and recognizes as true. Enjoy this spaciousness to unfold your cramped brain; and invite even more creative solutions, inspiration, and innovative ways of looking at reality and current-day problems to circulate through your mind and thoughts. Allow the ego-mind to take note of this data-gathering process that is driven less by logical thought, empirical data, and hard facts, as is predominantly taught in school, but instead prioritizes wisdom, big-picture clarity, and knowing, gathered and tagged as true through direct felt-experience, which is more than enough to serve as the guiding principles to navigate life.

Allow the ego-mind to take stock that your soul is better suited in the role of visionary. The ego-mind provides concrete and often dichotomous information to keep you physically safe and healthy, and together, your ego-mind and your soul are in the best position to decide on an optimal course of action. Give your ego-mind an expanded view of how long your ancestors have been forced to focus more on physical survival and all of its modern-day mutations. Has this focus undermined your ability to hold space for a larger and deeper truth that is better aligned with your greatest potential and well-being, both on the physical and spiritual levels? Can your ego-mind entertain paradoxical, cyclical, and spiral thought, instead of just linear thought, when reconsidering challenges and fears? What once seemed guaranteed safe may now seem suffocating, stifling, and forgoing important opportunities for growth and adventure; and what once seemed too risky and dangerous may now seem like an enticing opportunity that's ready to be reexamined, digested, repurposed, and transformed into something better.

Give your go-getter tendencies the opportunity to sit back and relax by resting your head against the tree trunk and giving life a chance to meet you halfway instead of chasing it so much. Notice what happens when your ego-mind trusts your inner experience of being safe, whole, and abundantly full, purely based on felt-sensations, rather than roaming through life hungry, empty, and constantly needing to acquire proof and permission that it's safe to trust, relax, and enjoy life, only to discover that these feelings are shallow and short-lived. Reflect on the unwavering presence of your ethereal and earthly ancestors and parents, sun and Earth, and the fact that they have never abandoned you, not even for a second. Recognize that they are two living beings that are deserving of your total surrender and trust. Notice what it feels like in your body when considering running your most important decisions and challenges by them from now on and allowing them to cradle you in their warm womb. Remember that you are a beloved child of nature and a nature spirit. All that you need to do to renature yourself is re-member your true nature.

Allow each of these insights and teachings from your Sacred Ancestral Tree guide and Air guide to sink in and take root in the depths of your consciousness and the cells and bones of your body. Know that this is your most updated and upgraded self and that you will notice shifts within yourself and in all your relationships with others for the next days, weeks, months, and years to come. Slowly retrace your steps and find your way back into the room or setting that you're in. Notice the chair that you're sitting in, stretch a bit, and bring your mind and attention fully back into the here and now. Notice your surroundings, wiggle into your body, bring all of your energy and attention back to the space you are in, and open your eyes slowly.

Alchemy Action Steps: Set daily intentions with clarity.

We are used to being gaslit and lied to, mined for our attention and buying power, and manipulated into spinning our hamster wheels as quickly as we can with false promises that this will actually get us somewhere over some rainbow faster. In reality, this mindless activity is preventing us from ever being still and conscious enough to realize that we will never really get ahead of ourselves or the pack within this capitalistic matrix and grind. We may know this but the allure of sexy objects and distracting facades continues to make this pursuit of the promised land irresistible. As you walk through life this week, drastically change your perspective toward having no choice about going through the motions of life, and explore what actual choices you do have, even if for now it is just in how you perceive (your) reality. See where you are able to pause, question, and pivot. Gather data and note what it's like to trailblaze in a brand-new direction.

CHAPTER 10

Step 3: Fire

Tired of Putting out Fires and Emitting Toxic Fumes of Resentment but Dismissing Personal Warming Signals and Burnout?

Objective of the Fire Guide and Protection Teachings: To gain a visceral sense of where we begin and end, and to set clear energetic, emotional, and physical boundaries that will remedy default patterns and common struggles around imploding and/or exploding our life energy, by learning to metabolize pain imbalances. By recognizing burnout, resentment, and personal warming signals, the Fire Protection guide helps us to fight toxic energy, internalized blame, and harm and to expel them out of our sanctuary like a fever. This is what boosts our vitality and immunity, and fuels our courage to pursue our passions and soul callings.

TOPICS:

Boundaries are your best friend: how to be kind and wild, soft and strong

The root cause of our love–hate relationship with healthy anger: what it is and isn't

We are mirrors whose brightness is wholly derived from the sun that shines upon us.

—C. S. LEWIS

We cannot steal the fire. We must enter it.

—RUMI

From the perspective of Chinese medicine, modern life generates excess heat. In Western terms, this is a result of sympathetic overdrive—too much cortisol and adrenalin—that sets the stage for inflammation. The solution is to restore the inner terrain, supporting host resilience. By nourishing the yin (moisture, blood), the overstimulation that produces excess yang (heat) is tempered.

—CHINESE MEDICINE WORKS

Our earliest prehuman ancestors were trailblazers in their own right. Around 2.5 million years ago, they learned to harvest fire from lava streams[1] in Africa and greatly accelerated their brain development by cooking food and freeing up time to enhance their survival strategies. Fire not only protected them from wild animals; it also protected them from cold, from dangers lurking in the dark, and from poisonous and disease-carrying insects, pests, and bacteria. A strong inner Fire is synonymous with a strong immune system, and just as an outer Fire needs to be tended to with constant care, a strong inner Fire needs similar tending to, making sure that there is a steady flow of Air (inspiration) without the risk of it getting blown out (stormy winds) and enough wood to feed it that's not too wet or dry (Earth and Water in balance, representing grounding, emotional regulation, stability, and action). A healthy inner Fire is cultivated by making sure that we no longer ignore personal warming signals (resentments and frustrations) and have plenty of Water (soothing, self-care, emotional support, and resources) nearby to contain the Fire should it get out of hand.

FIRE BOOSTS OUR IMMUNITY

The Fire in our heart center is tended to by each of the elements and requires our support of their efforts. Notice the connection between your Air element, inspiration, boosting the vitality of your inner Fire, your passion, and vice versa. Notice how your body naturally gains vitality and clarity and defends itself from pathogens and harmful attacks when oxygenated, especially when you don't meddle with this process and override it with your usual stories. Your body responds to misaligned energy by heating up and concentrating its defenses through an army of orchestrated killer T-cells and white blood cells that produce pain, inflammation, and fevers that have only one objective—to expel the foreign particles and restore your ecosystem's health and equilibrium. As peace- and harmony-loving creatures, we unfortunately undermine this gift by splitting intense emotions into good and bad categories, and pegging anger and rage as negativity and hate. Our knee-jerk response, when mistreated, is to fight hate with compassion and love, not more hate, just as Dr. Martin Luther King Jr. advised. But what happens when you're subjected to hatred and inequalities that don't ease up but take the form of relentless psychological, emotional, and life-threatening physical harm and trauma? Your anger will naturally start to intensify based on the severity of the threat. Do we honor or squash this energy? Turn it inward? How do we embrace it to boost our immunity, just like a fever does, without imploding or exploding—i.e., punishing ourselves or lashing out at others?

HEALTHY SELF-DEFENSE AND ANGER ARISE OUT OF LOVE, NOT HATE

There is far more to love and hate than meets the eye. Similarly, there is far more to anger than imploding and exploding. These unstable patterns are usually due to a lack of energetic boundaries and a tendency to polarize positive and negative emotions in the same way we have pegged black and white, light and dark, good and bad into opposites. We'll miss a lot of nuanced lessons and the multidimensional nature of reality that trauma, fear, isolation, pain, and disconnection are attempting to teach us if we continue to do so. A good number of modern-day corporations, organizations, and systems are run by leaders and supporters who are highly invested in exploiting and dominating us through abuse of political, military, police, and economic power. We, sensitive souls, have big reactions to these imbalances in an attempt to realign the whole (and ourselves). These misaligned systems, situations, and individuals evoke outrage, fear, and helplessness and our most intense objections. These emotions are totally appropriate and shouldn't be shut down or squashed in any way. As a matter of fact, it's necessary to feel the intensity of these emotions to alchemize the imbalances with energy that matches them. The trick is being able to do so without going haywire, short-circuiting, or being afraid that you'll spontaneously combust in the process, which many of us fear doing more and more these days. This reactivity makes us very susceptible to manipulation and mind control. Although it's true that we can't fight hate and divisiveness with more hate and divisiveness, we won't be able to reform these systems with just a soft glow of love and light either. Double-minded strategies and practices entail getting ourselves into optimal shape, clarity, and health to meet today's astronomical challenges—the ongoing threat of powerful leaders in every industry who will do all that they can to manipulate and dominate us to maintain status-quo power and privileges by sabotaging the rights, power, and privileges of those they deem less than themselves. Before we can catalyze change, we need to focus on our wholeness first, by learning to fiercely protect ourselves and our energy in our respective sanctuaries. When we feel safe and buffered, we're much better prepared to deal with pushback and obstacles along our path toward liberation.

OUR AMYGDALA: MORE THAN THE BRAIN'S FEAR CENTER

The amygdala is commonly known as the brain's fear center, but this may be more of a cultural myth than a universal truth. "Scientific facts" often take on a life of their own. Scientists make legitimate and exciting new discoveries, with the best tools available to them in their time, and these findings get verified, modified, cited, and, eventually, repeated without question. Over time, insights get simplified for nonscientists, and translated into the plain language of introductory textbooks. If they get repeated often enough, for long enough, some of these facts even seep into the popular culture. So it is with the amygdala, often held responsible for our primitive and reptilian impulses. This common notion about the amygdala is not entirely wrong. But two psychological scientists are arguing that it's rather simplistic and incomplete. A more accurate view, according to neuroscientists William Cunningham and Tobias Brosch, is that the amygdala appraises the world much more broadly, looking not just for threats but for anything that might be important to furthering one's goals and motivations. "Fearsome stimuli might indeed be relevant—almost certainly are—but so too might unusual, interesting, ambiguous, and even positive stimuli, depending on the person and the situation. In short, uncertainty is more arousing than what's familiar. Some subjects respond more to positive and negative stimuli than to neutral stimuli; others mostly to negative stimuli; and still others to positive information. In other words, amygdala activation may not have the same meaning for everyone; it may instead reflect the psychological state of the individual."[2] I would add that it could reflect the psychological state of a cultural and social group, as we are still so much like monkeys: monkey see, monkey do.

RARE COURAGE AND SOUL AUTHORITY

It was bone chilling and at the same time extraordinary to hear (firsthand while standing at the exact site) how a gonini—a massive harpy eagle with a wingspan as wide as seven feet and looking like a dinosaur raptor—had snatched up a small toddler a few years ago from a patch of cleared communal Maroon farmland while her parents were busy farming. These goninis prey on small monkeys, sloths, and other small animals and tragically lasered in on a child that day to feed itself and its young. Their seven-inch spread of talons, larger than a grown man's hand, are found lying around in the wild, perhaps as a reminder of their presence and the danger they pose. The grief about this event was real, but there was also a palpable deep acceptance of mystery's ways, including death. I understood for the first time how immense our speciesism is when I stood there face to face with people where it was completely absent. There was no hatred or anger toward this gonini, no expressed desire to hunt or kill it, or a sense of terror living in such close proximity to these predators. It wouldn't be that hard to get a gun or have one with them for protection, but there were very few signs of fear or death anxiety to warrant such action, even after such a traumatic event. In their presence, I experienced a deep knowing of how futile this would be. Danger and the risk of dying were ever-present, but this led to more alert and, ironically, to more relaxed living provided that our ego-mind feels held and safe in its rightful, proportional, and aligned place within the arms of Mother Nature.

LOW DEATH ANXIETY LEADS
TO FULL-THROTTLE LIVING

After this horrific incident, all that the villagers did was build a cover for small children to hide under when their parents were too busy to protect them. They weren't being stupid or spiritually bypassing the terrible pain this incident caused. Their response was merely one of the extraordinary and rare examples of what living in harmony with nature for centuries looked like in this particular Maroon village near Kayana. There seemed to be very little opportunity, benefit, or space to fester in good versus bad ego-judgments and neuroses within this community. Life was too much in flux and too full of surprises, requiring their full-bodied and sober presence and responsiveness. Feedback on whether or not they made an aligned or misaligned move came almost instantly from their environment and demanded swift and continuous adjustments. The Maroons' low death anxiety is paradoxically connected to their refined sixth sense and their skills in carefully balancing life and death on a continuous basis. From birth on, they learn to notice subtle signs and clues of animal tracks for food and to avoid danger lurking everywhere. This evolved inner state involves shrinking themselves to a humble size so that they can more accurately discern how to navigate their environment and be fully present instead of shut down amid ongoing stimulation and daily life-threatening situations.

BEHIND THE ARMOR AND FACADE

Right now, default self-blame and self-loathing cause us to hold up a facade and hard, protective armor around our heart, vulnerability, and sixth sense. We "defend" ourselves against hearing hard truths, and we don't take more responsibility where we can and must. This is not the formula for fierce boundaries or how to stand in your soul authority when challenged or tested. I firmly believe that if we use our wits and our natural human genius, and fill up with our own energy and collective determination, we can meet modern-day challenges and dangers with more presence and fierce compassion. Tough love and firm limits—e.g., strategic interventions, decisive leadership, and laser-focused policies—have proved to be most effective in dismantling rigid systems that are invested in upholding their privileges and pecking order. We are most equipped to do this when our own soul authority and natural genius are operating at full throttle. No one will ever truly get ahead by using divide-and-conquer scare tactics; and the quicker this reality sinks in, the better off we will be in liberating ourselves from oppressive, fragmenting systems and transforming and repairing them from the inside out, starting with ourselves. It's illuminating to compare our behaviors and attitudes with those of people from entirely different parts of the world. It's the fastest way to get a fresh perspective on a situation and to gain self-awareness, something my rich multicultural environment allowed me to do on a daily basis while growing up. Maroons most certainly dispel the myth that our existential angst and modern-day fears and anxiety stem from past encounters with predators and are hardwired in our amygdala.

CONFIRMATION BIAS

We're often told that our skittish behaviors and hypervigilance helped us to survive and are the reason why we are now stuck with a fight-flight-freeze response that we can't do anything about. This kind of thinking creates a closed feedback loop of confirmation bias. Those using imbalanced power, aggression, and domination out of fear interpreted and created their life experiences and environment in a similar skewed fashion, reinforcing the need to rely on their imbalanced methods to survive. Those with an unwavering conviction to remain in balance, and to tap the depths of their soul authority, also did so. They remained in balance with nature and their surroundings and, interestingly, also felt reinforced. The Maroons show that it is possible to be in ego-eco-aligned soul authority and to walk the planet with the lightest of footprints while living among dinosaur-size eagles, piranhas, crocodiles, snakes, poisonous frogs, bullet ants, and lots of other dangerous predators and creatures. Their choices feel as natural to them as ours feel to us. This is the thing: We are always "right" and will succeed in justifying whatever our trauma-body or our truth-body wants us to do. The key is in discerning what part of us is in charge: our heart or our hurt. In the Maroons' case, the heart is leading and helping them to make wiser and more aligned choices that we can learn from.

Allow yourself to consider these aspects of your human potential and most ancient and courageous ancestry—there is so much collective shame that's been stuck in our psyches and bones because of the cowardice, greed, disconnection, and so on of our more recent and recorded past. Any one of us who goes further back will encounter ancestors who lived bravely and harmoniously with nature and other animals. Against all odds, our planet is still blessed by a handful of people, tribes, and living traditions similar to these. These tribes and cultures have survived this long, and would continue to do so if it weren't for their modern-day brothers and sisters, us, slowly killing them off by encroaching on their sacred lands and ways of life. We can support them by honoring the aspects within ourselves that long to live in alignment with nature, and by boosting our courage, integrity, and humility by facing and dealing with modern-day dangers with greater presence, wisdom, maturity, and agility.

REFLECTIONS FROM PRACTITIONERS ON WORKING WITH THE FIRE ELEMENT

I'm constantly confronted with tricky family binds, but instead of indulging in circular conversations (usually about politics), I let Fire guide me. This results in a peaceful flexibility as opposed to rigidity, stubbornness, and ultimately tears. With Fire, I'm permitted to create space within myself for the full effect of triggers, emotions, and fears. They simply just run their course. I allow my fire to heat up, burning foreign and toxic narratives or imbalances—like a fever eradicating some virus. Consequently, any lingering pain from my childhood or potential bitterness and disappointment is alchemized and rebirthed as something vital: boundaries. In a sort of spiritual chemical reaction, creative solutions begin to sprout from ashes where my fire has burned. The boundaries that guide and protect me are modeled by the healthy, comforting warmth that is Fire.

—Valerie Vargas, EdD, special education
teacher and artist

I went into trance attempting to meet my four elemental guides ... instead I was greeted (repeatedly) by dragons. Though my experience went "off-script," I was, in the end, guided to where I needed to be, both in regard to the elements and in regard to key elements of myself. Later on, I came to encounter more dragons, as well as other guides, to aid me in my alchemical dance with the fire of PTSD. With the help of Loraine, my dragons, the phoenix, and Kali Ma, I was able to transform the trauma—threatening at times to burn through the forest of my heart—into a kind of hearth: a place of warmth and solace. I was able to transform my pain—my sacred inner "fire"—into a source of life rather than a threat to my own.

—Michelle Present, artist, writer, and peer
specialist

Meditation Script for Fire

Imagine sitting at the base of your Sacred Ancestral Tree in your inner sanctuary and leaning your back against the trunk. Feel its sturdy support light up your spine, letting you know that the tree has your back and is strengthening your courage and backbone. Rest your head against the trunk of the tree. Open your crown chakra above your head to receive inspiration and guidance from the sky, and open your base chakra to ground and root nourishment from the earth into your body and sanctuary.

Feel the sun on your body, warming you all over, keeping the temperature of your ecosystem within a soothing, stable, and ideal range, both within your human body and within Earth's ecosystem. Fire and magma are the heart, womb, and blood vessels of Gaia, which has an inner core of about the same temperature as the sun. It has created mountains and ridges on Earth's surface and has spewed out—over millions of years—water vapor, mineral-rich land mass, and fertile soil, thereby turning what once was a water world into the beautiful life-giving planet we get to enjoy and cherish today.

As you lean against your tree and soak up the sun, see if you can tell where your body begins and ends, and where to draw this boundary that gives your parasympathetic nervous system the most peace. Especially for those of us who have thin skin, this is easier said than done. Feel your energy field expand and contract, and imagine your energetic boundaries around your entire sanctuary protecting you from harm and unseen energetic imbalances and attacks. Be as bold as you need to be. Most of us are living in too cramped of a space.

Notice how often these boundaries and our protective inner fire—our frustrations, anger, and rage in response to social mistreatment and injustices—were ignored and dismissed, or used to justify violence and punishment throughout history. How did this play out in your ancestry and culture whenever you or someone else challenged oppressive customs and harmful privileges? An implosive and explosive pattern that looks like a wave probably developed and replaced the sturdy and stable boundary that your Fire element prefers. In the imploded state, you may feel depleted, helpless, depressed, anxious, ashamed, inferior, and guilty. It's the result of internalizing the blame, rejected emotions, and anger that were projected on us, or often, the result of inheriting this imploded state that our ancestors passed down to us. In the exploded state, we project unacceptable and hard feelings onto others, or we funnel them into workaholic or frenzied activity so that we don't need to digest and metabolize them, passing the pattern along to the next generation.

With the help of your Fire guide, serving as an emotional and energetic fever of sorts, push this harmful, imbalanced pattern out of your energy field and give yourself as much space as needed until you feel reset, spacious, and at peace. You may need to expand further out and take up more inner space than any of your ancestors have ever done. Keep going until you are able to rest the implosion–explosion pattern on the bark of your Sacred Ancestral Tree and seal your field and sanctuary with the energetic boundary that first appeared when asking Fire to set your aligned boundary.

Remember that it's heat, not light, that transforms. This is how you set a true boundary without bypassing unresolved issues. If a part of you is still attached to this pattern—which is the case with many of us, in more ways than we realize—go back to steps 1 and 2, and work some more with your Sacred Ancestral Tree guide and Air guide to unpack and unravel the false control that this implosion–explosion pattern promises you. When you feel clear about the samsaric runaround and double-bind that this pattern is trapping you in, work again with Fire to reset new energetic boundaries with this misaligned core belief. You may need to use this fire and heat to alchemize old and limiting beliefs (the mental order of the past) into a higher form and spiritual order. Do this as often as you need to until you feel realigned and rooted in the throne of your truth-body.

Allow each of these insights and teachings from your Sacred Ancestral Tree guide and Fire guide to sink in and take root in the depths of your consciousness and the cells and bones of your body. Know that this is your most updated and upgraded self and that you will notice shifts within yourself and in all your relationships with others for the next days, weeks, months, and years to come. Slowly retrace your steps and find your way back into the room or setting that you're in. Notice the chair that you're sitting in, stretch a bit, and bring your mind and attention fully back into the here and now. Notice your surroundings, wiggle into your body, bring all of your energy and attention back to the space you are in, and open your eyes slowly.

Alchemy Action Steps: Say yes or no with courage.

The time has come for us to upgrade and become energy efficient on all levels of our existence. We cannot neglect our inner appliances. *Are yours energy efficient?* The ultimate goal of my Soul Authority system is to help you to become as energy-efficient, balanced, and integrated as possible in the quickest, most organic, authentic, and sustainable way that is humanly possible. What does being energy-efficient have to do with soul authority? How often do you give your power away, and remain in a tug-of-war with someone or some system that is unwilling to give it back? Are you perhaps still stuck in one of these dynamics, not realizing that it's your birthright to fully own your power and your authority? That you don't owe anyone any explanation or apology to protect what's yours? That you can walk away from any situation where your authority and wholeness are not honored and celebrated? Wouldn't you be much more efficient in getting your soul purpose and true work done if you weren't busy all day in managing these repetitive spin cycles that did nothing other than waste energy and damage your inner wiring? Confusion around this is the weed, and every piece of root of this confusion that is still scattered around will grow into another power struggle at some point. How can you pull weedy patterns out at the root level by setting clear and no-nonsense energetic boundaries?

CHAPTER 11

Step 4: Earth

Paving over Unresolved Problems with Quick Fixes Instead of Pulling Them out at the Root?

Objective of the Earth Guide and Grounding Teachings: To keep track of our organic growth in physical ways and to measure our progress and mastery of all aspects of our being, including our spiritual development. By connecting with and rooting in the true self, the Earth Grounding guide provides nourishment, structure, and stability, has our back, and allows the ego-mind to realign itself to Mother Nature's integrity, rhythms, and slow pace. This embodied wisdom helps us to take action, shift from analysis paralysis to patience, stop comparing ourselves to others, and enjoy the blooming of our flowers and the sun-ripening of our fruit in our own time.

TOPICS:

How to heal and compost pain and trauma into new growth and beginnings

Earth has your back: the magical and magnetic powers of your assertions and actions

> *This beautiful, bounteous, life-giving planet we call Earth has given birth to each one of us, and each one of us carries the Earth within every cell of our body.... We need to realize that the Earth is not just our environment. The Earth is not something outside of us. Breathing with mindfulness and contemplating your body, you realize that you are the Earth. You realize that your consciousness is also the consciousness of the Earth. Look around you—what you see is not your environment, it is you.*
>
> —THICH NHAT HANH

You are not your body nor your mind. Every experience you have happens in your consciousness. Your body and your mind are the metabolism of experience in consciousness.

—DEEPAK CHOPRA

The ultimate goal of grounding is not static peace and calm but greater inner strength to compost pain and more space to support your dynamic growth.

—LORAINE VAN TUYL

Welcome to the Earth element. Put on your seatbelt. Here is where you get to practice integrating what you have learned into physical, tangible form and take greater action.

If you're unsure about proceeding, you're not alone. Many of our convictions don't align with our actions because of common, baseline splits between our mind, heart, body, and soul. Instead of these parts of ourselves working together, it seems as if they each have their own agenda and are trying to outdo one another. There is an explanation for this. As we became more settled, advanced, industrialized, and "civilized" hundreds to thousands of years ago, so became the need of leaders to divide and conquer us, undermining our integrity and soul authority, and turning us into good and manageable subjects, serfs, peasants, enslaved people, and pawns to make them richer and more powerful. Our ancestors were more often than not manipulated into adopting a particular version of reality that was created for egocentric, patriarchal, and exploitative reasons, and had no other choice but to play by the rules of the game. Questioning or stepping out of the social matrix of the time was not an option and was severely punished through torture, exile, public shaming, discrimination, and so on. The only way that those at the bottom of the ranks could escape these oppressive repercussions was by competing for higher ranks or starting over somewhere else far away. Unfortunately, their past trauma followed them when crossing the ocean and settling in the New World. Creating a just and fair society may have sounded nice to our pioneering and trailblazing ancestors, but they didn't possess the know-how, life experience, opportunities, and skills to make this happen. Most were more drawn to overcompensate for lingering feelings of inferiority by taking advantage of the many ways they felt superior, by oppressing more vulnerable "others," and by establishing a more socially secure position at the top of the ranks.

THE AMERICAN DREAM

Over the generations, the American Dream of being free and everything we could be in the New World got conflated with a competitive, dominating spirit that is as much about winning and filling an inherited void as it is about true equality, fairness, and freedom. When stuck in our individual silos and working on ourselves and our professional development, it's easy to lose sight of the many inconspicuous ways that society has influenced us, and that we, in turn, have influenced society. Today's methods of social conditioning are so sophisticated and smooth that we don't realize that our limited, egocentric beliefs and stunted potential were spread around by an unnamed, social pandemic. Many of us have caught the bug without even realizing it. We tend to 100 percent blame ourselves when we feel ungrounded, overwhelmed, foggy, insecure, or confused. Deep down, we know better but don't dare to trust our truth and power. We've unwittingly become the foot soldiers and marketers for organizations, companies, churches, and businesses, some well intended with quality products and ideas, some not so much. A whole lot of them are just contributing to superfluous consumerism and are finding ways to make a living the best way they know how within industrialized, modern societies. Harboring self-doubt and a fragmented, not-good-enough inner state makes it easier to manipulate and sell us all kinds of feel-good ideas, products, pills, entertainment, ads, news, food, substances, tips, and programs to distract, numb, and soothe our suffering and to supposedly better ourselves, our businesses, and our lives. Sadly, we can't tell anymore if we are paving over deeper problems and shortchanging root solutions that are trying to emerge, or creating problems where there are none and imagining a nagging voice that doesn't really exist. Our culture of instant relief and instant gratification has heightened this challenge. Because of the fortification of our egocentric self, we confuse our trauma-body with our true self, and we haven't used our wise and expansive mind and muscles enough to gain more clarity.

As a result, we are not able to confidently differentiate healthy growing pains from unhealthy prejudices, fear of change, and unmetabolized dirty pain. We don't know when it's wise to "trust our gut" and "follow our heart" or when not to. We wonder if undigested, old hurt is tainting our perspectives and causing us to overreact in an explosive, controlling manner, or if we are afraid of facing hard truths because we have a limited bandwidth and intolerance for growing pains. Either way, our usual methods are keeping us stuck and small. A constricted, false self more easily falls for tempting solutions that often lead to serious problems—e.g., substance abuse, gambling, chronic blaming, overwork-ing, rationalizing, and many other serious modern-day addictions. The cathartic high and release that these addictions provide us can easily steamroll over the many negative repercussions, natural consequences, and dis-ease they simulta-neously cause, such as relational conflicts, financial problems, health concerns, and emotional instability. How do we navigate through this entangled laby-rinth to get to the authentic self?

HUMILITY AND BEING OF HUMUS—EARTH

There are striking parallels between you and your Earth Mother, who is as alive as you are and is fueled by a similar self-regulating life force. Your skull and skeleton are made of solid, strong, and dense bone, like the layered canyons, mountain ranges, granite formations, and crystal caves of Earth. These structures are pro-tecting your most vulnerable organs, fluids, and marrow and give your body its stability, immunity, and vitality. Feel Earth's gravitational forces and your corre-sponding weight and physical density pulling you down, as if weighing you down with rocks. This is not to hold you back and hinder your progress, but to make it easier for you to slow down and anchor in space and time so you can be pres-ent, connect with, and metabolize your life experiences and emotions with the help of your body's heat, passion, and protective boundaries. They are all working together nonstop to reveal what you need for optimal health.

It takes great respect, surrender, and humility (being of humus—earth) to clearly hear and receive guidance that comes through from mystery and nature, especially regarding situations that involve a lot of pain and that cause us to feel ashamed, powerless, lost, and vulnerable. This is precisely the reason we keep falling for the fat, juicy carrot of empty promises that causes us to keep going—instead of dropping into the body—whenever it's dangled in front of us. Our rational ego-mind has difficulty grasping paradox, holistic harmony, and the dynamic forces that orchestrate ego-ecosystem alignment. Because we can't decipher the ambig-uous feelings and mixed sensations that we feel when we are getting closer to our true self, we default to logical thought and reason. If alignment doesn't feel 100 percent good, it must be bad. The ego-mind is also adamant about staying in control and is terrified about giving up power—vulnerability being one of the misleading "bad" feelings. The only way to get out of this vicious cycle is by hack-ing it: stop playing by the usual rules and blindly trusting all that we are used to doing to feel better. Feeling better may not always correlate with getting better. It is very challenging in modern-day societies to recognize when we are dangerously spinning further and further away from our core. Peeling the layers back can help to reveal and amplify the magnetic and, eventually, irresistible pull of the truth.

WHY THE TRUTH TRANSCENDS FEELING GOOD OR BAD

Discovering the truth doesn't "feel good" in every moment, but on a deeper level of our being we feel reintegrated, redeemed, and reestablished in the central thrones of our being when aligned with our truth. Unfortunately, our stubborn ego-minds are capable of pulling an endless number of denial tricks and blinders over our eyes that cause us to avoid taking responsibility for ourselves, our past, and our future potential. It's difficult for our minds to fully absorb the potent truth of who we are and to cultivate the tremendous response-ability and sacred co-creative powers we possess. We tragically either resist, fight, or take for granted the wondrous forces of nature that energize our bodies. Sadly, our disconnected and fear-driven efforts to keep up with and control modern life cause us to objectify, pave over, and reduce life, Earth, and ourselves into concrete and flat versions of reality. Once stuck in this rut, it's easy to forget the reason why we are here now and why we were granted this incredible gift of life in such a close relationship with Mother Earth, herself a miracle child of the cosmos who's generously offering us a glimpse into the light, sparkly stardust, and elemental magic that's buried in each of our own souls. Each breakdown, crisis, and illness offers us a new opportunity to disintegrate and compost our outdated and disconnected ways with renewed hope.

SPIRITUAL COMPOSTING

The spiritual composting process can be a turnoff because it's messy, it's icky, and it makes our lives feel out of our control. All organic composting processes involve some rotten, smelly, creepy, and crawly aspects, but once it's all done, beautiful rich fertile dark soil will feed new life and make our efforts worthwhile. The more we concentrate and intensify our assertions and alchemy action steps with conscious intention, the more we will crystallize them in more solid form and attract synchronistic guidance toward us. It's a process that is as natural and magical as a bone healing and sealing a fracture once it's reset. Serendipitous signs provide us reassurance, validation, guidance, and purpose-related opportunities that similarly seal fractures within our disconnected self and fragmented soul. Mother Earth and the Universe have our backs. Their primary function is to help us expand and grow by materializing an ego-eco reality that is increasingly more aligned with our true nature, wholeness, and well-being.

FILL YOUR SANCTUARY WITH YOUR PRESENCE

A neglected garden is much less hardy and immune to invasive weeds and discarded seeds blown over by the wind than a mature, fully grown garden is. Lack of presence creates a vicious cycle where a false self serves as an empty shell and ends up inviting in exactly what we fear. The more we consciously tend to and embody the totality of our powerful energy field and true nature, the more grounded, resilient, and robust we will feel and be, not leaving space for harmful thoughts or self-doubt. To get a fuller sense of this, reflect for a moment on all living matter—all plant and animal species, including ourselves—that is nourished by and nourishing the planet. Our bodies are 100 percent organic and miraculous physical expressions and extensions of Mother Earth, the result of billions of years of evolution of the simplest of single-celled organisms into one of the most brilliant, advanced, and conscious biological organisms alive today. We are wired to thrive, and we do so when our ego-minds don't interfere and try to outsmart life but choose to align with it. This is difficult to do and sustain, but the grounding and rooting practices in the meditation section have worked wonders for many people and will offer you new inroads and shortcuts to anchor in your core self and soul's home base.

REFLECTIONS FROM PRACTITIONERS ON WORKING WITH THE EARTH ELEMENT

I used to feel like a balloon with a long string, tied to a rock. Should a strong gust of wind come by, I feared it would easily seize me up and uproot my only tether to this world. I feared that one day I might float away from this place. Now, I find I am more like the rock—or rather, I am a distant cousin to the rock. I am a boulder. I cannot be pushed, moved, rocked, or blown away by a gust of wind. I have cracks, crevices, and imperfections exactly as a boulder should. Where my boulder-self ends and Earth begins is difficult to discern. The Earth element brazenly demonstrates the right to take up space on this planet. The right to be imperfect and tenacious, substantial and rooted. I'm no longer fearful of being so easily blown away. I'm grounded, present, and don't see that wavering.

—Valerie Vargas, EdD, special education
teacher and artist

I listened to this meditation while falling asleep one night, and another evening while I was doing qigong. I really resonated with needing that grounding in self and feeling of the "earth" as tender and strong, and especially to enjoy all of the senses in a beautiful way. I think I got really distant from just enjoying the feeling of being alive at some point last week due to emotional overwhelm and dissociation, and this meditation really helped pull me back to that moment-to-moment enjoyment of life. I will have to continue listening to it to continue learning more! When I came to see Loraine, I was often really exhausted all the time. I had headaches, sometimes migraines, dizziness, stomach and digestive pain and food sensitivities (irritable bowel syndrome), chronic bacterial vaginosis or yeast infections, and chronic pelvic pain. I kept having medical tests done, and nothing physical was showing up that Western doctors could figure out how to treat. I actually saw an acupuncturist the spring before I started meeting with Loraine, and she expressed surprise that I and other relatively healthy young women would come in and appear energetically and physically as though they were getting chemo.

It was really painful to be in my body. I couldn't do breathing meditations because even my breath felt painful, but no medical cause or relationship. Now I would say almost all of those things are gone. Occasional dizziness or headaches when I overdo it, but now I know it's my body telling me so. My breath is relaxing to focus on, and I'm just tired because I have a baby that wakes me up at night. I would say symptoms sometimes emerge more as red flags or indicators that something is imbalanced, but also my feeling about them is so different. I now am like, oops, I'm off balance—body, thank you for the reminder to ground, rest, relax, and reconnect with myself.

—Audrey Cohen, LSW, social worker

Meditation Script for Earth

Imagine sitting at the base of your Sacred Ancestral Tree in your inner sanctuary and leaning your back against the trunk. Feel its sturdy support light up your spine, letting you know that the tree has your back and is strengthening your courage and backbone. Rest your head against the trunk of the tree. Open your crown chakra above your head to receive inspiration and guidance from the sky, and open your base chakra to ground and root nourishment from the earth into your body and sanctuary.

While in your healing sacred garden, notice how intimately your five senses are linked to the elements within your inner world. They help you to perceive the energy of the elements and experiences outside of you and to link these with the elements and sensations inside of you. Deepen your awareness of these interconnections. As you explore your sanctuary, smell the fresh scent in the air, hear the gentle rustling of leaves, and feel the soft breeze on your skin. Notice the warmth of the sun on your cheeks and how beautiful it is when it rises up and illuminates the world each morning. Imagine taking a bite into the plump berries and flavorful vegetables from your luscious garden while admiring the stunning scenery around you. Hear the nearby brook babbling as you get nearer, and splash some refreshing cool water on your face.

These are the kinds of things that we don't only enjoy seeing, hearing, tasting, feeling, and smelling, but that actually enhance many aspects of our physical health. Forest and nature bathing are practices that are highly valued in Japanese culture because of these health benefits. Research has shown that we can reap many of the benefits of nature bathing just by staring at images of nature or imagining ourselves immersed in the woods.[1] We underestimate our body's self-healing potential and forget that it's a powerful self-adjusting ecosystem and microcosm that's wired to harmonize our imbalances as long as we support, instead of sabotage, our natural genius.

Enjoy this dynamic process of slow growth, and trust that your flowers will blossom and that the fruit of your labor will sun-ripen in their own time. We often want to grow and develop faster, but take a moment to reflect on how much you have already grown throughout your lifetime but hardly registered. Has it really sunk in that the body that encases you is not the same body that encapsulated your life energy when you were an infant, a toddler, a child, an adolescent, and a young adult? Those may seem like changes too slow to notice, but our nails, skin, and stomach lining have much shorter life spans ranging from days to weeks. It's still easy to take them for granted. Our fat cells and bones live ten years on average, while some of our cells—our brain, tooth enamel, and eye lenses—are with us for life. When we tally the number of clothes and shoes we've gone through, it's easier to conceive of the trillions of cells that have been replaced and recycled into new cells and forms of ourselves throughout our lives. Being fixated on a false or distorted sense of self causes us to underappreciate the brilliance and natural genius of our ecosystem. Most of us feel a bit overwhelmed and vulnerable when attempting to re-member neglected parts of ourselves and trying to occupy more of ourselves and wholeness. Being more dense causes sensations to get more intense.

Remind yourself not to identify with a fleeting state, like today's weather, when your energy and emotions get more intense. Nothing about you is permanent; your energy is in constant flux in an attempt to establish and maintain equilibrium. Your Sacred Ancestral Tree will help you hold and ground all parts and bleed-throughs of your powerful energy field for you—the seen and unseen, your past, present, and future selves, your newly emerging leaves and the ones dropping or already composting on the ground, your neglected cries and the neglected cries of your ancestors passed down through the generations. Knowing who we truly are at the core—as we shift from an egocentric self understanding to a soulcentric self—and grounding this clarity with the help of the Earth element offers us the spaciousness, protection, and physical support to correct imbalances with greater ease and fewer chances of short-circuiting in the process.

Allow each of these insights and teachings from your Sacred Ancestral Tree guide and Earth guide to sink in and take root in the depths of your consciousness and the cells and bones of your body. Know that this is your most updated and upgraded self and that you will notice shifts within yourself and in all your relationships with others for the next days, weeks, months, and years to come. Slowly retrace your steps and find your way back into the room or setting that you're in. Notice the chair that you're sitting in, stretch a bit, and bring your mind and attention fully back into the here and now. Notice your surroundings, wiggle into your body, bring all of your energy and attention back to the space you are in, and open your eyes slowly.

Alchemy Action Steps: Take aligned action with conviction.

Do you know when your ego-mind is in charge when you go about your day? When you are expanding in soul consciousness or constricting in fear? How about when you are imploding or exploding to manage unhealed and unresolved wounding? Are you growing in a spiral shape, feeling more in your element and soul authority every time you come around full circle, like a tree coming back to life after a still and chilly winter; or are you more like a broken record, confined by the perimeters and arc of the same story line when triggered? If you notice your ego-mind feeling threatened or overwhelmed in your interactions with others, wanting to crunch data or shut down instead of take a risk, ask it to sit back and relax, as if watching a movie. Practice being aware that you are safe in your seat. This mental trick—imagining that you are observing your life from a distance—has helped many to strengthen their double-minded practice and muscles. Notice how this distance makes it easier for you to become an observer and to decharge the intensity of painful and challenging situations while remaining submerged in life.

Invite your highly developed brain to trust your natural genius and to settle into your expanded, soulcentric self. Notice that your usual egocentric self—your identity, professional roles, your way of relating to others, your story, and your mindset—matters, but your egocentric self is a smaller subset of your soulcentric self. Allow both experiences of yourself to coexist. You may notice that they are contradicting one another and in conflict in some areas of your life, and are aligned and in partnership with one another in other areas. Notice the strength of conviction within yourself when your soul and ego take aligned action. To gain more clarity and courage on how to get realigned, hold back on actions that are not aligned, and work with your Air and Fire guides when you get a chance. You'll feel your sense of integrity become more solid as you deliberately lay each new building block, which paradoxically will allow you to vigorously flow your Waters without getting flooded. It may help to commit to your actions and plans by blocking your endeavors into your schedule. The ones that my tribe in particular have trouble with are rest, setting intentions, daydreaming, reverence, meditation, pleasure, movement, creative expression, and other forms of self-care and deep listening.

CHAPTER 12

Step 5: Water

Unable to Keep Your Head above Water or Prone to Compulsively Rescue Others Downstream Instead of Stopping the Dumping Upstream?

Objective of the Water Guide and Circulation Teachings: To offer soothing comfort, circulation, sensual pleasure, and clarity by interpreting our needs and e-motion—our energy in motion. By aligning to the flow and cycles of nature, the Water Circulation guide helps us to detox our systems, clear what no longer serves us, release tension, hydrate what's dying and brittle, and transport nutrients. The integration of our heart, mind, body, and soul depends on the alchemical reactions and the accurate translation of messages, needs, and emotions—that are carried through tears, sweat, blood, urine, saliva, and spinal and sexual fluids—into language.

TOPICS:

How to clear emotional dams and transform fear of flooding and drowning into creative flow

How to identify and nurture subtle and intense emotions without over-identifying with them

Grief is an uncompromising teacher, but it can take you to depths within yourself and teach you things nothing else can.

—ISA GUCCIARDI

Be wild; that is how to clear the river. The river does not flow in pol- luted, we manage that. The river does not dry up, we block it. If we want to allow it its freedom, we have to allow our ideational lives to be let loose, to stream, letting anything come, initially censoring noth- ing. That is creative life. It is made up of divine paradox. To create, one must be willing to be stone stupid, to sit upon a throne on top of a jackass and spill rubies from one's mouth. Then the river will flow, then we can stand in the stream of it raining down.

—CLARISSA PINKOLA ESTÉS

It is said that Grandmother Moon watches over the waters of the Earth. We see this in her regulating of the tides. Grandmother Moon controls all female life. Much of water life spawns according to the cycles of the moon. It is said that Grandmother Moon is especially close to women because she governs the woman's cleansing cycle of menstrua- tion known as moontime. Just as Grandmother Moon watches over the waters of the Earth, it is said that women watch over the waters of the people.

—INDIGENOUS COUNCIL ON EDUCATION AT
NORTHERN COLLEGE

It's incredible that about 70 percent of the human body is made up of water and, coincidentally, about 70 percent of Earth, our beautiful blue and green planet, is also covered by water. Some scientists believe that Earth was born "wet."[1] They claim that billions of years ago, water vapor was released out of volcanoes and minerals in ancient rocks in the Earth's mantle and, at one point, turned our planet into a water world. Fire and magma caused tectonic plates to shift and rise into protruding land mass, continents, and distinct oceans. Evap- oration, condensation, and rain created freshwater ponds, lakes, and waterways and an oxygen-rich and ozone-protected environment that has sustained and nourished plants, animals, and ecosystems that we, humans, are a part of today. Water, oxygen, and cloud cover continue to play a large role in regulating the weather, temperature, rain, airstreams, humidity, and sunrays to make life on Earth as optimal, moist, fertile, and sustainable as possible for millions of life forms around the globe.

WATER: THE WEIRDEST LIQUID
ON THE PLANET

According to Alok Jha, author of *The Water Book,* water possesses the most impressive and mind-blowing qualities of all liquids. The more scientists examine the properties of water, the stranger it seems. We keep studying it because we're made of it and, likely, feel unsettled that this innate part of us is still such a mystery. Apparently, water breaks all the rules of a framework that chemists developed in the nineteenth century to describe the behavior and qualities of liquids. Here are just a few of water's incredible properties. By association, they also describe our mysterious core elemental makeup:

> Ice floats because water expands when it freezes. This seems like a small and inconsequential curiosity, but this anomaly—one of water's plethora of strange and unique behaviours—has shaped our planet and the life that exists on it. Because bodies of water freeze from the top down, fish, plants and other organisms will almost always have somewhere to survive during seasons of bitter cold, and be able to grow in size and number. Over geological time, this oddity has allowed complex life to survive and evolve despite the Earth's successive ice ages, periods when fragile life forms would have otherwise been wiped out on the desiccated, frozen ground and—if water behaved like a normal liquid—in solidified seas, too.[2]

Another very unusual and much appreciated characteristic of water is this: "All of the water on Earth should exist as only vapour: part of a thick, muggy atmosphere sitting above an inhospitable, bone-dry surface. A water molecule is made from two very light atoms—hydrogen and oxygen—and, at the ambient conditions on the surface of the Earth, it should be a gas."[3] These incredible traits have significantly benefited us and our bodies. For instance, "Water is not only attracted to itself but will stick to almost anything else it comes across. It is the closest thing we have to a universal solvent, able to tear apart other compounds."[4] Because of this bizarre property, water circulates particles, cleanses, and detoxes us on all levels of our being—physical, biochemical, and energetic. It is able to interact with different substances, and it favors structures that support nature's delicate and complex forms: "Water can dissolve a wide variety of nutrients and other ingredients and move them around our bodies. The basic molecules of life—DNA, proteins, molecules that make up cell membranes, etc.—wouldn't work without water. The billions of protein molecules inside your body only fold into the right shapes to do their jobs because their interaction with water nudges them into the correct three-dimensional formats."[5] Proper circulation throughout our body enhances not only our physical health, but also our overall sense of well-being, mental clarity, and wholeness.

WATER IS LIFE

Long before we had advanced instruments for scientific study, our ancient ancestors and wise elders already understood how powerful, magical, and essential water is to our well-being. Some of their teachings have survived the ethnocide of the last few centuries but are holding on by a thin thread. The Lakota phrase *Mní wičhóni* ("Water is life") was the rallying cry that united millions of Native and non-Native protesters around the world. They wanted to put an end to the controversial construction of the Dakota Access Pipeline (DAPL) on sacred lands and were outraged and concerned because a potential oil spill would threaten the water supply and cultural resources of Natives at the Standing Rock Sioux Reservation. For Native Americans, water not only sustains life, it is sacred.[6] It cannot be separated from our environment. It's an integral part of our makeup and Earth's physical structure. For water to remain clear and safe for all life, it needs structural support and protection that allows it to flow and circulate freely. Water's main role in our body is very similar to its role on Earth: to circulate and recycle particles, oxygen, nutrients, and toxins. Water is integral to all inner processes, from the breakdown of the food that we eat, to the shedding of the lining of our stomach and uterus, to the elimination of waste and what we no longer need through our urine, sweat, menstrual blood, and fecal excretions. All of these cycles are vital to our functioning and well-being, and will shut down within days if not provided water.

The parallel cycles between menstruating cis-females and nonbinary people, Grandmother Moon, and Mother Earth and her oceans perhaps tops all when it comes to the mysteries and the wonders of human life. It's beyond uncanny that the average length of a human's menstrual cycle is the same length as the moon's 29.5-day waxing and waning cycle.[7] The moon's gravitational pull generates the ocean's tides, which affect the reproductive cycles of fish and ocean plants and their migration patterns during ebb and flow, making it easier for animals, including humans, to fish for food. Floating plants and animals ride the tidal currents between the breeding areas and deeper waters, which enhances their survival. The tides circulate phytoplankton and nutrients from greater ocean depths to the surface. This aids photosynthesis, provides food for fish and marine animals, and clears pollutants from the water and carbon from the atmosphere. These deep-cleansing, pro-creative, and transformational cycles mirror what happens in our wombs every month. A series of even more complex processes happen when humans conceive. The amniotic fluid of all mammals, including that of humans, is remarkably similar to seawater. Both fluids contain the same salts in almost exactly the same proportions, suggesting that amniotic fluid quite likely resembles the ancient homes, the seas, of our earliest marine ancestors. We are water babies and, to this day, are protected by it, develop and swim in it, and practice all organ functions in water for nine months before we're born.

ROCKING US THROUGH THE UPS AND DOWNS OF LIFE

Over the course of millions and billions of years of evolution, Earth's powerful harmonizing principle has favored the dynamic ebb and flow of life over an ideal, fixed state. It's not difficult to see that life would lose its vitality and would feel stale and static without the contrasts. Ironically, making space for opposites and contrasts is what creates inner harmony. The moon's gravitational pull on the Earth plays an important role in holding our planet in place and regulating its variations in climate and weather.[8] Without the moon stabilizing our tilt, it is possible that the Earth's tilt could fluctuate too wildly. There would either be no tilt (which means no seasons) or too much of a tilt (which means extreme weather and even ice ages). The planet is more resilient, diverse, and fascinating because of this restraint and the ability to safely hold and support the ups and downs of water and life. The moon's influence on the Earth's tides produces the biggest waves on the planet and causes the sea to approach and retreat along shores around the world. It seems to be Mother Earth's way of rocking and comforting us. Imagine sitting on a beach and looking at an ocean that didn't have any waves. It could probably cause us to feel emotionally stifled. We love watching and listening to the rise and fall of crashing waves because they normalize and soothe the ups and downs in our life. Life force circulates through our veins as it circulates through Mother Earth's Water and Air ways. When we trust and rest in our true nature, we feel at peace. Our heart and lungs expand and contract in alignment with the forces, seasons, and cycles of nature.

MOONTIME AND SACRED FEMININE CYCLES

Ancient and Indigenous cultures have honored the cycles of the moon through-out time and have considered it to be a divine honor to intimately experience these powerful balancing forces and life-death-rebirth cycles in their bodies. According to the Indigenous Council on Education at Northern College, a young person's first menstrual period was a big deal and was ceremonialized in meaningful ways:

> When a young woman had her first moontime, her aunties or grandmothers would take her to a small lodge where she could be close to the natural world. The young woman is sacred at this time. She is now able to give life. Her mother, grandmothers or aun-ties would give her the teachings about her new life. She would be taught about her role as a woman in the community.... The moon-time is considered a time of power, second only to the ability of the Great Spirit to give life. Some teachings say that when women are on their moontime the Creator comes closer to them. The moon-time is a ceremony of life for women and a time for renewal. The moontime is a time for women to relax and take it easy. All the chores are done by other family members. It is a time for women to think about themselves, their family, their relatives or anyone they think needs help. It is a time of reflection.[9]

They believed that the moon cycle was a reminder of the powerful gift of being able to bear life, resembling the Creator, something that the Maroons in Suriname also believe. Both cultures treat it as a time for menstruating members to cleanse themselves mentally, physically, emotionally, and spiritually by tuning inward and relying on their connection to nature to deepen their reflections and wisdom.

THE LOSS OF INTUITIVE GUIDANCE
AND RITES OF PASSAGE

Studies by Ioannis Ilias and colleagues about dreaming and the menstrual cycle indicated that their participants dreamed more frequently and had more vivid dreams during the premenstrual and menstrual phases of their cycles.[10] It supports ancient claims that we are more intuitive during our moontime, and that the "veil" between the worlds of the seen and unseen, and the conscious and the unconscious, is much thinner, enabling us to serve as a sacred channel to divine guidance for our tribes and communities during our moontime, if we want to. Tragically, these rites of passage and cultural teachings have in some Western European regions been chastised for centuries. Many modern-day cultures no longer celebrate or honor this sacred time because it revealed and challenged what was hidden in the shadows. Wise women who spoke their truths were often ostracized and accused of witchcraft because they often challenged problematic social norms at inopportune times—nearly always. How has loathing and despising this powerful, creative process that's so tied into our core human essence—regardless of our own physical sex and gender identity—affected us over the generations? Most menstruating girls and women are troubled by these internal cycles when they have their period (and not because of gender dysphoria and the painful monthly reminder of being misgendered). Even those of us who identify as girls and women were taught to view this time as a nuisance for interfering with our path in life and success, as defined by patriarchal values and egocentric norms. From the get-go, preteens learn to associate their periods with feeling inferior, abnormal, embarrassed, vulnerable, and bloated, and with messy inconveniences, moodiness, PMS, bitchiness, and body aches.

Because so many of us lack the support, knowledge, and skills to translate our emotions and inner experiences into meaningful messages, we may not even realize the range of loss that we are grieving for ourselves and humanity when we feel sad, pained, distressed, angry, and empty during our periods. Instead, we feel particularly on edge and vulnerable about slipping up and appearing overly emotional at work and at home right before and when menstruating. We likely developed "true nature" dysphoria after all these attempts to disconnect us from our core self. We may fear being perceived as inadequate, unprofessional, or a problem rather than an oracle of sorts, more attuned than usual to the imbalances all around us during this special time. This is now hurting all of us, just as racism hurts all of us at the deepest soul levels, regardless of our racial identity and appearance.

Being publicly shamed, punished, and ostracized for expressing and listening to our emotions caused us to shun and mistrust our innate sacred wisdom. In the last few centuries, the lack of reverence for the sacred Waters and mysteries that reside within us has heightened the exploitation of human bodies for profit, power, and pleasure. Women's bodies, BIPOC's bodies, trans bodies, children's bodies—not even our own bodies are off-limits to abuse and being beaten into submission by our harsh superegos. We mine and mistreat our own minds and bodies for information, resources, control, and energy in exchange for money, status, respect, achievement, and success, even if it makes us feel sick and exhausted. Overtime pay is in many industries often enough compensation in exchange for dis-ease and is justification for working ourselves to the bone. Sometimes, respect and admiration for "sucking it up" and being a tough cookie is enough of an incentive to disrespect our boundaries and feelings. We similarly exploit and mistreat other animals and the Earth. The world is struggling as a whole because we, as a species, have lost our intuitive ability to deeply connect with and read the healing messages and energy brought to us by Water. By overidentifying with and favoring good over bad emotion, we are obstructing Water's free-flowing and healthy circulation through our bodies, especially our emotional bodies. This blocks the natural metabolism of loss and grief, causing us to miss the creative opportunities for healing that are embedded in them. Our Fire element is struggling to fiercely protect us and our immunity because of all the excessive moisture.

ALIGNING UPSTREAM VERSUS RESCUING DOWNSTREAM

As sponges and hollow bones, highly sensitive souls and trailblazers like us often struggle at first with our nuanced, complex, intense energy-in-motion—our emotions.

- We fear that we'll drown if we open the floodgates or cry us a river.
- We cringe when others get emotional, and we try to rescue them as soon as they hint at pain.
- We dam and control our emotional life force at every corner, and at the same time wonder why our creative well is so dry and our flow so clogged up and weak.

Meditation and grounding guidance help us improve our emotional regulation skills. We are often taught to watch thoughts go by like sailboats and clouds to shut off our mind chatter and to activate our relaxation response. Shutting off the monopolizing egocentric voice of the trauma-body is an excellent start to reconnect and realign with our true nature. After consciously creating more space and structural support for our full range of feelings, we need to invite old, stuck trauma and short-circuited patterns back into the streams of our expansive truth-body. Embracing and integrating these feelings with compassion and curiosity, and thoroughly excavating their messages, will effectively discharge ruminating thoughts and will allow our minds to naturally return to an inner state of peace and homeostasis. Clearing limiting thoughts, undigested trauma, and energetic constrictions that block healthy circulation is most imperative during this process.

REFLECTIONS FROM PRACTITIONERS ON WORKING WITH THE WATER ELEMENT

It's not just rejuvenation, revitalization, or healing that occurs when my parched lips find relief among fresh water—it is a far more complicated orchestration of love. I didn't initially understand how this type of love worked, though water surely taught me with the same determination, pace, and manner it uses to shape a rock over time. Water soothes the sharp edges of my diffidence, washes through crevices, and fills any empty vessels it finds. Through this, I learn forgiveness, healing, and wholeness. In my most challenging moments, I am suspended and cradled by the water beneath my feet underground, above my head in the atmosphere, and inside my own body. Like steady waves, I'm rocked and soothed by the movement of this omnipresent element. Cleansed, forgiven, and soul quenched, I breach the surface of my own pain to continue my healing journey.

—Valerie Vargas, EdD, special education
teacher and artist

With the help of the elements, and in particular water, I can cry again without getting splitting headaches. Before, I was so emotionally backed up that every time I emoted with tears, I got a migraine. Now, I can cry freely! And this month, the hormonal wave broke so gently upon me, it was like a quiet song being hummed to me from far away and getting closer and closer with each day. No flu-like symptoms, no crashing depression. I am in total awe that such powerful body changes can occur alongside such deep internal healing work!

—Sarah Ginnan, writer, content marketer

When I feel the ego-mind's conditioned me to avoid writing, I simply wave my magic elemental intention and move water to a flowing brook around my sanctuary that I "hear" and feel as me, as I sit in my cave entrance, my fire gentle and strong behind me, my tree strong and leafy just outside where I sit, and my dragons circling above. And it's the water, the flowing and inviting babbling, that causes the whole scene to harmoniously dissolve into my writing space. I actually sense the water still flowing, a kind of sweet, refreshing boundary. And the resistance is gone. And I'm so happy and balanced as I start writing, which has a real impact on the authenticity and fluidity of my characters and plot.

—J. R. Schumaker, author of *Diana's Dragons: The Awaited*

Meditation Script for Water

Imagine sitting at the base of your Sacred Ancestral Tree in your inner sanctuary and leaning your back against the trunk. Feel its sturdy support light up your spine, letting you know that the tree has your back and is strengthening your courage and backbone. Rest your head against the trunk of the tree. Open your crown chakra above your head to receive inspiration and guidance from the sky, and open your base chakra to ground and root nourishment from the earth into your body and sanctuary.

Explore how water runs through your sanctuary. Are you near a brook, stream, or river? Can you hear the crashing sounds of a waterfall or ocean waves in the distance? Or are you near a quiet lake that's fed by clear streams and melted runoff from snow-capped mountains? Notice the drifting clouds above. Reflect on their formation and the interplay of heat evaporating moisture and water from trees, vegetation, lakes, and oceans into vapor and clouds; cooler temperatures and wind circulating these clouds; and land and mountains aiding with their buildup and precipitation once they've turned heavy and dark, eventually releasing tension and cleansing rain that soaks into the ground.

While hydrating the earth, water also bonds with and redistributes minerals to enhance the growth, transformation, recycling, and composting of all organic matter and organisms. Water enriches our ecosystems with nourishment, delight, ease, and comfort, and regulates us and each of our cycles on its way back to the ocean. Changing a key aspect within any of these ecosystems can create a trophic cascade, a complex, ecological process that starts at the top of the food chain and cascades down the trophic levels to affect all life. Recent examples of trophic cascades are reminding us how harmful our limited, reductionistic ego-minds can be when we disregard and try to override the mysterious cycles of life on the planet with our human logic and affinity for polarizations.

Take this example involving whales. Whales eat massive amounts of fish and krill. At one point, Japanese politicians encouraged the killing of whales, drawing a logical inference that fewer whales would mean more fish and krill. The opposite happened. As the population of the great whales declined, so did the krill and fish populations. And when the whales reemerged, the populations of fish and krill bounced back. How can we make sense of this? Whales feed in the dark depths of the ocean, then return to the photic zone at the surface, where there is enough sunlight for photosynthesis to occur. They release fecal plumes that are rich in nutrients, iron, and other minerals that are scarce in surface waters. These poop plumes fertilize microscopic, one-celled phytoplankton, which, in turn, are food for krill, fish, and marine mammals, including whales. Whales' diving also stirs the waters, vertically mixing and redistributing plankton and nutrients where they are needed. Phytoplankton photosynthesize and produce the majority of oxygen in the air that we breathe. They also sequester huge amounts of carbon, which eventually gets stored at the bottom of the ocean. The oceans, not the forests, are by far the largest heat and carbon sinks, oxygen producers, and climate regulators. Whales play a vital role in keeping the oceans healthy through regular mixing and circulation of undertows, layers, and currents of various depths.[11]

We similarly need to dive far beneath the shallow waters to access sustainable root solutions of depth and substance. Many wondrous cycles of transformation happen within our bodies and go unnoticed. Some of these cycles are biologically wired by ultradian, circadian, and infradian rhythms, such as our breathing, eating, sleeping, and resting, and hormonal, libido, and menstrual cycles, and affect energy levels, moods, and physical and cognitive functioning. All are aided by water, and without water would collapse within days of dehydration. Other patterns are emotionally driven and are triggered by memorable and painful situations from the past. They may be related to special events, such as birthdays, holidays, and anniversaries or may be idiosyncratic to you and activated by significant losses of meaningful people in your life. Supporting these cycles of transformation, healing, and grieving requires emotional agility and balancing, which can't happen when we have rigid attachments or aversions to certain emotions or story lines.

Limber joints, strong vitals, and the absence of obstructions, constrictions, and stagnations in qi circulation promote our health, resilience, and wellness, not just on a physical level but on all levels of our being. How can you become more present and supportive of all of your moving, metabolizing, and alchemizing parts? While disintegrating and composting our old forms, it's easy to freak out and disrupt the dissolution process. We tend to short-circuit and shoot out of our bodies when our emotions get intense, our hearts begin to soften, a knot forms in our throat, our eyes moisten, and we're getting closer to decoding the messages held within our feelings. Holding sacred space for your complete unfolding, and refraining from prematurely aborting the process, especially when feeling vulnerable and powerless, is super important.

When we prematurely release steam out of this pressure cooker or cauldron—right when it's getting hotter and better able to break down and alchemize raw emotion, it's as if we're poking holes in our chrysalis. The cracks and energy leaks that result abort the process and allow harmful and parasitic energy to come in. Aligning your mind, heart, body, and soul will help you to make contact with your sacred healing well and kickstart the flow of water and fluids in your body—e.g., tears, sweat, saliva, and blood—as you melt frozen parts of yourself.

Your guides and higher self will attempt to seal these leaks and cracks with your conscious energy—your wise emotions. When you're crying and grieving losses that you fully acknowledge, you are in essence applying energetic glue to severed parts of yourself to restore your brilliant interconnectedness and wholeness. Just reflect for a moment how many different types of messages tears can hold. They can signal frustration, sadness, despair, being moved, appreciating beauty, feeling loved, connecting to deep mystery, and feeling scared and overwhelmed. Our ability to interpret the energy that flows through the intricate web of emotions within our bodies and ecosystem is nothing short of genius and provides us boatloads of information and guidance on how to align our egos with our true nature. This enhances your unfolding potential so that the love and healing energy from the immortal Source of your well-being can continue to flow freely throughout your body.

Allow each of these insights and teachings from your Sacred Ancestral Tree guide and Water guide to sink in and take root in the depths of your consciousness and the cells and bones of your body. Know that this is your most updated and upgraded self and that you will notice shifts within yourself and in all your relationships with others for the next days, weeks, months, and years to come. Slowly retrace your steps and find your way back into the room or setting that you're in. Notice the chair that you're sitting in, stretch a bit, and bring your mind and attention fully back into the here and now. Notice your surroundings, wiggle into your body, bring all of your energy and attention back to the space you are in, and open your eyes slowly.

Alchemy Action Steps: Soothe your heart and soul with compassion.

Explore your relationship to your feelings, your flow, your intuitive interpretation of your energy, and your ability to surrender and viscerally emote in your everyday life. How has your trust in your body's wisdom, intuition, and emotions been compromised? How have dirty pain patterns—short-circuiting, avoidance, dissociating, freezing, or shooting out of your body—blocked your Water flow and caused either drought or emotional flooding? How can the elements of Air, Fire, and Earth help support your truth, reclaim the power of your Water element, and cultivate greater trust in mystery, your vulnerability, and your deepest self? How can they help you to reach groundwater, your sacred healing well, with greater ease and openness? Make it okay again to choke up in public or even to let your tears flow freely if need be? Our tendency is to shut down and diminish our moment-to-moment intuitive awareness so we can function more effectively, but superficially, in our fast-paced, concrete world.

How can you reclaim the flow of Water (your e-motion) as soothing, cleansing, and healing, rather than a painful, shameful, or negative emotion and element? It will require trusting and surrendering to a mysterious, wondrous process that we can't control. We may not feel better during this composting and purging process, but this is how we ground in our deepest truths and get better at the root level. Explore your relationship with water outside of you and all the ways it helps ease and soothe your inner water cycles. Do you enjoy listening to raindrops or ocean waves? Enjoy sipping herbal, calming tea? Do you like getting all loosey goosey in a warm bubble bath or jacuzzi, or prefer a massage therapist or lover to get your body and muscles supple, relaxed, and juicy? When did you last have a good, cleansing cry, grieving the many losses of recent months and years that you may have powered through? When was the last time you allowed yourself to be moved by a beautiful and inspiring story, sunset, or gesture of affection, really giving yourself the space and time to fully take in awe, joy, and pleasure? Make that time now, and sense how much more alive you feel when blood, sweat, tears, saliva, and sexual fluids start to move more freely through your ecosystem.

CHAPTER 13

Step 6: Heart Compass

Is Your Inner Compass Giving You the Runaround Instead of Guiding You to True North?

Objective of the Heart Compass Guide and True North Teachings: To offer us a felt-sense of agency and greater self-trust in how and where to embody and anchor in our soul authority. After connecting with each of the prior six directions, the Heart Compass guide helps us to trust our connection to the seventh direction: our Creator within and our sense of True North. This enhances our effectiveness when doing mundane daily tasks as well as when engaging in healing endeavors, creative projects, activism, and other meaningful missions. At the nexus where the elements converge, our Heart Compass feels most powerful, regenerative, and catalytic, similar to the ways in which luscious lava erupts and mixes with air and water to form fertile, dark soil, birth new possibilities, and feed life's amazing diversity and interdependent complexity.

TOPICS:

How to dethrone your trauma-body with your truth-body and ground in self-love

Fierce compassion versus compassion fatigue: guerrilla self-care and serving others from the inside out

Self-trust is the first secret to success.

—RALPH WALDO EMERSON

If braving relationships with other people is braving connection, self-trust is braving self-love.

—BRENÉ BROWN

Within you, as within each one of us, there is an unbroken tie to the universe, an unending tap that flows with love. But it is as though most of us are standing on the cosmic hose that is sending love our way, while we scratch our heads bewildered, wondering where all the love has gone. When we are developing self-love, we need to look within at the ways in which we are blocking the flow to feel love, to feel loved.

—PARVATI

Navigating life and personal relationships is harder than ever in the twenty-first century. Especially highly sensitive trailblazers can feel overwhelmed and get misguided by the many unnamed imbalances and shiny objects that are woven into every aspect of society today. I remember having a much less complicated connection to Source, my Sacred Heart Compass, and my old soul as a wise young child. I enjoyed the vast uncluttered space in my mind and felt free to be spontaneous, authentic, and curious. I could also tell that my free-spiritedness was getting more encroached upon by external forces and powerful influences the older I got. Growing up, I was considered to be a tomboy and daredevil because I often ventured into domains that were usually monopolized by boys and for no good reason off-limits to girls. My mother and some of my aunts and cousins worried that my many cuts, scrapes, and insect bites would toughen and permanently scar my legs, but I was having too much fun—climbing to the top of trees, crawling into dugouts, flying on (and sometimes off) my bike, chasing my brother and other boys, and exploring bugs, animals, plants, trees, and the natural world around me—to care. Why would anyone give up what was most exciting about being alive just to have soft, smooth legs? What for? To attract a boyfriend? You might as well saw them off, preserve them in a glass case, and lock me up, I thought. I don't know how I knew, but I could immediately tell—thanks to my Sacred Heart Compass—the difference between a concern that was truly for my own good and one that was the result of biased social rules, conformity, and appearances.

How come no one worried about the legs of boys? If their chances of finding true love later in life weren't ruined because of some scars on their legs, why would they be for girls?

I concluded after some deliberation that if something like that could scare away a boy, then so be it. Being coupled with a partner in some distant future was the least of my concerns. Who would want to be tied up with someone who'd treat you like a porcelain doll and expect you to act like one anyway? I wasn't fascinated only with nature and the creatures around me. I was curious about my own body and even more so about the cuts, bruises, scrapes, and bites that people thought of as ugly. They were far more interesting to me than oppressive social norms, because they were like a portal to mysteries that you could delve into and unfold layer upon layer. For instance, have you ever asked yourself how wounds magically healed all by themselves? Or what caused bleeding to stop? Why did cuts and scrapes hurt more for a while before they got better? Why did rubbing a bruise cause it to get lighter? How did my attitude and physical tension—panicky or calm—impact the sensations of pain and the sharp sting of iodine and alcohol? Was it better to clench your jaw or stay relaxed? Why did the wounds get so itchy after they scarred? At what point could you pick at an itchy scab without causing it to bleed again? My well of curiosity was bottomless. This is how my deep examination of emotional hurts and healing began. I discovered that it was just as layered as physical wounding and could be conveyed through as many different kinds of cries and expressions of pain. I also realized that for my emotional wounds to heal as quickly as possible, I needed to resist picking at the scabs, and to trust that my body knows what to do, just like it does with physical wounds.

PAIN AS A COMPASS GUIDE

After watching a documentary on Indigenous customs, my father told me that some Indigenous tribes in the jungle required their adolescent daughters to go through an ant test (by placing their hand in a calabash of fire ants or other aggressive ants). This was a part of their initiation into adulthood right after their first menstrual bleeding. I was beyond intrigued and intuitively picked up that there was more behind this ritual than learning to withstand physical pain. I had an inkling that learning to transcend the grip of the five senses was of the essence in this practice, and I grokked that the intention of this cultural ritual was not to hurt or punish them. It was to liberate them. Even though I'd barely skimmed the surface of this deep well of wisdom, it awakened wise consciousness that had been asleep in my old soul. I vividly remember the life-changing insights that trickled in, such as realizing that pain was not the enemy. Pain was protective and useful. Without pain, we could hurt ourselves very badly (e.g., some people born with congenital analgesia even die in childhood because they are not able to feel pain and are unable to develop agility and to brace themselves from injuries and burns). I'd developed equanimity and spacious curiosity in regard to physical pain, but I was a total wuss when it came to emotional pain and conflict. Like most children, I split people into the classic good guys versus bad guys categories around moralistic issues, and I relied on this dualistic worldview to guide my heart compass. The overwhelming and constant emotional pain it caused indicated to me that something was off. It slowly sank in that I needed to adjust my perspective.

UNRAVELING MY GOD-COMPLEX

I couldn't stand it if the bad guys were winning: e.g., a teacher spanking and humiliating "lost cases" in front of everyone; a bully teasing and picking on someone smaller; a relative with a sharp tongue calling my cousins names; my mother not getting my deepest heartache and threatening to give me reasons to cry. I'd even gotten in a fight with a boy when I was in the first grade, taking it upon myself to punish those who weren't playing fair and were getting away with it. They had a God-complex—thinking that they were entitled to more and better than the rest of us, breaking and bending rules, and bossing people around. I didn't have a God-complex. I was convinced that I was just trying to stop them from exercising theirs, but one day I had an epiphany that I was no different from them. I began to understand how these polarities and my sensitivity and reactivity to other people's pain (often reminding me of my own) were causing me to go in circles rather than toward my True North. It clicked that the reason Indigenous people taught their children high tolerance for physical pain was to teach them equanimity and curiosity toward emotional pain as well. I realized that nonjudgmental spaciousness around emotional pain was providing my Sacred

Heart Compass with information and sensations that felt more trustworthy because I was grounded in my truth-body. I didn't feel a need to control my feelings or feel victimized or manipulated by them. On the contrary, I was eager to hear what they had to say.

We would not be able to grok our True North path in life if it weren't for polarities helping us to become aware of higher consciousness that transcends them. Loving or hating one extreme over another had been the problem, because it caused me to operate from a place of unmetabolized pain that heightened the inner drama between split parts. I didn't use any of these fancy terms to describe my insights, but I understood that when my dad said, "The body is weak, the spirit is strong," I needed to tame my impatient God-complex and naive impulse to eliminate all bad in the world. I realized that I could quiet my screaming heart by breathing stillness into my body. This made more room for my wise spirit to shine through, as role-modeled by the girls who were bravely passing the fire ant test. This early exposure to the ways of the Indigenous Surinamese rooted and fortified my commitment to embrace clean pain and get to the bottom of it. I learned to detect and enjoy my growing sense of fulfillment, wholeness, and inner strength each time I digested it and accessed root solutions instead of getting derailed by dirty pain, and judgmental and avoidant patterns.

TRUSTING YOUR SACRED HEART COMPASS

In an interview with author, teacher, and tarot muse Tania Pryputniewicz, she asked me deliciously provocative questions pertaining to my memoir and self-trust. She nudged me to dig deep and to describe how I developed and sustained trust in my Sacred Heart Compass, and what helped me to access my truth as I got older and life got more complex. When she asked me point-blank, "Where and how did you find the strength to trust yourself?" I said:

> Let me begin by saying that I love this question because trust is such a layered and complex process and skill that I think everyone, but especially healers, seers, seekers and psychics, grapple with as part of their initiation, training, and ongoing growth, starting at really early ages. I believe that everything begins and ends with

trust in ourselves, soul, and sacred guidance, which directly trans-
lates into trusting others, trusting love, trusting adversity in life,
trusting nature, and the nature of reality and the Universe. I started
to experiment with trust as a child because it made me feel better
and less distraught when I got warmer and closer to my truth—not
because I'd consciously deliberated that self-trust was an important
first stepping stone.

There are different kinds of self-trust to develop, depending on
one's gifts, and there are also different domains to master. As an
intuitive empath, my strengths and passion have always been in
deciphering relational dynamics with souls in bodies using Earth
wisdom and my own body's natural wisdom and sense of harmony
as a template. I could make very subtle and clear distinctions as a
young child decades before words like trust, self-awareness, and
shamanism entered my vocabulary, usually while daydreaming and
wandering in my neighborhood or in the rainforest by myself.

It was almost as if I could see a halo above certain events, traditions,
people, information, and beliefs as a child that spoke to my soul yet
tended not to be noticed or valued as much by others. I felt a calling to protect these experiences and the sacred by keeping them a
secret and burying them in my mind like a treasure. I was drawn to
freedom fighters and stories about rebel slaves, who planted opposing seeds and ideas in my soul—to liberate others with this info,
despite the risks, instead of keeping it a secret. The self-doubt that
developed over the years were several layers out, related to who to
trust with this, what to do with it, and how to manage this gift that
I knew was out of the ordinary and sacred.[1]

OUR SELF-LOVE AND TRUE NORTH

It's confusing and discombobulating when our devotion to our highest good is
most threatening to many others. You start doubting their love for you, and you
start doubting your intuition and ability to take care of yourself. You may even
start doubting your perception of reality. Remember that people behave this way

when their own highest good and clean pain cycles are also the most threatening to them. This is due to the double-bind we've been talking about all along. They are still trapped in it because advocating for their own self-love often requires heading in a True North direction, fraught with increasingly more obstacles and resistance to test their resolve and reveal unfinished business. This tends to disorient our egocentric selves and spin us around in dirty pain cycles—involving self-doubt, denial, avoidance, self-blame, despair, scapegoating, etc.—causing us to divert clean pain cycles that lead us closer to our True North and higher integration. To make matters worse, we've most likely received confusing messages from well-intended friends, counselors, and guides in regard to self-love. It often gets mixed up with related, but more egocentric ideas, such as self-esteem and self-confidence. Parvati, author and founder of the Marine Arctic Peace Sanctuary, explains the difference between self-esteem, self-confidence, and self-love really well. She says, "Self-love is different from self-confidence or having a strong self-esteem, though they can be related. We are self-confident when we feel certitude in our ability to discern or act. Self-esteem involves a quiet assurance in our place within the whole, a feeling of being a valuable and welcome part of the universe. Self-love involves the ability to treat ourselves with understanding, kindness, patience, and gentle perseverance. Deeper still, self-love involves our ability to know that our true nature is love and that our human destiny is to embody that love and express it in all we do."[2]

REGENERATION AND CREATIVE REBIRTH

Taking it to the next level requires embracing organic, spiritual composting cycles in our bodies and fully supporting and surrendering to the natural purification and harmonizing powers that our bodies possess. Earth's regenerative and detoxing processes have parts that are not pretty, but this is the only way in which the rotten and painful aspects of ourselves and life get composted and transformed. It's imperative that we each learn to surrender to these healing processes without imploding in shame, guilt, self-loathing, and not-good-enoughness. It is possible for us to get more comfortable with the worms and vultures that are cleaning up the mess, and to not overidentify with them, the stench, or the grossness of the process. Decomposition is an integral part of our healing and growth cycles, and it's Earth's greatest "clean pain" secret in purifying dis-ease and folding the dead back into the cycle of life. We cannot love or heal the Earth without loving and healing our bodies, true nature, and mysterious essence in the same radical way. Our good intentions and lofty ideals will not ground and take root if we bypass these processes and remain rigid about our tendencies and gravitation toward splitting all of life, not just our emotions, into good versus bad buckets. Consciousness will remain as superficial as our judgmentalness if we do so; and before we know it, we're back to sowing new seeds, because nothing took hold. Therefore, slow down and observe your inner climate like a hawk. To have the seeds of self-love and clean pain patterns sprout and take root within yourself, your inner climate needs to be infused with the utmost gentleness and love. This is how the delicate seedlings and saplings you're cultivating will get hardy enough to withstand rougher weather and conditions.

TRUE NORTH LEADS TO DIVERSITY, HARMONY, AND SIMPLICITY

Remember John and Molly Chester from the Biggest Little Farm,[3] and how much care, patience, and energy it took to restore it into a fully functioning organic farm? Because of the extreme swings—from snails to ducks, ladybug swarms to ravenous coyotes, parched dry land to flash floods and raging wildfires—it was hard to trust their consultant Alan York, a traditional farming expert who encouraged them to be patient. He insisted that natural ecosystems "regulate themselves through diversity" and that this "diversity would lead to simplicity." This sounded ludicrous at the time. Things seemed to get more complicated each time a new factor was added to the equation. What Alan meant was that nature and wildlife were already in harmony and would balance the needs of the farm the more these two aligned and merged into one. Molly and John indeed needed to do less—just carefully observe and make minor, creative adjustments—when nature began to take over in their ambitious renaturing journey. Then the day arrived when nature did what it does best: maintain harmony and equilibrium on its own. After a few years, signs that Alan had been right began to emerge. Each new species that wandered, slithered, or flew in, or was purchased and introduced into the ecosystem of the farm, helped to balance all other forms of life and establish a sturdier equilibrium.

ANOTHER TROPHIC CASCADE: HOW WOLVES CHANGED RIVERS

Fortunately, most of our ecosystems are not as arid and neglected as the Biggest Little Farm initially was. Based on what I've seen in my practice and courses, my guess is that most of us need only a single critical adjustment, like what occurred at Yellowstone National Park. Thirty-one wolves were reintroduced into Yellowstone between 1995 and 1996 and have caused a massive trophic cascade.[4] Gray wolves were deliberately hunted by visitors, nearby residents, and the federal government backed by Animal Damage Control programs starting in 1907 supporting owners of livestock. After the last pack, two pups, had been killed in the 1920s, the elk population exploded and grazed their way across the landscape, killing young brush and trees. As early as the 1930s, scientists were alarmed by the degradation and were worried about erosion and plants dying off. Yet again, an egocentric human intervention guided by superficial judgments about what's good (elk) or bad (wolves) for us was terribly off when considering the big picture and the highest good of all involved. Apparently, the reemergence of wolves triggered a nonlinear, regenerative, and reciprocal effect among animals and plants, one that will take decades of research to understand. Biologists and ecologists are enjoying a rare and very unique opportunity to study what happens when an ecosystem becomes whole again. By adding wolves back into the equation, they are discovering how incredibly complex nature's networks are. One change can ripple direct and indirect consequences throughout the ecosystem and affect the landscape.

Researchers have now determined that wolves are the primary reason for elk mortality. The wolves are not only regulating the elk population, they are showing how the overpowering, hegemonic presence of any one species can compromise the health, diversity, and vitality of all. Remarkably, the presence of wolves also indirectly changed the rivers. When elk and also deer stopped munching their way through the valleys and gorges, where wolves could easily hunt them, the vegetation was able to recover. This increased biodiversity and provided food and shelter for a larger variety of plants and animals. Riverbank erosion and collapse decreased due to the regeneration of forests. When the rivers started to meander less and become more fixed in their course, the channels deepened and small pools formed.

Many of our personal ecosystems would similarly benefit by reintroducing one key element: wolf energy (i.e., Fire guides, boundaries, vitality, immunity) would be my first choice. I believe that our ecosystems have been similarly depleted and robbed of our "bad" and wild nature by early settlers, colonizers, and the domestication and modernization of daily life within Western industrial society. With the help of Air guides, we are gaining more clarity and consciousness about how detrimental this has been to our well-being. By realigning Air and Fire, wisdom, fierce boundaries, and protection, Earth is able to restore and to provide solid ground to support the flow and circulation of our Water—i.e., emotional regulation, cleansing, and grieving. This naturally resuscitates the magnificence of many forms of life, including innate self-love and reverence, that were desecrated and compromised. Most importantly, when we reintroduce fire and protective boundaries, we will eventually experience fewer emotional flash floods. Instead of flailing and drowning in our emotions, we will feel guided, empowered, and protected by them, which in turn will enhance our sense of agency, the actions we take, and the health of the soil we will be cultivating and grounding in. This will in turn produce more moisture for vegetation on the land, less drought, and a more balanced ecosystem.

SELF-TRUST AND GUERRILLA SELF-CARE

We are layered, complex, and culturally conditioned by what we inherited through the generations. We can be most trusted with the parts of ourselves that we have confronted, metabolized, integrated, taken responsibility for, and are conscious of. In deciding who we can trust, it's less about discerning who is a good person with good intentions versus a bad person with bad intentions. Most of us get tempted by the illusion of a moral dichotomy. I believe some intuitive street smarts and guerrilla tactics give us more useful insights when it comes to setting protective boundaries for ourselves. Because we are multidimensional beings, our trust in others needs to be multidimensional. For example, I would step in a helicopter and trust Prince William with my life. I even believe that he would take great risks to save mine if put in that situation. I trust that he is an excellent and caring father doing all within his power and consciousness to fulfill his understanding of that. I believe that he loves his brother Prince Harry and sister-in-law Meghan, the Duke and Duchess of Sussex. Do I trust that Prince William is capable of personally or institutionally supporting their best interests and mental health by honoring their experiences and accusations of racism within the royal family and Great Britain? No. A few days after Oprah's interview with Prince Harry and Meghan aired, revealing very disturbing patterns of oppression and racism that caused the couple to move to the United States, Prince William defensively stated, "We're very much not a racist family," when a journalist asked him if the royal family is racist.[5] Ironically, he and his wife Kate were visiting a school in East London that had recently reopened following a national lockdown and was rolling out a mental health project that Kate had launched three years previous. Does William mean to hurt Harry and Meghan? No. Is he capable of gaslighting them and harming their inner peace and happiness if he believes that the truth will put his power and denial in jeopardy? Yes. He therefore needs to be "mistrusted" and be held as much at bay as needed until he has faced some of his inherited and denied demons. The people I work with are similarly layered. Every person in my direct family is similarly complex, not able to face the truth about some aspects of themselves. It's easier to like and love them when we and they know which parts are not fully metabolized. Radical acceptance and self-trust entail knowing what parts of ourselves to set limits with and mistrust—i.e., making discernments between the multidimensional interplay of dirty pain versus clean pain processes, truth versus trauma, heart versus hurt, and higher soulcentric self versus lower egocentric self motivations.

The untrustworthy and raw parts of ourselves that are not fully processed are protected by a defensive, egocentric self that can act like a cornered animal. Space and fierce compassion can help with gently approaching and broaching touchy, off-limits topics with this wounded part of ourselves. Our devotion to our deepest truth fosters trust in our relationships with others, provided that they do similar work, nondefensively, and have good self-awareness. Our commitment to renaturing and grounding ourselves in our truth-body also develops self-trust, regardless of what others do or don't do, because it's so much easier to detect the islands within them that need work when we are intimately familiar with our own. These disconnected, denied, and undigested raw parts of ourselves and others need to be held with clarity and healing love until they are ready to be unfolded and the hurt that is still tightly wrapped up in them can be alchemized. Connecting to our truth-body and self-love with the help of the elements provides us the best support to fall apart and to unravel the egocentric wounds that are monopolizing our inner climate. If you are feeling quite confident about the foundational setup provided by your sanctuary, you are now ready to fortify it by invoking more angelic, animal, archetypal, ancestral, and ascended masters and teachers to boost your connection with each of the seven sacred directions and to take in more of their magical healing powers. This is how you will alchemize lifelong karmic patterns into a liberating dharmic path of meaning and truth.

REFLECTIONS FROM PRACTITIONERS ON WORKING WITH YOUR SACRED HEART COMPASS

Loraine reminds us that in our deepest moments of personal and spiritual rejection lie the seeds for self-love. We learn that by confronting our obstacles and trusting the process, we have the potential to awaken beautiful parts of ourselves otherwise left untested and dormant.

—Tania Pryputniewicz, author and teacher

I was an avid collector of disorders and insecurities for nearly twenty years. Loraine knew that she, herself, could not find the secret locations of the pain that had become disunited within me—a different temper than I had previously experienced. It was through many sessions of guided hypnotherapy and aided self-discovery that I began to harness the tools in order to piece my shattered selves together again. I had not simply found an ailment, then had Loraine heal it. Loraine has given me my own tools to fix any issue I might potentially confront. With Loraine's help, I was able to unite a majority of my fractured selves. It is amazing how complete and balanced I feel today, and I still continue to grow and use the tools she provided. And though there are hundreds of differences I can discuss between myself a couple years ago and today, the result of Loraine's guidance is as follows: I am happy—finally—and have manifested a dream job that nourishes my soul and mission.

—Valerie Vargas, EdD, special education
teacher and artist

I did a journey today. There were stars streaming out of my hands, and roots growing out of my feet. I saw Earth as just one tiny cell of trillions living within a giant organism that is space. Then, my phoenix guide took my heart out of my chest, pecked all the rotten bruised bits out, and healed the tissue with its tears before replacing it in my chest. We lit a fire of sage and fed it the rotten bits, with me breathing in the healing smoke. At the end of the journey, I was given a handful of rough precious stones. I ground them up into a powder and dusted it all over my body, dancing and alchemizing the shame of self-hatred.

—Sarah Ginnan, writer, content marketer

Meditation Script for Your Sacred Heart Compass

Imagine sitting at the base of your Sacred Ancestral Tree in your inner sanctuary and leaning your back against the trunk. Feel its sturdy support light up your spine, letting you know that the tree has your back and is strengthening your courage and backbone. Rest your head against the trunk of the tree. Open your crown chakra above your head to receive inspiration and guidance from the sky, and open your base chakra to ground and root nourishment from the earth into your body and sanctuary.

While connected with your Sacred Ancestral Tree, feel your inherent worth and wholeness. Notice that the size, length, thickness, or thinness of your branches and trunk don't make you better, more beautiful, or more valuable than the tree next to you. The color and wrinkles of your bark, whether you're male, female, or nonconforming, and how much fruit or how many flowers you bear don't make you superior over other trees or entitle you to more privileges, safety, acceptance, or resources in life. You engage in healthy competition for sun and soil, but this involves searching for, absorbing, and fully occupying your space and your own vessel with the energy and nourishment they provide you. You see no benefit in undermining or harming other trees. As a matter of fact, you like and need their company. You actually fare better as part of an intricate social network of diverse trees versus being by yourself or surrounded only by trees of your own kind. The more you stretch and grow, the more you inspire the trees around you to do the same.

As a tree, our human inclination to overexert and exploit ourselves, others, and our Earth Mother in ways that constrict our own true nature and deprive us of vital energy and nutrients to "get ahead" is and feels unnatural. Your tree self and true nature don't have an egocentric desire to see or treat yourself and other sentient beings as objects or commodities to accumulate wealth, status, markers of success, achievement, or power. It's clear that this kind of ego-mind separation makes you more vulnerable to dis-ease and mistreatment because you're intentionally obstructing the flow of life energy and self-love through your body. This severely compromises your integrity and leaves empty spaces and cracks for pathogens, maladaptive patterns, and energetic parasites to occupy your body and sabotage your optimal health.

Connect with each of the elements—Air, Fire, Earth, and Water—and have them supplement your energy field with supersoul food wherever you could use a bit of extra support. Deepen your embodied felt-sense of your wholeness, and amplify feelings of self-love that are already flowing through your body. Let your natural genius loose, and see what kinds of guides and guidance are antsy to come through for you. You can work with one element at a time and invite a dream team of guides from each dimension to step up and offer you their teachings, if that feels right; or you could sit back and allow them to do their harmonious dance without directing it in any way. If the process doesn't flow, you may need to come out of the meditation and try these advanced techniques another day, or you may just need to slow things down and digest a charged chunk in smaller, bite-size pieces. You have all the time in the world. All that matters is accessing the powerful healing powers of the present moment deep now, and if this doesn't happen, explore your reactivity to your inner blocks. This may very well be the neglected gift most in need of unpacking. Remember, this is a marathon, so pace yourself. Actually, it's more like showering or brushing your teeth. It really doesn't matter how well of a job you did on Sunday or yesterday. You will need to do it all over again today and tomorrow. Be present with the process, and practice your spiritual hygiene rituals on a regular basis to reap the most benefits.

Allow each of these insights and teachings from your Sacred Heart Compass to sink in and take root in the depths of your consciousness and the cells and bones of your body. Know that this is your most updated and upgraded self and that you will notice shifts within yourself and in all your relationships with others for the next days, weeks, months, and years to come. Slowly retrace your steps and find your way back into the room or setting that you're in. Notice the chair that you're sitting in, stretch a bit, and bring your mind and attention fully back into the here and now. Notice your surroundings, wiggle into your body, bring all of your energy and attention back to the space you are in, and open your eyes slowly.

Alchemy Action Steps: Transform self-doubt into confidence.

How well are you able to hold onto the reality of your true nature when immersed back into the elaborate human dramas and oppressive social systems that we are part of? Imagine having a terribly stressful day that sweeps you up like a whirlwind. The energy and sensations that your five senses pick up are most likely dramatically different from what you experienced when you were having a calm day in your protective sanctuary. Instead of everything feeling and looking peaceful, your day looks in total disarray with lots of loose pieces swirling around, making you feel scattered. The sound of tense voices all around you is creating a palpable feeling of doom and gloom that hangs heavy over your head and makes your mind foggy.

When dealing with the highs and lows of life, our ego-mind tends to overidentify with the fleeting weather in our inner sanctuary rather than remain grounded and draw strength and guidance from our true nature to reestablish equilibrium. This causes us to adopt a rigid and distorted egocentric self that undermines the harmonizing genius and dynamic wholeness of the body. This exercise will help you keep the distance and nonjudgmental neutrality that are needed to better harmonize your inner space:

Reconnect to your truth-body and feel your Sacred Heart Compass beat where each of the four directions and four elements intersect. You are like a mini-Earth, a microcosm and ecosystem that can do incredibly complex balancing acts involving an intricate network of many converging and symbiotic dimensions. Notice how essential each of the elements—Air, Fire, Earth, and Water—are in sustaining your life and enhancing your well-being. They inspire, energize, ground, and soothe your mind, heart, body, and soul in the same way they dance with one another within the optimally balanced atmosphere of the Earth. These elements are just as mysteriously aligned and attuned to one another within your body, harmonizing disruptions that are mostly caused by misguided egocentric agendas and beliefs. Try to feel and translate the harmonizing energy and guidance that's moving through you. Don't judge, question, scrutinize, or doubt the creative answers and solutions that pop into your mind. Give them each the benefit of the doubt and a chance to deliver their message.

CHAPTER 14

Step 7: True North Living

Are You Breathing, Healing, Loving,
and Leading with Soul Authority or
Taking Yourself Too Lightly
(or Too Seriously)?

Objective of True North Living and Impact and Visibility Teachings:
To live our lives in ways that energize our deep knowing that we are,
at our core, pure light and love. By treating ourselves and others like
Mother Earth's miraculous offspring and dynamic works of art, this True
North guide helps us to continuously dissolve, recalibrate, and reorganize
the creative life energy that moves through us, as well as to transform
people, systems, and organizations around us. Like a spiral, we shift into
more highly integrated and ego-eco-aligned expressions of consciousness
in increasingly greater likeness of our Earth Mother and the Universe's
all-encompassing and ever-expanding wisdom. The more we deepen and
expand our sense of soul authority, the more we inspire others to discover
and embody their own.

TOPICS:

Get out there and share your message, because it is and isn't about you

Why renaturing your denatured mind heals our nation, humanity, and the Earth

I've come to believe that each of us has a personal calling that's as
unique as a fingerprint—and that the best way to succeed is to discover
what you love and then find a way to offer it to others in the form of

service, working hard, and also allowing the energy of the universe to lead you.… Your life is not static. Every decision, setback, or triumph is an opportunity to identify the seeds of truth that make you the wondrous human being that you are. I'm not talking just about what you do for a living. When you pay attention to what feeds your energy, you move in the direction of the life for which you were intended. Trust that the universe has a bigger, wider, deeper dream for you than you could ever imagine for yourself.

—OPRAH WINFREY

Resistance will unfailingly point to True North—meaning toward that calling or action it most wants to stop us from doing. We can use this as a compass. We can navigate by resistance, letting it guide us toward that calling or action that we must follow before all others. Rule of thumb: the more important a call or action is for our soul's evolution, the more resistance we will feel toward pursuing it.

—STEVEN PRESSFIELD

The vision is True North for the soul. It is a permanent intuitive compass direction for a human being. Every person inevitably strays from the path. Life is an endless experiment and course correction. The vision brings one back to the true path.

—THOMAS G. BANDY

Did your kids enjoy playing "opposite day" when they were younger? When my daughter was about seven years old, she was really into it. She would claim that the grass was blue and the sky was green, and when I looked confused, she'd blurt out, "Got you! It's opposite day!" Musings over the color of the sky and grass often led to more pointed questions such as "How do you know that the blue your eye sees is the same blue my eye sees?" and after a few more questions that deviated us from this original topic, she would ask, "Why are we talking about this again?" The questions that preoccupied her mind ventured beyond the usual "But why?" questions and explorations of children her age. As fun, educational, and endearing as this was, it was not what got her most excited. She got the biggest kicks out of getting an emotional rise out of me. She loved to drop a bomb on me like "Mom, I hate you" with a dead-serious look. She'd wait to see the utter shock and pain on my face, then exclaim, "It's opposite day!" and run toward me with outstretched arms and a big smile to comfort my broken heart. It was her way of experimenting with her emotional range and transcending opposite feelings with agility. It seemed to loosen her attachment toward—and bias against—any one emotional state. She could embody, draw, and playact almost any emotion so well—even with just a fork and a spoon or two sticks at her disposal to serve as puppets—that I'd run to her rescue multiple times, thinking she'd gotten in a bad fight with her brother or had gotten hurt. Nope, she was just practicing her sad cry or mad bickering or scared scream, and really seemed to enjoy finessing her craft, both at home and during musical theater and dance practice and performances. Although I was one to avoid the limelight rather than crash stages starting at age one, my daughter's knack for tracking conversation topics and comparing her inner states with those of others reminded me of myself when I was younger. I was similarly captivated by the depths of my consciousness and was constantly comparing notes with others for a reality check and True North guidance to see if I was headed in the right direction. My daughter's soul-searching paid off. She's now almost eighteen, and it doesn't surprise anyone that she plans on studying philosophy mixed with healing and performing arts in college. Interestingly enough, she can still spin off in self-doubt, not sure if this is the right career direction for her, when she bumps into one of her "islands."

RECONNECTING OUR DISCONNECTED ISLANDS

We, social creatures, need to be able to cross-check our sense of integrity with more than one trustworthy mirror that can reflect our layered, complex selves and our interconnected reality back to us. This is how to detect and heal the desolate "islands" within our inner self that I mentioned in the last chapter— referring to Prince William's unmetabolized ego-defenses hindering the cultivation of interpersonal trust—which is needed to intimately connect with others as well as our true selves. We turn our soul's unresolved karma into a transformational dharmic journey by radically accepting, alchemizing, and reintegrating all parts of ourselves. Our pain and struggles become the fuel for our journey toward our True North, a path that is backed by Mother Earth and the Universe. Simply put, consciousness supports the physical manifestation of our ego-ecosystem alignment and will accelerate this embodiment with signs and opportunities that serve our dharmic path—the path of our highest truth and the greater good.

As a child, I thought of my islands—my touchy trigger points and lost or confused soul parts—as puzzle pieces that had no place in the world, no social box in which they seemed to belong. Unbeknownst to me, this is the kind of aura that our soul purpose often emanates while orbiting around humanity's neglected islands in need of reclamation. Our soul purpose is like a mysterious treasure trove that draws us in and sometimes whispers sweet nothings in our ear. It typically takes us a lifetime to excavate, decipher, and retrieve all of our unclaimed soul parts; but from the start of the journey, we experience moments of ecstatic bliss when tasting our wholeness and the inner peace that we savor when sitting by a warm, central hearth at home. And we can simultaneously also experience terror and fear of failure, alienation, persecution, or humiliation at the thought of falling short or not completing our mission.

FRINGE EXPERIENCES AND TRUE NORTH

When examining my deserted islands through a wide-angle lens, I saw that they had to do with fringe experiences on the cutting edge of our collective (un)consciousness. I was curious about the exact topics that were considered improper, superstitious, scary, or too something else. If you had similar experiences in childhood, it's a sign that you are a bona fide consciousness pioneer and transformation trailblazer. We were born to make sense of these outlying, shadow experiences and interweave them back into our social fabric. Most of us know this before having any clarity about how this will translate into a career or job. I, for instance, knew how to attract and work with spirit guides and knew who they were without anyone explaining this to me. Stories about and by Anne Frank, Helen Keller, and Joan of Arc offered me hope, comfort, clarity, and reassurance. Each one was an important lighthouse that guided me out of my dark silo. They helped me to feel less alone about my peculiar soul-purpose inklings that had started to bleed through at a young age. Even though I didn't have much (current) life experience, their struggles and solutions resonated with and validated what was percolating inside of me. And as fellow old souls, they showed me that it was perfectly human and normal to mysteriously know things that adults somehow didn't know or were afraid to admit to themselves.

SPIRIT GUIDES: THE KEEPERS AND WAYSHOWERS OF TRUE NORTH

Spirit guides color outside of the lines and help us flesh out and materialize what we have trouble embodying. They are not concerned about our age or any other identity label. They are here to remind us that consciousness is timeless and doesn't discriminate. For instance, Anne Frank found her voice at age thirteen. She kept a diary in hiding and secrecy to help her deal with the horrendous mistreatment of Jews by the Nazis. Her precocious insights were shared with the world thanks to her brave words and writing, something that I knew in my bones I'd also do one day. The important lesson was that she never lived to see her impact, but it didn't stop her from doing what she knew she came here to do. While her words were inspired by the world's collective (un)consciousness, she addressed her diary, Kitty, as her dear friend. She first and foremost was motivated by a desire to heal her own heartache. Her first lines read, "I hope I will be able to confide everything to you, as I have never been able to confide in anyone, and I hope you will be a great source of comfort and support." Much later, when she heard a broadcast urging people to document their lives under Nazi rule, she was ready to heed the call and rewrote her diary.

Helen Keller saw things that others with perfect sight were not able to see. I too saw the invisible with my intuitive sight and heart. She didn't need to have a word for water to trust that she knew its life-giving essence intimately. In her world, the tangible and concrete didn't override subtle reality and what she knew to be true in her heart. She gave me permission to do the same. Joan of Arc disguised her true self and controversial source of divine guidance to help lead her country to freedom. She understood that anyone could become a freedom fighter and leader, regardless of gender and age, but that not everyone, especially not those dependent on their patriarchal powers, would support these progressive notions. Joan understood that her soul authority was much more powerful than their pompous posturing. She was connected to a Source of life energy that transcended life and death, and because of that she was perceived as a dangerous threat in need of execution. Because of Joan's story, I felt steadfast in my unwavering devotion to my soul authority. I was able to allow this steadfast knowing to guide me until I discovered in a past-life regression decades later that I had a near-death experience right before I was killed. I had the epiphany that I was made of eternal love and light and that there was nothing to fear. I could not die, and I was able to successfully pull this wisdom into this life, first through dreams, then through intense transcendental ego-death experiences.

HUMAN TROPHIC CASCADES

Each of these courageous young women caused a human trophic cascade by feeding our hungry souls superfoods that humanity had been deprived of. They helped me to grasp that my *eigenwijze* passions, dreams, caution, and insights pertained to soul-purpose calls that were already ringing in at a young age. These pieces of information were the most challenging to integrate because they involved out-of-the-box and inexplicable processes, such as my past-life gains, my premonitions about the future, and pure awareness of and objections about social dynamics that most people preferred to keep in the closet, in their blindspot, or in the dark shadows. While the inexplicable aspects of our mysterious callings may very well be the hardest for us to wrap our minds around, I've come to understand, and still regularly observe, that our logical brains get tripped up the most by the concept of *paradox*—an integral part of all things soul purpose related.

OPPOSITE DAY

Following our True North can feel like being trapped in a pinball machine. Although our True North direction is not really changing course, the amount of agile shifting and resilience that's required to absorb and harmonize the bombardment of information and blows that we're receiving from all corners of the world during these times of 24/7 virtual connection can make us feel be-wild-ered, overwhelmed, and filled with self-doubt and uncertainty about the concrete life plans we thought we had. Western and Judeo-Christian moral influences have over the centuries reduced paradoxical and holistic worldviews into good–bad gospel truths and rigid polarities. Because of these historical and ongoing influences, an egocentric heart compass is now misguiding many of us without our awareness or informed consent in almost every major region of the world. It makes total sense that a labyrinth path, guided by dynamic, circular wholeness and paradoxical wisdom, would be challenging to walk when everyone around us seems to be walking down a beautifully paved, straight path.

I often share my "It's opposite day!" stories with my clients when they get thrown off by this kind of unraveling and don't know how to read, ride, and alchemize their resistance, emotions, and life energy. The first thing I do is remind them of the guidance of their Sacred Ancestral Tree. It's tempting to take surface impressions and feelings at face value, especially if they haven't done deeper self-exploration and soul integration that shifted their center of authority. They can also feel disillusioned if they unexpectedly get stranded on an "island" or in a trauma bubble that's popping up to help illuminate and fuel the journey ahead. This is why we initially spend a good amount of time working with the Sacred Ancestral Tree guide—learning about the spiral growth patterns that are facilitated by the seasons, embracing nonnegotiable life-death-rebirth cycles, and understanding that your unique egocentric self is a side dish and a subset of your soulcentric self and a microcosm that works best when aligned with an overarching macrocosm—to dislodge the conceptual mind from predictable and confining tracks that block more complex forms of guidance.

Our True North is often not a linear direction that just straight up feels good, and our pursuit of it is also not a heady, intellectual endeavor. It's more like feeling our way through the dark until our guides illuminate the way. It's normal and common to trigger some old trauma and dirty pain resistance when we approach our soul purpose. Our potent potential initially causes us to shrink in fear. Our purpose feels big, raw, and daunting, because it often involves the death of a limiting belief, thought, or ego-mind pet affinity that we've grown quite attached to or a coping pattern that has kept us safe. Boats docked at a harbor are safer than at sea, but there is a trade-off for this safety. The closer we get to understanding what we are here to do, the more likely that we'll light up, expand, and feel antsy to embark on our mission. Our souls feel nourished by the deeper meaning of our purpose on Earth and want to get going. It gives us the incentive to take risks, complete a stunted posttraumatic growth or grief cycle, and spiritually evolve into the next phase of our development.

TRUE NORTH CALLINGS

Remember my earlier comment about our free-floating inner islands often being related to our soul callings? They are not only soul parts in need of healing and integration but often portals into a deeper calling that point directly to our True North. This is how I detect islands within myself. After connecting to my Sacred Heart Compass (make sure you're aligned with your Sacred Ancestral Tree guide and each of the elements), I lean my back against the tree and have my compass needle scan my field by making sweeping rotations. You could also face North and ask your guides what's waiting for you beyond the horizon, but I usually have more success when the path trails inward like a labyrinth. When you are embodying your truth-body and are grounded in your soul sanctuary, you are occupying "the safe and just inner space for humanity" inside of the ring, and neither imploding or exploding your energy beyond your boundaries. When you detect a blip on your radar, you are most likely tuning into some imbalance or pain point within your trauma-body that is causing you to spin out of bounds. Using the Implosion–Explosion Diagram, check to see if the emotional state associated with it falls on the collapsed, imploded end or more on the inflated, explosive, and overextended end of the polarity.

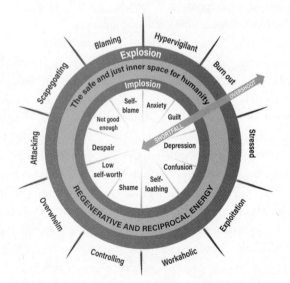

Implosion–Explosion Diagram (Van Tuyl, 2021)

Then take a look at Kate Raworth's Overshoot Doughnut,[1] and see which of your feelings and implosion–explosion pattern is the result of a shortfall in social foundation or an overshoot in ecological ceiling that you, your family, your ancestors, or your community were hurt by, worried about, or struggled with because of your identity, prejudice, or other factors.

The Overshoot Doughnut (Raworth, 2017)

Notice if you feel passionately drawn to learning how your inner states may have been shaped by your external experiences in or out of "the safe and just space for humanity" in the Doughnut. What have you learned or done to rebalance yourself, and what groups of people, animals, ecosystems, or problems pull on your heartstrings for help? What would you like to teach or pass down to others as your legacy?

REFLECTIONS FROM PRACTITIONERS ON WORKING WITH YOUR TRUE NORTH GUIDE

I am at a crossroads, wondering which direction is True North. I sit for a while and contemplate the following questions: "Which path will hurt less?" and also "Why does it seem like the harder path is the one I am supposed to choose?" Lastly, I ponder, "Does it always have to hurt?" I am eventually assured by a familiar sensation and unseen forces, pushing me towards something that feels better than anything: Love. The answer to my questions unfolds like fog clearing up with the sun—suddenly, drastically, and without boasting. The answer turns out harmless. The answer becomes easy. In sitting with the tangled knots that are my fears, I discovered that the fears had more entangled stories within them. I was intimidated and daunted by the task and seemingly inevitable pain that came with the untangling of those feelings; however, that changed when I trusted in the guidance of my Sacred Heart Compass in alignment with my elemental guides. I followed that compass, that guidance, and was led through the most peaceful path. This does not mean the path was without brambles and scratches. Rather, the path had those things and potentially even more. The fact is, if the right path has those things, then it becomes worth it. The compass doesn't serve as a path without pain. The heart's compass tells you that it is worth it.

—Valerie Vargas, EdD, special education
teacher and artist

After creating a grounded, elementally balanced inner sanctuary, I was pretty much like, "How was I living without this?" I was able to invoke my muse, at will, to feed the flow of my fiction. I could then grasp the essence of my villain with much greater ease and clarity. Then, I passed the ultimate test when the most challenging person from my past tried to push all the old buttons. I was so in my authority. I had that strong tree behind me, I had my own mentor voice in my head, I had my elements at my disposal. It was amazing. Today, all of the wondrous inklings of what the sanctuary is—a microcosm of the Oneness—came together in a bodily experience. As soon as I felt the predictable resistance to writing, I remembered my soul sanctuary, and as I put myself there, everything started to kind of tingle. My body felt lighter, but grounded at the same time. This state is my writing environment. My computer on the desk, my bulletin boards, my sticky notes, my characters and story, and my being aren't just *in* the sanctuary, we *are* the sanctuary. I can't believe how smoothly I just settled into my creative heart and mind. Resistance just disappeared like wet sand beneath a flowing stream. I mean, I believe it because I'm living it, but wow, I've been freed! Since working with Loraine, I live so much more from my center than I ever thought possible. Sometimes, I just stop and smile and marvel. I'm so grateful.

—J. R. Schumaker, author of *Diana's Dragons: The Awaited*

I just started seeing a young woman in her twenties, Maria Pascal, who gave me permission to use her brilliant journeys as a teaching example. You can record her transformation as a guided orientation and visualization exercise to get your own creative juices going if you like, or just read it. It may inspire your guides to take you on a similar journey tailored to your unique needs. Interestingly, Maria's guides didn't want her to lower the temperature. They wanted her to raise it and to learn to work more skillfully with Fire. I've seen many of my other clients work with Fire in the same way. Shoveling snow like good neighbors is unfortunately not enough these days to alchemize our unmetabolized, deep-seated hurts and dirty pain patterns in need of transformation. Only a hot cauldron will do. As you will see, Maria is a bona fide trailblazer, a prodigy whose guides and younger selves found me online just in time to make it into my book. They were excited to share their wisdom and natural genius, and to show you how to tie all the piecemeal steps together into a compact, elegant whole.

Her journeys portray how to work with your Sacred Ancestral Tree guide and each of the elements to transform your old self into a new form. She showcases how to trust your Sacred Heart Compass, follow your True North, and recruit a dream team of guides. She even did some advanced techniques when healing her relationship with her father and ancestors. Her journeys also reframe our sense of reality and mental order—in "opposite day" fashion. Societal lack of space and lack of understanding of her natural genius and creativity led to some of her neurodivergent gifts being misdiagnosed as a disability rather than a superpower. This is often what happens when our deficits, fears, limitations, and unrealized potential are projected onto sensitive, creative, and neurodivergent others—pathologizing them—while at the same time neglecting their true challenges. This is incredibly confusing and frustrating. Maria was famished and took to my Soul Authority teachings like a duck to water after minimal preparation or prompts from me. I primarily held space for her, and observed her guides take her on a life-changing pilgrimage over the course of just four sessions, alchemizing her karmic pain into a clear dharmic path guided by liberating truths and callings that she was ready to commit to. This is the fastest any of my clients has been able to cover so much healing ground with these tools. I'm certain that this is no coincidence but a purposeful gift for all of us.

After gathering all the necessary information I needed from Maria during our first session, we set up and entered her sanctuary in the second session. The blip she detected when scanning her field pertained to a seven-year-old self who'd felt shunned and misunderstood by her peers. She was able to escort this younger self, who was stuck in a trauma bubble scene, as I call it, into her sanctuary. (Never force this. Have them test out the waters if they are not sure if they'll like it. They can always return to their old setup. Some experience Stockholm syndrome symptoms and feel guilty about abandoning the troubled people who've kept them hostage.) Her seven-year-old self felt safe and comforted in the sanctuary and was met by a large black cat with green eyes that reminded her of her independent free spirit who was especially curious about mystery.

In between our second and third session, Maria said that a five-year-old abandoned younger self had popped up and nudged her to speak up to her partner during conflict, something she typically doesn't do. When we entered her sanctuary during the third session, we learned that this younger self had retreated from the world and had been hiding in a dark, damp cave in her inner sanctuary all these years. The five-year-old had felt small, scared, and invisible, as if she wasn't a person with needs and feelings. This was because whenever they were fighting, her father had threatened to leave her mother and take Maria with him. Maria said that the cave represented safe, mother energy that she'd been holding onto out of fear that she'd suddenly lose her mother. Her father, who was from a traditional and patriarchal culture, died a few years earlier. Because of her unresolved feelings toward him after these fights, she had not been able to appropriately grieve him when he died almost two decades later.

Maria said that her younger self had remained hidden in the cave, afraid that others would also judge her as "deformed and abnormal." Another big hurt that she remembered was caused by a prejudiced comment that a guidance counselor once made. She bluntly said that she didn't think Maria was cut out for UC Berkeley, because of her autism diagnosis. Maria did get in and is currently doing well as a bright and dedicated student working on her honors thesis with plans to pursue her graduate studies in sociology with a specialization in disabilities.

The counselor's painful and derogatory remark hexed Maria and gave her an "inferiority complex." To prevent being found out as an "impostor," she "overcompensated" by pressuring herself to "be perfect." No matter how well things went, they never went perfectly well, which caused her to still feel inadequate and insecure in spite of her accomplishments and being a leader in her community. There was a sacred fire in front of the cave, and Maria used it to light a torch to find and retrieve her younger self. She handed her five-year-old self the torch, which empowered and emboldened her. The fire made her feel warm, dried the dampness around her, and offered her light and clarity. It gave her the courage to get up and explore. She examined the contours of the cave for a bit, but soon shifted her attention. I couldn't help but think that in traditional talk therapy, one could spend years talking about and describing the inner contours of the cave.

Maria recognized that she was famished, and she felt as if she'd just awakened from a long hibernation. The aroma of food cooking over the fire outside tantalized her to venture outside. Food, water, and sunshine nourished her body and soul, and she started to feel more energized and stronger. She took an honest look at herself and concluded that she "wasn't deformed or abnormal, neither on the inside or outside," as others had insinuated. She decided to burn all of the harmful experiences and patriarchal ancestral patterns that were passed down through her father's line and that had hurt her in the fire. It cleared what had stood in the way of their emotional connection, and disentangled her energy from his. She was able to forgive and grieve him without the interfering blocks, and she sent his soul off in peace.

After completing these three advanced processes, directed by her natural genius and Sacred Heart Compass, she wondered what to do with the ashes. She didn't want them to go to waste. She had the epiphany that taking care of what's right in front of her from now on will help her feel safe and nourished. She felt more solid and robust after fertilizing her tree with the ashes, then decided to plant and fertilize a vegetable and fruit garden in an open field nearby. She called her seven-year-old self and had her and the cat join her. She was encouraged to take all the time she needed in the sanctuary to make up for lost childhood years and to nourish deficient, hungry parts with all the supersoul foods that she'd been deprived of. Maria reported that these journeys had helped her "phenomenally." She had struggled with horrible test anxiety for years and said that previous therapy felt "superficial" and "temporary" compared to the deep shifts and root soul remedies she was enjoying now. During her recent exams, her level of anxiety for the first time felt "in the normal range," and this improvement felt to her like a permanent shift.

The following week, she reported that her roommate had tested her by being "disrespectful," "refusing to communicate" about issues, and "mocking" her. This made Maria feel "small, invisible, and unsafe" in her own space. She celebrated that there was a moment when she had a "flashing thought" wondering if she deserved this mistreatment, but right away realized that "no one deserves this mistreatment." This was quite remarkable and unusual. She had successfully healed her bruised ego and was able to factor it out with relative ease. This incident would have spun her in a tailspin in the past by making it too much about herself, something that most of us do without realizing it. The more we try to prove or defend ourselves, avoid pain, or redeem our worth, the more we get trapped in ego-ecosystem misalignments. When Maria exercised her soul authority, her roommate's assaults were "surprisingly not penetrating very deep" in her psyche.

She was also able to set and maintain firm mental and energetic boundaries, seek support, and receive reassurance from others that this had nothing to do with her. She was happy that she and her partner were "supporting one another beautifully" through this ordeal. She noted that she wasn't able to detect any other younger selves in need of attention or help, but felt that her five-year-old and seven-year-old selves felt a bit vulnerable due to the recent altercations. I sensed that they were ready and eager to recruit more guides. When we entered her sanctuary, Maria noted that there was now a ring of smooth stones around the circumference of her Sacred Ancestral Tree. The seven-year-old self had laid them there and painted them to mark off her sacred space. Apparently, her five-year-old and seven-year-old selves had already connected to a good number of guides and wanted to get her up to speed so they could become better partners. Maria commented,

> Oh, there's a fox scurrying around the perimeter that I didn't notice before. There are a lot of fox holes, and the fox is closely connected to earth because of the burrowing. There's a falcon at the top of the tree. Falcon has a lot of wisdom and sight, giving me a much larger view of my surroundings. Oh, and there's a bear in the cave. It's a she. The five-year-old with the torch wanted a companion in the cave. In terms of a Water guide, there is a stream nearby. Let's follow it. It leads to a big lake that I didn't even realize was here. This place is pretty amazing.

> There are a lot of salmon in the river area of the lake. A big part of what they represent is change. They travel in accordance to their breeding cycles, and it represents how they live and die and the cycle of life. The cat loves the salmon, of course [*laughs*]. Butterflies are a big part of the ecology. I saw them as soon as the five-year-old with the torch came out of the cave, and freedom was the first thing that came to mind. I definitely feel that they represent her journey. She was in a cocoon and then suddenly emerged.

> Near the lake is a tortoise, earthy and secure in its shell. I feel better now, knowing the guardians. They want me to know that this place is sacred and to keep it free of toxins. This is why the five-year-old still carries the torch even though she doesn't need it. It cleanses the toxins. And why the seven-year-old put the rocks around the tree. The seven-year-old is bringing up the painting. I have historically been a very creative person—drawing and painting regularly—but all that stopped during the pandemic. I haven't

tapped into this side of myself, and I haven't made the space to do it. She is saying that through creativity you nourish the place and help things grow, because things naturally decay. You need creativity and being a creator to keep the cycle going. Creativity is kind of like fungus. That's why the paint is on the rocks on the ground. It's recycling something that's painful or dead into something beautiful.

I notice that the younger selves are so much more articulate. It was hard for them to speak, and they are now able to convey information and their needs to me and I'm able to convey information to them so much easier. They were sort of lost before, and now they have this whole team. They can communicate their needs, which they weren't able to before. The five-year-old wants to build a house. She said they had been meeting at the front of the cave, and they need a new home base. Hmm, I think she wants one made of wood. I need to find her some wood.

This upgrade paralleled what was going on in her concrete life, and inspired her to take appropriate practical action. It often takes a while for the younger selves and the adult self to get on the same page and form a well-oiled partnership. This journey could require lots of dialogue, soul and power guide retrievals, soul-part exchanges, and ancestral healings to free the ego-mind from wounded mind control. Maria held onto her truth so successfully that it felt like her guides had turbocharged us to this endgame—her soul's mission—and were ready to rock and roll.

"How do your younger selves feel about sharing their wisdom in my *Soul Authority* book?" I asked her.

"They are all for it and excited about helping a lot of people. Hmm, they want to include other younger selves that want to contribute. I just wanted to put that out there."

The younger selves in need of a retrieval didn't have painful, dense, or karmic parts and patterns stuck in the shadows. That's why none showed up when we did a body scan earlier. These younger selves have high-vibrational, dharmic wisdom stuck in the shadows and are ready to emerge out of the darkness into the light of day.

"These younger selves may want you to write your own book that's been inside you and is now ready to emerge," I said. "Have you ever considered writing one?"

"I definitely have, based on my own research, and I might include some of my reflections in it to give my research a narrative. The self with the cat wants the book to be illustrated [*chuckles*]. I think that would be fun and would reach a lot of people."

Meditation Script to Activate Your True North

Imagine sitting at the base of your Sacred Ancestral Tree in your inner sanctuary and leaning your back against the trunk. Feel its sturdy support light up your spine, letting you know that the tree has your back and is strengthening your courage and backbone. Rest your head against the trunk of the tree. Open your crown chakra above your head to receive inspiration and guidance from the sky, and open your base chakra to ground and root nourishment from the earth into your body and sanctuary.

Fully relax underneath your Sacred Ancestral Tree, and ask all four of your elemental guides to harmonize your inner climate and to balance your ecosystem, working together as one interconnected whole. You're now ready to string the ABC's you've learned together and experience the sum total being greater than its parts. You are not only going to create words with these letters; you are going to create sentences and eventually stories, poetry, and songs. And with enough practice, you will develop the muscle memory to swiftly drop into this dimension where your creativity and natural genius are celebrated. Don't direct the process; just feel what's happening in your body as the elements balance and counterbalance your energy, doing whatever is needed to move along stuck emotions and give the melodies inside of you an outlet of expression.

Take note how the elements guide, activate, and temper one another and you. Air could mean that you need more mindful breathing and inspiration to inflate your depleted spirit. Fire could indicate that you need firmer boundaries around your sacred healing well to protect vulnerable emotions. Earth could be slowing you down so you can gather scattered parts and give composting the time it needs, while Water could mean that you need more physical activity, sweat, and flow to burn and digest constipated issues, tension, heartaches or body aches, and stress.

Two of my clients who are quite serious about and dedicated to their soul purpose both received guidance to lighten up. The work of one involves transitioning incarcerated BIPOC back into society, and the other one oversees biotech research that breaks down environmental pollution and explores ways to improve COVID-19 vaccine manufacturing. They are carrying heavy loads and received guidance that in order to be more in their soul authority and ego-ecosystem alignment, they needed to become more carefree, have more fun, experience more pleasure, and do more frivolous projects that excite them. It wasn't what they'd expected or were used to hearing from mentors.

One received the green light to follow her hunch and move to another country, where life is simpler and where she would no longer feel trapped in traffic and in the capitalistic grind. She needed to be more immersed in nature. The other one needed to regularly experience a sense of free-dom and adventure by going on road trips and camping with her dog and cat. When your soul and the elements, rather than your ego-mind, are in charge, any insight or sensation is fair game. Have you beaten your body and soul into submission and need to ease up? Or do you need to take yourself more seriously by working through ego blocks, clearing resistance, and finally embarking on your most important soul mission?

Don't be afraid of peeling back your layers and encountering creepy, crawly creatures and worms. They will help you to metabolize and break down what's in need of composting. Breathe in your sacred heart center, and let your compass needle scan your field. What imbalances does it detect? Are these associated with a younger self who needs to be escorted into your sanctuary? Have your yin and yang elements been out of whack? Water and Earth are traditionally associated with feminine energies, while Air and Fire are traditionally associated with masculine energies. Have rigid messages around gender-appropriate behaviors or sexist pressures stunted the free flow and the chemistry between your elements?

Have you concluded that you are not smart enough or lack the chops to be successful, because the way you think, feel, or process information doesn't fit the conventional mold or what's considered to be top-notch? Do you need more courageous Fire to reignite your inhibited passions and creativity? Or do you need to ground more and to drop deeper into your body to touch your sacred healing well? To feel humbled by mystery, and to well up with tears of awe? What do you need to stay in your soul's sweet spot—in the safe inner ring of the implosion–explosion ego-ecosystem model—to stand your ground and remain centered while venturing into the imbalanced world? Confronting shortfall- and overshoot-related problems all around us can be taxing, challenging, and scary. It can cause us to lose sight of our True North or to not dare to look at it at all. Has past trauma left parts of you paralyzed or frozen? Could a waterfall help thaw your heart and body, and help you to feel and grieve? Or would sitting by a crackling fire fill you with loving warmth and empower the daring rebel in you?

Remember that your inner core is like the inner rings and core of your Sacred Ancestral Tree. Traumatic experiences were always buffered and absorbed by your outer bark. When they were not, you created new bark over exposed areas. Your mind may not have fully registered that you survived the blows. As you grew and expanded, so did your bark, all the while remaining on the outside of you. What you feel inside of you are not current wounds, but the energetic imprints and reminders of past harshness. They are your age lines and the rings of wise life experience.

We enjoy optimal well-being when we are in our element and fully occupy our safe and just inner space for humanity. Entering your sanctuary naturally evokes these feel-good balanced states and backlights imbalances—intense ego-attachments and indignant aversions—in need of harmonizing. Explore your sanctuary and see if any of your elemental guides or other guides—from the animal, ancestral, angelic, archetypal, or ascended masters realms—have some lessons, information, or healing ceremonies that they would like to share with you at this time. Repeat this pilgrimage and enjoy these discoveries as often as possible.

For now, allow each of these insights and teachings from your Sacred Ancestral Tree guide and True North guide to sink in and take root in the depths of your consciousness and the cells and bones of your body. Know that this is your most updated and upgraded self and that you will notice shifts within yourself and in all your relationships with others for the next days, weeks, months, and years to come. Slowly retrace your steps and find your way back into the room or setting that you're in. Notice the chair that you're sitting in, stretch a bit, and bring your mind and attention fully back into the here and now. Notice your surroundings, wiggle into your body, bring all of your energy and attention back to the space you are in, and open your eyes slowly.

Alchemy Action Steps: Fulfill your soul's mission with commitment.

This last section is a bonus visualization that will work like a suggestion hypnosis script if you read it slowly. It will prime your mind, heart, and soul to fully embody your ego-ecosystem alignment with authority so you feel as confident and committed as possible when doing your transformational work.

Start recording here:

When you embrace, embody, and exercise your soul authority, not only do you feel radiant and centered in your power, but you can't help but bring out the best in others. You will attract guidance, mentors, healers, and opportunities to you as well as students and clients who want to learn from you. When your sacred healing well is filled, it will overflow and automatically nourish others. Everyone around you will perk up and notice the vitality and soothing energy that will ripple out from you. Their dormant soul authority will light up and spontaneously start to tingle because of your brilliance and infectiousness. People will feel loved, be at ease, and become realigned in your presence without any effort from you. Their higher self and their soul will feel uplifted by your clarity, care, and confidence; and their neglected longings and desire to make a meaningful difference will start to stir or get stronger when near you. Your powerful way of being and running energy through your system will clear debris and will open channels of possibility in them. All of this will get your and their juices flowing. Without fully understanding why, they will want to bask in your energy, stay connected, and tell people about you and your ideas. All of these soul authority benefits will help you to become more clear and more effective in executing your mission and influencing whomever you are meant to guide with your powerful message, vision, and frameworks. You will inspire other sensitive leaders, trailblazers, and change agents with your fresh, sustainable, and holistic perspectives and methods. Your courage, convictions, practical solutions, and game-changing visions, shared in your books, your blogs, or public speaking forums, will strike a universal chord and will offer many people a place of community and belonging. Each and every day, these fans, supporters, clients, and students will help you define with increasing clarity what you were born to do. Your magnetic presence, compassion, strong convictions, and ability to connect will keep on attracting your ideal people and tribe. Harnessing your magnetic soul authority to serve others—whether your children, students, colleagues, clients, readers, or listeners—will cause them to:

○ Trust your leadership and seek out your guidance.

○ Appreciate your authentic and vulnerable sharing about life challenges and growth opportunities.

○ Feel safe and forthcoming about their struggles around you.

Here are a few concrete examples and ways in which you will be able to implement Soul Authority skills in your personal and professional endeavors:

○ Turn your inner critic into an inner mystic and a guiding voice (rather than a berating one).

- Recognize narcissistic, sabotaging, and harmful patterns in yourself or others.

- Be less manipulatable, gullible, and impressionable.

- Experience deep soul transformations and fulfillment.

- Transform hiding and hurting into healing and leading.

- Shift self-centeredness into a desire to be of service to all sentient beings.

- Rediscover your unique gifts and superpowers, and understand why they matter.

- Clear symptoms of psychological and emotional despair, anxiety, irritability, insomnia, and overwhelm.

- Regulate and reduce many stress-induced physical ailments: inflammation, headaches, back pain, hormonal imbalances, tense muscles, irritable bowel syndrome, rashes, swelling, and breakouts.

- Balance heart and mind, and connect feelings with facts.

- Speak and write about yourself and powerful transformative experiences with more clarity, authority, authenticity, and vulnerability.

- Feel motivated and committed to eat healthy, sustainably farmed and raised food; and exercise regularly to enhance your sense of well-being, play, perseverance, and vitality.

- Improve conflict-resolution skills, set limits with challenging people, and cultivate work, school, friend, and family environments where openness, support, and laughter are the norm.

- Offer your child(ren) conscious and effective parental guidance, structure, and discipline that makes it easy to enjoy quality time together; and foster a relationship of mutual respect, fun, and growth.

- Experience deep trust, intimacy, and safety in your romantic relationships by being fully present, differentiated, and honest about your needs.

- Confide in and connect with friends during times of hardship and times of joy, when in need of a break, or when just wanting to celebrate life, relax, and enjoy their company.

- Thrive in your professional endeavors and career by doing stimulating, creative, and risk-taking work; and feel recognized and generously compensated for your original ideas, designs, programs, books, solutions, and contributions.

- Sustain your focus and transform yourself and the world from the inside out with unstoppable momentum.

- Develop trust in your experiences, insights, and intuition even if others are in disagreement.

- Gracefully transition and integrate all parts of yourself into your new butterfly self and highest expression.

- Speak about and commit to your mission with ease, joy, and confidence.

Imagine mastering this level of soul authority and naturally touching each person in your life with your essence and gifts just by being your most aligned and potent true self. The sky will be the limit in terms of what you will be able to accomplish during this intense transformational age, because of your exponential impact on others, inspiring them to guide those they are called to lead in similar ways. The more skilled and consistent you get in harmonizing and protecting your private ecosystem, the faster you will renature your mind, empower yourself, and harness your fullest potential. And the more effective you will get in supporting symbiotic relationships and mysterious interconnections within your outer environment, helping to heal and restore our nation, our Earth Mother, and all of her children.

Notes

CHAPTER 1

1 Lee Carroll and Jan Tober, *The Indigo Children: The New Children Have Arrived* (Carlsbad, CA: Hay House, 1999).

2 adrienne maree brown, ed., *Pleasure Activism: The Politics of Feeling Good* (Oakland, CA: AK Press, 2019).

3 Steve Taylor, "The Self Is Not an Illusion," *Psychology Today*, April 2017, www.psychologytoday.com/us/blog/out-the-darkness/201704/the-self-is-not-illusion.

4 Taylor, "The Self Is Not an Illusion."

CHAPTER 2

1 "Revealed: Most Forested Countries in the World," *CEO World*, published September 20, 2019, https://ceoworld.biz/2019/09/10/revealed-most-forested-countries-in-the-world/.

2 Loraine Van Tuyl, *Amazon Wisdom Keeper: A Psychologist's Memoir of Spiritual Awakening* (Phoenix, AZ: She Writes Press, 2017), 317.

3 *The Secret of the Golden Flower: A Chinese Book of Life*, trans. Richard Wilhelm (London: Lund Humphries, 1947), 18.

4 *The Secret of the Golden Flower*, 13, 18.

5 Brooke Medicine Eagle, *Buffalo Woman Comes Singing: The Spirit Song of a Rainbow Medicine Woman* (New York: Ballantine Books, 1991), 277.

6 *The Secret of the Golden Flower*, 9.

7 Leslie Gray, "Deviance and Discipline in Shamanism," filmed September 2011 at 28th International Conference on Shamanism, Healing, and Transformation, San Rafael, CA, video, 43:40, www.woodfish.org/articlesmedia/videos.html.

CHAPTER 3

1   Resmaa Menakem, *My Grandmother's Hands: Racialized Trauma and the Pathway to Mending Our Hearts and Bodies* (Las Vegas: Central Recovery Press, 2017), 165–166.

2   Resmaa Menakem, "Somatic Abolitionism," website homepage, accessed May 26, 2021, www.resmaa.com.

CHAPTER 4

3   "Thomas Jefferson: Liberty & Slavery," Jefferson's Monticello, Smithsonian National Museum of African American History and Culture, accessed May 27, 2021, www.monticello.org/slavery-at-monticello/liberty-slavery.

4   Jeff Jacoby, "'All Men Are Created Equal' Is Not Hypocrisy But Vision," *Boston Globe*, July 4, 2010, http://archive.boston.com/bostonglobe/editorial _opinion/oped/articles/2010/07/04/all_men_are_created_equal_is_not _hypocrisy_but_vision/.

5   Jacoby, "'All Men Are Created Equal' Is Not Hypocrisy But Vision."

6   Jerry D. Stubben, "The Indigenous Influence Theory of American Democracy," *Social Science Quarterly* 81, no. 3 (September 2000): 716–731, www .jstor.org/stable/42863999?seq=1.

7   G. Keith Parker, *Seven Cherokee Myths: Creation, Fire, the Primordial Parents, the Nature of Evil, the Family, Universal Suffering, and Communal Obligation* (Jefferson, NC: McFarland & Company, 2005), 13.

8   "The American Indian Holocaust," *Living the Native Life*, published September 24, 2012, http://livingthenativelife.blogspot.com/2012/09/the -american-indian-holocaust-known-as.html.

9   Ron Rosenbaum, "The Shocking Savagery of America's Early History: Bernard Bailyn, One of Our Greatest Historians, Shines His Light on the Nation's Dark Ages," *Smithsonian Magazine*, March 2013, www .smithsonianmag.com/history/the-shocking-savagery-of-americas-early- history-22739301/?fbclid=IwAR1L6JPah9xJvdD7W1Eoll2EkHTUMaK zKz9_A3EAUsgYX29n4U6zVGSvw5o&page=1.

10 "Origins of Thanksgiving," American Indian Movement Grand Governing Council, published November 23, 2005, www.aimovement.org/moipr /thanksgiv.html.

11 Christine Nobiss, "Thanksgiving Promotes Whitewashed History, So I Organized Truthsgiving Instead," *Bustle,* November 16, 2018, www.bustle .com/p/thanksgiving-promotes-whitewashed-history-so-i-organized -truthsgiving-instead-13154470.

12 Fred Lucas, "4 Key Moments from Trump's Speech on History, Critical Race Theory," *Daily Signal,* September 17, 2020, https ://hdv6t3yp3awaiboqs4sr3qfvxa-adv7ofecxzh2qqi-www-dailysignal-com .translate.goog/2020/09/17/4-key-moments-from-trumps-speech-on -history-critical-race-theory/.

13 Jonathan Holloway, "Isn't 400 Years Enough? The Failure to Appreciate Black History Leaves Our Nation Incomplete," *New York Times,* February 10, 2021, www.nytimes.com/2021/02/10/opinion/black-history-month .html.

14 Alison Durkee, "More Than Half of Republicans Believe Voter Fraud Claims and Most Still Support Trump, Poll Finds," *Forbes,* April 5, 2021, www.forbes.com/sites/alisondurkee/2021/04/05/more-than-half-of -republicans-believe-voter-fraud-claims-and-most-still-support-trump -poll-finds/?sh=5f476b591b3f.

CHAPTER 5

1 DeNeen L. Brown, "'Almost Blasphemous': Trump Plans Rally in Tulsa, Site of Race Massacre, on Juneteenth," *Seattle Times,* June 11, 2020, www .seattletimes.com/nation-world/almost-blasphemous-trump-plans-rally -in-tulsa-site-of-a-race-massacre-on-juneteenth/.

2 Russell Cobb, "Trump Rally in Tulsa, a Day After Juneteenth, Awakens Memories of 1921 Racist Massacre," *Folio,* University of Alberta, June 19, 2020, www.ualberta.ca/folio/2020/06/commentary--trump-rally-in-tulsa -a-day-after-juneteenth-awakens-memories-of-1921-racist-massacre.html.

3 Cobb, "Trump Rally in Tulsa, a Day After Juneteenth."

4 Burgess Owens, "Tulsa Is the Right Place for a (Post) Juneteenth Trump Rally," Opinion, *Wall Street Journal,* June 19, 2020, www.wsj.com/articles /tulsa-is-the-right-place-for-a-post-juneteenth-trump-rally-11592605459.

5 Taylor Lorenz, Kellen Browning, and Sheera Frenkel, "TikTok Teens and K-Pop Stans Say They Sank Trump Rally," *New York Times,* June 21, 2020, www.nytimes.com/2020/06/21/style/tiktok-trump-rally-tulsa.html.

6   "Keti-Koti (Dag van de Vrijheden) [Cutting Chains Day of Freedom],"
     July 1, 2021, www.beleven.org/feest/keti_koti.

7   Simon Romero, "Suriname, South America's Hidden Treasure," *New
     York Times*, September 16, 2011, www.nytimes.com/2011/09/18/travel
     /suriname-south-americas-hidden-treasure.html.

8   "What Do Benin, Belgium, Suriname and Brazil Have in Common?
     They Head a New List of the Most Diverse Countries in the World,"
     Corporate Travel Community, Global Diversity Index data published May
     20, 2019, https://corporatetravelcommunity.com/what-do-benin-belgium
     -suriname-and-brazil-have-in-common-they-head-a-new-list-of-the
     -most-diverse-countries-in-the-world/.

9   Loraine Van Tuyl, "'Ala kondre' (All Countries), but 'na fraga' (No Flag)?
     A Multidimensional Analysis of the Experiences of Surinamese 'Doglas'
     (Multiracials) in the Caribbean," PhD diss., 1999.

10   "Suriname Election: Convicted Murderer Dési Bouterse Is Replaced by
     Ex-Police Chief," *BBC News*, reported July 14, 2020, www.bbc.com/news
     /world-latin-america-53394785.

11   Kate Raworth, *Doughnut Economics: 7 Ways to Think Like a 21st Century
     Economist* (London: Penguin Random House, 2017), 63.

12   "What on Earth Is the Doughnut?" Kate Raworth: Exploring Doughnut
     Economics, website homepage, accessed May 30, 2021, www.kateraworth
     .com/doughnut/.

13   "What on Earth Is the Doughnut?" Kate Raworth: Exploring Doughnut
     Economics.

CHAPTER 7

1   *The Secret of the Golden Flower*, 24.

CHAPTER 8

1   Steven Crandell, "Ancestor Deficit Disorder," Spiritual Directors Interna-
     tional, published July 27, 2017, www.sdicompanions.org/ancestor-deficit
     -disorder/.

CHAPTER 9

1 Aylin Woodward, "Tool-Wielding Monkeys Push Local Shellfish to Edge of Extinction," *New Scientist*, September 19, 2017, www.newscientist.com /article/mg23531441-900-toolwielding-monkeys-push-local-shellfish-to -edge-of-extinction/#ixzz6wIwkf0KF.

2 "Macaque Cons Squirrel into a Free Meal," video clip of the Nature mini -series *Secrets of Survival: Primates*, PBS, November 4, 2020, www.pbs.org /wnet/nature/macaque-cons-squirrel-free-meal/23243/.

3 *Secrets of Survival: Primates*, Nature mini-series, episode 1, PBS, premiered November 4, 2020, www.pbs.org/wnet/nature/about-primates-secrets -survival/23112/.

4 "Alpha Gorilla Is Dad of the Year," video clip of the Nature mini-series *Secrets of Survival: Primates*, PBS, November 4, 2020, www.pbs.org/wnet /nature/alpha-male-wins-best-gorilla-dad-hl7n8a/23286/.

5 Jane Goodall, *Through a Window: My Thirty Years with the Chimpanzees of Gombe* (Boston: Mariner Books, 1990), 243.

6 *The Biggest Little Farm*, directed by John Chester (FarmLore Films, 2018), www.biggestlittlefarmmovie.com/.

7 Elie Wiesel, *Night*, trans. Stella Rodway (New York: Hill & Wang, 1960).

8 "Serfdom," Wikipedia, last modified August 12, 2021, https://en.m.wikipe-dia.org/wiki/Serfdom.

9 Robert A. Scott, "Life in the Middle Ages," *Miracle Cures: Saints, Pilgrim-age, and the Healing Powers of Belief* (Oakland, CA: University of California Press, 2012), 9–11, https://content.ucpress.edu/chapters/11633.ch01.pdf.

10 "Time Clocks," Kentucky Geological Survey, last modified August 1, 2012, https://www.uky.edu/KGS/education/clockstime.htm.

CHAPTER 10

1 Michael Medler, "How Fire and Lava May Have Made Us Who We Are," filmed July 16, 2015, at TEDxWWU, Western Washington University, Bellingham, WA, video, https://youtu.be/qv6kcj6Uv2Y.

2 Wray Herbert, "Fleeing the Brain's Fear Center," *Association for Psycho-logical Science*, January 9, 2012, www.psychologicalscience.org/news/full -frontal-psychology/fleeing-the-brains-fear-center.html.

CHAPTER 11

1   Daniel K. Brown, Jo L. Barton, and Valerie F. Gladwell, "Viewing Nature Scenes Positively Affects Recovery of Autonomic Function Following Acute-Mental Stress," *Environmental Science and Technology* 47, no. 11 (April 2013): 5562–5569, www.ncbi.nlm.nih.gov/pmc/articles/PMC3699874/.

CHAPTER 12

1   Mike Wall, "Earth May Have Been Born Wet," *Space*, October 2020, www .space.com/earth-born-wet-meteorite-study.html.

2   Alok Jha, "Water: The Weirdest Liquid on the Planet," *Guardian*, May 11, 2015, www.theguardian.com/global/2015/may/11/water-weirdest-liquid -planet-scientists-h2o-ice-firefighters.

3   Jha, "Water: The Weirdest Liquid on the Planet."

4   Jha, "Water: The Weirdest Liquid on the Planet."

5   Jha, "Water: The Weirdest Liquid on the Planet."

6   Rosalyn R. LaPier, "Why Is Water Sacred to Native Americans?" Perspectives, *Open Rivers: Rethinking Water, Place & Community*, no. 8 (Fall 2017), https://editions.lib.umn.edu/openrivers/article/why-is-water -sacred-to-native-americans/.

7   Winnifred B. Cutler, "Lunar and Menstrual Phase Locking," *American Journal of Obstetrics and Gynecology* 137 (1980): 834, www.athenainstitute .com/sciencelinks/lunarandmenst.html.

8   "The Moon's Influence on Us," Lunar and Planetary Institute, Universities Space Research Association (USRA), accessed May 30, 2021, www.lpi.usra .edu/education/explore/marvelMoon/background/moon-influence/.

9   "Moontime," Indigenous Council on Education at Northern College, accessed May 30, 2021, www.northernc.on.ca/indigenous/moontime/.

10 Ioannis Ilias et al., "Dream Recall and Content versus the Menstrual Cycle: A Cross-Sectional Study in Healthy Women," *Medical Sciences* (Basel) 7, no. 7 (July 21, 2019): 81, https://pubmed.ncbi.nlm.nih.gov/31330877/.

11 "How Whales Change Climate," *Sustainable Human*, published November 30, 2014, video, https://youtu.be/M18HxXve3CM.

CHAPTER 13

1   Loraine Van Tuyl, "Amazon Wisdom Keeper and Spiritual Awakening: An Interview with Loraine Van Tuyl, PhD," interview by Tania Pryputniewicz, published October 19, 2017, www.taniapryputniewicz.com/2017/10/amazon-wisdom-keeper-and-spiritual-awakening-an-interview-with-loraine-van-tuyl/.

2   Parvati, "How to Connect with the Amazing Power of Self-Love Right Now," *Thrive Global,* April 2, 2018, https://thriveglobal.com/stories/how-to-connect-with-the-amazing-power-of-self-love-right-now/.

3   *The Biggest Little Farm.*

4   "How Wolves Change Rivers," *Sustainable Human,* published February 13, 2014, video, https://m.youtube.com/watch?v=ysa5OBhXz-Q.

5   Adela Suliman, "Prince William Says Royals 'Not a Racist Family' after Harry and Meghan's Oprah Interview," *NBC News,* March 11, 2021, www.nbcnews.com/news/world/harry-meghan-interview-prince-william-denies-royal-family-are-racist-n1260627.

CHAPTER 14

1   "What on Earth Is the Doughnut?" Kate Raworth: Exploring Doughnut Economics.

About the Author

Loraine Y. Van Tuyl, PhD, is a licensed clinical psychologist and shamanic ecopsychologist who has distilled thirty years of well-rounded and diverse professional experiences into an elegant and seamless integration of modern psychological expertise, ancient healing practices, and nature wisdom. *Soul Authority,* her cutting-edge magnum opus, addresses the most critical and salient social and mental health crises of our times. It is informed by her life-long commitment to guiding and supporting the anti-racist and anti-sexist activism and soul missions of hundreds of transformation trailblazers in psychology, holistic health, academia, the arts, renewable energy, economics, social justice, social work, and spiritual entrepreneurship. Van Tuyl has written extensively about her renaturing, ego-eco healing system as a contributing author for *Thrive Global, Rebelle Society, Elephant Journal,* and *Medium,* and has presented her work at the UC Berkeley Counseling Center, the American Center for the Integration of Spiritually Transformative Experiences, the Association for Transpersonal Psychology, the Native American Health Center, and the Mind & Life Institute.

About North Atlantic Books

North Atlantic Books (NAB) is a 501(c)(3) nonprofit publisher committed to a bold exploration of the relationships between mind, body, spirit, culture, and nature. Founded in 1974, NAB aims to nurture a holistic view of the arts, sciences, humanities, and healing. To make a donation or to learn more about our books, authors, events, and newsletter, please visit www.northatlanticbooks.com.